WHEN EGYPT WENT BROKE

A NOVEL

I0667605

HOLMAN DAY

1st WORLD
LIBRARY
Literary Society

When Egypt Went Broke

Holman Day

© 1st World Library, 2007
PO Box 2211
Fairfield, IA 52556
www.1stworldlibrary.com
First Edition

LCCN: 2007934129

Softcover ISBN: 978-1-4218-9649-6
Hardcover ISBN: 978-1-4218-9749-3
eBook ISBN: 978-1-4218-9549-9

Purchase *"When Egypt Went Broke"*
as a traditional bound book at:
www.1stWorldLibrary.com/purchase.asp?ISBN=978-1-4218-9649-6

1st World Library is a literary, educational organization
dedicated to:

- Creating a free internet library of downloadable ebooks

- Hosting writing competitions and offering book publishing
scholarships.

Interested in more 1st World Library books? contact:
literacy@1stworldlibrary.com
Check us out at: www.1stworldlibrary.com

1ˢᵗ World Library Literary Society

Giving Back to the World

"If you want to work on the core problem, it's early school literacy."

- James Barksdale, former CEO of Netscape

"No skill is more crucial to the future of a child, or to a democratic and prosperous society, than literacy."

- Los Angeles Times

"Literacy... means far more than learning how to read and write... The aim is to transmit... knowledge and promote social participation."

- UNESCO

"Literacy is not a luxury, it is a right and a responsibility. If our world is to meet the challenges of the twenty-first century we must harness the energy and creativity of all our citizens."

- President Bill Clinton

"Parents should be encouraged to read to their children, and teachers should be equipped with all available techniques for teaching literacy, so the varying needs and capacities of individual kids can be taken into account."

- Hugh Mackay

CHAPTER I

T. BRITT STARTS TO COLLECT

Tasper Britt arose in the gray dawn, as usual.

Some fishermen, seeking bait, stay up late and "jack" angleworms with a bull's-eye light. The big worms are abroad on the soil under cover of the darkness. Other fishermen get up early and dig while the dew is holding the smaller worms near the surface of the ground; in going after worms the shrewd operator makes the job easy for himself.

Tasper Britt—"Twelve-per-cent Britt"—trimmed his slumber at both ends—was owl and early bird, both, in his pursuit of the pence of the people, and got 'em coming and going.

He was the money boss for the town of Egypt, and those who did not give him his per cent nickname called him "Phay-ray-oh"—but behind his back, of course. To his face his debt slaves bespoke his favor obsequiously. Seeing that nearly every "Egyptian" with collateral owed him money, Mr. Britt had no fault to find with his apparent popularity. He did believe, complacently, that he was popular. A man who was less sure of himself would not have dared to appear out, all at once, with his beard dyed purple-black and with a scratch wig to match. Men gasped when they came into his office in

Britt Block, but men held their faces measurably under control even though their diaphragms fluttered; the need of renewing a note—paying a bonus for the privilege—helped supplicants to hold in any bubbling hilarity. Therefore, Mr. Britt continued to be assured that he was pretty generally all right, so far as the folks of Egypt were concerned.

Mr. Britt dyed after Hittie died. That was when he was past sixty-five.

It was only the familiar, oft-repeated instance of temperament being jounced out of a lifelong rut by a break in wedlock relations.

Hittie was his yoke-mate, pulling hard at his side with wages of food and drink. The two of them kept plodding steadily in the dry and rocky road all the years, never lifting their eyes to look over into pastures forbidden. Perhaps if Hittie had been left with the money, after the yoke had been sundered, she would have kicked up her heels in a few final capers of consolation, in order to prove to herself, by brief experience, how much better consistent sainthood was as a settled state.

In view of such a possibility—and widows are not altogether different from widowers—it was hardly fair in the folks of Egypt to twist every act of Widower Britt to his discredit and to make him out a renegade of a relict. He did go through all the accepted motions as a mourner. He took on "something dreadful" at the funeral. He placed in the cemetery lot a granite statue of himself, in a frock coat of stone and holding a stone plug hat in the hook of the elbow. That statue cost Tasper Britt rising sixteen hundred dollars—and after he dyed his beard and bought the top piece of hair, the satirists of Egypt were unkind enough to say that he had set his stone image out in the graveyard to scare Hittie if she tried to arise and spy on his new carryings-on.

Mr. Britt had continued to be a consistent mourner, according to the old-fashioned conventions.

When he arose in the dawn of the day with which the tale begins and unwound a towel from his jowls—for the new Magnetic Hair Restorer had an ambitious way of touching up the pillow-slip with color—he beheld a memento, composed of assembled objects, "sacred to the memory of Mehitable." In a frame, under glass, on black velvet were these items: silver plate from casket, hair switch, tumbler and spoon with which the last medicine had been administered, wedding ring and marriage certificate; photograph in center. The satirists had their comment for that memento—they averred that it was not complete without the two dish towels to which Hittie had been limited.

Mr. Britt inspected the memento and sighed; that was before he had touched up his beard with a patent dye comb.

After he had set the scratch wig on his glossy poll and had studied himself in the mirror he looked more cheerful and pulled a snapshot photograph from a bureau drawer, gazed on it and sighed again. It was the picture of a girl, a full-length view of a mighty pretty girl whose smiling face was backed by an open sunshade. She was in white garb and wore no hat.

"Vona," said Mr. Britt, talking out as if the sound of his voice fortified his faith, "you're going to see this thing in the right way, give you time. I'm starting late—but I'm blasted wide awake from now on. I have gone after money, but money ain't everything. I reckon that by to-night I can show you honors that you'll share with me—they've been waiting for me, and now I'll reach out and take 'em for your sake. Hittie didn't know what to do with money—honors would have bothered her. But with a girl like you I can grab in and relish living for the rest of this life."

Then Mr. Britt went over to the tavern to get his breakfast.

By eating his three meals per day at the tavern he was indulging his new sense of liberty. He and Hittie always used to eat in the kitchen—meals on the dot, as to time. The tavern was little and dingy, and Egypt was off the railroad line, and there were few patrons, and old Files cut his steak very close to the critter's horn. But after the years of routine at a home table there was a sort of clubman, devil-may-care suggestion about this new regime at the tavern; and after his meals Britt sat in the tavern office and smoked a cigar. Furthermore, he held a mortgage on the tavern and Files was behind on the interest and was eagerly and humbly glad to pay his creditor with food. In order to impress a peddler or other transient guest the creditor was in the habit of calling in Files and ordering him to recook portions.

In his new sense of expansion as a magnate, Tasper Britt took his time about eating and allowed men with whom he had dealings to come into the dining room and sit down opposite and state their cases.

That morning Ossian Orne came in and sat at the table without asking for permission to be admitted to such intimacy. He came with the air of a man who was keeping an appointment, and Mr. Britt's manner of greeting Orne showed that this was so.

Mr. Orne did not remove the earlapper cap which the nippy February day demanded; nor did he shuck off the buffalo coat whose baldness in the rear below the waistline suggested the sedentary habits of Mr. Orne. He selected a doughnut from the plate at Britt's elbow and munched placidly.

Landlord Files, who was bringing ham and eggs to a commercial drummer, was amazed by this familiarity and stopped and showed that amazement. He was more astonished by what he overheard. Mr. Orne was saying, "As your manager, Britt—"

Mr. Britt scowled at Mr. Files, and the latter slap-slupped on his slippered way; it was certainly news that Britt had taken on a manager. Such a personage must be permitted to be familiar. When Mr. Files looked again, Mr. Orne was eating a second doughnut. He was laying down the law to a nodding and assenting Mr. Britt on some point, and then he took a third doughnut and rose to his feet.

"I'll be back to-night, with full details and further instructions to you, Britt," declared Mr. Orne, who was known in the county political circles as "Sniffer" Orne. He combined politics with nursery-stock canvassing and had a way of his own in getting under the skins of men when he went in search of information. "If I ain't back to-night I'll report to-morrow. I may have to take a run over into Norway, Vienna, and Peru to make sure of how things stand generally."

He trudged out, stooping forward and waddling with the gait of a parrot ambling along on a pole; his projecting coat tail and his thin beak gave him a sort of avian look. The commercial drummer, overhearing his projected itinerary, glanced out of the window as if he expected to see Mr. Orne spread wings and fly. But Mr. Orne tucked himself into a high-backed sleigh and went jangling off along Egypt's single street.

The stranger, inquiring of Mr. Files, learned that Mr. Orne was not as much of a globe-trotter as he sounded.

"It's only the way the Old Sirs named the towns in the ranges about here when the land was took up. In this range we have Egypt and them other towns you heard him speak of. In the next range below are Jerusalem and Damascus and Levant and Purgatory Mills. If them unorganized townships to the north of us are ever took up and made towns of, it would be just like some whifflehead to name 'em Heaven, Hell, Hooray, and Hackmetack. But the name of Egypt fits this town all right," stated Mr. Files, disconsolately, and in his perturbation raising his voice.

"Files, don't run down your home town," rasped Mr. Britt.

"What has been run down as far's it can be run can't be run no farther," said the landlord. "And I 'ain't said why the name Egypt fits the town, for that matter." Britt's ugly stare was taking the spirit out of the landlord's rebelliousness.

"Suppose you do say!" counseled Mr. Britt, menace in his tones. "I've got a new and special reason, right now, why I demand that every citizen must uphold the good name of our town—especially a citizen in your position, first to meet all arriving strangers. Why does the name fit this town?" He banged the handle of his knife on the table.

Mr. Britt had reason for the heat which he was displaying and which caused the stranger to open his eyes more widely. Mr. Britt was fully aware that men called him "Phay-ray-oh" and that his statue in the cemetery was called "The Sphinx." He knew that since the town had gone on the down grade through debt and the decay of industries the inhabitants had begun to call themselves "The Children of Israel," and to say they were trying to make bricks without straw. In face, an itinerant evangelist who called himself "The Light of the World" had come to town and was trying to exhort the inhabitants into rebellion against conditions, and in his crack-brained hysteria was having some success in exciting

"The Children" to protest against the domination by Tasper Britt.

Mr. Files was not as handy with his tongue as he was with the mallet with which he pounded steak. He struggled with an inept reply about an old town having a dignified old name. He stuttered and stopped when Britt came and stood in front of him, chewing savagely on a toothpick.

"Files, I wasn't intending to make a formal announcement till my political manager, Ossian Orne, gets back with reports from the field. Not but what I expect that when it is known that I'm willing to accept political honor it will be given to me. But when I sit in the next legislature of this state as Representative Britt of Egypt, I propose to represent a town that ain't slurred at home or abroad. Hereafter, mind your tongue and advise others to do the same."

He stamped out. Landlord Files was left standing with an open mouth from which no speech issued.

"Emperor, or only a plain king?" inquired the bagman.

"You being a stranger, I can let out some of my feelings," returned Mr. Files. "Emperor, you say? He might just as well try to be one as to run for the legislature."

The drummer showed interest.

"That's what getting to be a widderer can do to some men," confided the landlord. He placed a smutty hand on the table and leaned down. "That legislature thing ain't the half of it, mister! He hasn't blacked his whiskers and bought that false mane simply so as to get into politics. He's trying to court the prettiest girl in this town."

"Aha!" said the drummer. "The old story! Cleopatra, queen of Egypt, is doing the job over again with the local Mark Antony!"

"Mebbe," admitted Mr. Files, his fishy gaze revealing that he had no personal knowledge of the parties mentioned. "It's the old story, all right. Widdereritis, and a bad run of it."

The bagman had a scarfpin in the shape of a horse shoe. His comment was in line with his taste in adornment. "Files, old scout, if a colt is put to harness so early that he can't get his natural fling in the fields, he'll have it at the other end of his life, when he's let run to pasture, spavin or no spavin. Why don't Egypt hold off and let Uncle What's-his-name enjoy his new hair and hopes?"

"He has known how to collect in the money that's due him," stated Mr. Files, "compound interest and all! He was only getting back his investments. But he has never put out any of the kind of capital that earns liking or respect or love. He has woke up to what he has been missing. He's trying to collect what he has never invested. And he can't do it, mister! No, sir, he can't!"

The drummer was a young man. He asked a natural question. "Isn't the girl willing to be an old man's darling?"

"You might go over to Britt's bank and ask her," suggested Mr. Files, crisply. "She's bookkeeper there. But you'd better not let that young fellow that's cashier overhear you."

"So that's it? Say, events in Egypt in the near future may make some of the mummies here sit up and take notice!"

"Shouldn't wonder a mite," agreed Mr. Files, beginning to gather up the dishes.

12   Holman Day

CHAPTER II

FIRST COLLECTIONS

That morning Mr. Britt did not dawdle in the hotel office with his cigar. He knew perfectly well that he merely had been making a pretense of enjoying that sybaritism, putting on his new clubman airs along with his dye and his toupee.

Among other curios in the office was a dusty, stuffed alligator, hanging from the ceiling over the desk. The jaws were widely agape and Mr. Britt always felt an inclination to yawn when he looked alligatorward. Therefore, the alligator offended Mr. Britt by suggesting drowsiness in the morning; Mr. Britt, up early, and strictly after any worm that showed itself along the financial path, resented the feeling of daytime sleepiness as heresy. Furthermore, that morning the gaping alligator also suggested the countenance of the open-mouthed Files whom Britt had just left in the dining room, and Files had been irritating. Britt scowled at the alligator, lighted a cigar, and hustled outdoors; he had the feeling that the day was to be an important one in his affairs.

Egypt's Pharaoh was able to view considerable of the town from the tavern porch. The tavern was an old stage-coach house and was boosted high on a hill, according to the pioneer plan of location. The houses of the little village straggled down the hill.

The aspect was not uninviting, seen under the charitable cloak of February's snow, sun-touched by the freshly risen luminary, the white expanses glinting; all the rocks and ledges and the barren shapes were covered. But under summer's frank sunlight Egypt was as disheartening a spectacle as a racked old horse, ribs and hip bones outthrust, waiting for the knacker's offices.

There were men in Egypt—men whose reverses had put them in a particularly ugly mood—who said out loud in places where Britt could not hear them that the money-grabber could not get much more than twelve-per-cent blood out of the nag he had ridden for so long, and might as well set knife to neck and put the town out of its misery.

Right behind Britt, as he stood on the porch, was a sheaf of yellowed papers nailed to the side of the tavern. Nobody in Egypt bothered to look at the papers; all the taxpayers knew what they were; the papers were signed by the high sheriff of the county and represented that all the real estate of Egypt had been sold over and over for taxes and had been bid in by the town as a municipality—and there the matter rested. Egypt, in other words, had been trying to lift itself by the bootstraps and was not merely still standing on the ground, but was considerably sunk in the hole that had been dug by the boot heels while Egypt was jumping up and down. Mr. Britt was not troubled by the sight of the yellowed papers; he owned mortgages and pulled in profit by the legal curiosities known as "Holmes notes"—leeches of particular drawing power. Mr. Britt did not own real estate. Egypt, in its financial stress and snarl of litigation, was a wonderful operating field for a man with loose money and a tight nature.

From far swamps the whack of axes sounded. Mr. Britt knew

Holman Day

that men were cutting hoop poles and timber for shooks; Egypt earned ready money with which to pay interest, getting out shooks and hoop poles. That occupation had been the resource of the pioneers, and the descendants stuck to the work, knowing how to do it better than anything else. There was not enough soil for farming on a real money-making scale. The old sheep, so cynics said, were trained to hold the lambs by their tails and lower them head downward among the rocks to graze. Poor men usually own dogs. But dogs would not live long in Egypt, the cynics went on to assert; the dogs ran themselves to death hustling over the town line to find dirt enough to bury a bone.

Mr. Britt could see his statue in the cemetery.

Down the street was a one-story brick building, the only brick structure in the town. Set into the front of this building was a replica of the statue in the cemetery. Britt had secured special rates by ordering two statues from the stonecutter. Britt possessed vanity. He had hidden it, begrudging the cost of gratifying it. The crust of his nature, hardening through the years, had pressed upon that vanity. The statues, his refurbished beard, and his rehaired head had relieved the pressure somewhat, but the vanity was still sore. In his new mood he was dreading a blow on that sore spot. He realized what kind of a grudge he was carrying around. A vague sense of an unjust deal in life is more dangerous to the possessor than an acute and concrete knowledge of specific injury. The vagueness causes it to be correlated to insanity. Britt, putting his belated aspirations to the test, hoped that nobody would presume to hit on that sore spot. He knew that such an adventure might be dangerous for the person or persons who went up against him.

He buttoned his overcoat, settled the cigar rigidly into one corner of his mouth, stared with approval at the stone image of himself in the facade of Britt Block, and walked to the edge of the porch.

Across the street sat a little building above the door of which was a sign inscribed, "Usial Britt, Shoemaker." That it was a dwelling as well as a shop was indicated when a bare and hairy arm was thrust from a side window and the refuse in a smoking iron spider was dumped upon the snow. Simultaneously it was shown that more than one person tenanted the building: a man, bareheaded, but with a shaggy mat of roached hair that served in lieu of a hat, issued from the door. The wanton luxuriance of the hair would have stirred envy in any baldheaded man; but Tasper Britt exhibited a passion that was more virulent than envy.

The man who came forth was "Prophet Elias." It was the newcomer, the religious fanatic, the exhorter against oppression of the people by usury, the fearless declaimer who named Tasper Britt in diatribe and was setting the folks by the ears.

The Prophet's morning greeting did not make for amity. He stood straight and pointed in turn to the visible statues and then to Tasper Britt, in person. "Baal, and the images of Baal!" he shouted. "Stone, all three!"

Then he stepped from the door and spread a prodigiously big umbrella—an umbrella striped in dingy colors and of the size of the canopies seen over the drivers of delivery wagons. The employment of such a shield from the sun in midwinter indicated that the Prophet was rather more than eccentric; his garb conveyed the same suggestion. He wore a frayed purple robe that hung on his heels when he came striding across the street. On a broad band of cloth that once had been white, reaching from shoulder to waist, diagonally across his breast, were the words, "The Light of the World."

Tasper Britt surveyed him with venomous gaze as he advanced. But Britt shifted his stare and put additional venom into the look he gave a man who came to the door and stood there, leaning against the jamb and surveying the scene with a satisfied grin. There was no need of the name "Britt" above his head to proclaim his kinship with the man who stood on the tavern porch. The beard of the Britt in the door was gray, and his head was bald. But he was Tasper Britt, in looks, as Britt unadorned ought to have been. There was something like subtle reproach in his sticking to nature as nature had ordained. And the folks of Egypt had been having much to say about Usial Britt putting this new touch of malice into the long-enduring feud between twin brothers—even though he merely went on as he had been going, bald and gray. But because Usial had taken to going about in public places wherever Tasper appeared, and unobtrusively got as near his brother as possible on those occasions, and winked and pointed to himself and suggested "Before using!" the malice was apparent.

Usial, in the door, stroked his smooth poll complacently and grinned.

Tasper, on the porch, shook his fist.

Prophet Elias marched close to the porch and struck an attitude. "Hear ye! Hath not Job said, 'The triumphing of the wicked is short, and the joy of the hypocrite but for a moment'?"

A man who was humped over a sawbuck in a nearby yard straightened up and began to pay strict attention. A driver halted a sled loaded with unshaved hoop poles, and listened. The commercial drummer came out on the porch.

"Look here, you crazy coot, haven't I given you fair warning about tongue-whaling me in public?" demanded the man who was pilloried.

"'Behold, all they that are incensed against thee shall be ashamed and confounded,'" quoted the Prophet, pounding his fist against the lettered breast. "'They shall be as nothing; and they that strive with thee shall perish.'"

Mr. Britt leaped off the porch, thrust the Prophet from his path, and strode across the street toward the man in the door. The brother did not lose his smile. He maintained his placid demeanor even when an angry finger slashed through the air close under his nose.

"I never intended to pass speech with you again, you renegade," stormed Tasper. "But I'm talking to-day for a town that I propose to represent in the legislature, and I won't have it shamed any longer by a lunatic that you're harboring."

Usial Britt lifted his eyebrows. "The legislature?" He puckered his lips and whistled a few bars of "Hail to the Chief."

Candidate Britt waggled the monitory finger more energetically. "You are sheltering and ste'boying on a crazy man who is making the rest of the people in this town crazy. If they hadn't grown loony they'd ride him out over the line on a rail."

The Prophet had arrived at Britt's shoulder. "'But God has chose the foolish things of the world to confound the wise; and God has chosen the weak things of the world to confound the things which are mighty.'"

"I don't guarantee my guest's brains," said the Britt in the door, "but I do vouch for the correctness of his memory when it comes to the matter of Gospel quotations. And a cracked record doesn't always spoil a good tune."

"I'll have him in the lockup as a tramp, or on the poor farm as a lunatic."

"You mean, that's where you would have him if the shelter of my roof didn't give him legal protection," returned Usial, calm in the face of wrath.

"'I was a stranger, and ye took me in,'" declaimed the Prophet.

"And I'm keeping you on," stated the cynical Usial, speaking for his brother's benefit, "because you're a self-operating, red-hot gad that is helping me torment yon pirate with texts after I had run out of cuss words. Go ahead, Prophet! Shoot anything. It's a poor text that will not hit him some place."

Obediently, the fanatic began to mouth Holy Writ in orotund. Tasper Britt raised his fist. But the devil himself shrinks before The Word. Britt did not strike. His face revealed his emotions; he could not bring himself to assault this fountain of sacred aphorisms.

He turned and marched away down the middle of the road, stamping hard into the snow.

One of the listeners was a man who came bearing a pair of shoes. Usial Britt took them from the man's hand. "You can have 'em to-morrow night."

"But there's only a little patch needed—"

"To-morrow night, I said. I've got other business for to-day."

He went into the house and slammed the door.

The Prophet set his umbrella over his head and went away on the trail of Egypt's Pharaoh.

Holman Day

CHAPTER III

MORE COLLECTIONS

There was a door in the middle of the facade of the low brick building; there were two windows on either side of the door. On the left-hand windows was painted in black letters, "Egypt Trust Company." On the right-hand windows was painted, "T. Britt." There was no legend to indicate what the business of T. Britt might be. None was required. The mere name carried full information for all Egypt.

Mr. Britt glanced in at the left-hand windows as he approached the door. Cashier Frank Vaniman was sweeping out.

When President Britt of the new Egypt Trust company went down to a business college in the city in search of a cashier, he quizzed candidates in quest of what he termed "foolish notions." Young Mr. Vaniman, who had supported himself ever since he was fourteen years old, and had done about everything in the ten years since then in the way of work, grabbing weeks or months for his schooling when he had a bit of money ahead, passed the test very well, according to Mr. Britt's notion. Young Mr. Vaniman had secured a business education piecemeal, and was a bit late in getting it, but Mr. Britt promptly perceived that the young man had not been hung up by stupidity or sloth. So he hired Vaniman, finding him a strapping chap without foolish notions.

Vaniman was cashier, receiving teller, paying teller, swept out, tended the furnace, and kept the books of the bank until Britt hired Vona Harnden for that job. Vona had been teaching school to help out her folks, in the prevailing Egyptian famine in finance.

But folks stopped paying taxes, and the town orders by the school committee on the treasurer were not honored; therefore, Vona gratefully took a place in the bank when Mr. Britt called her into his office one day and offered the job to her. He said that the work was getting to be too much for Frank. That consideration for hired help impressed Miss Harnden and she smiled very sweetly indeed, and Mr. Britt beamed back at her in a fashion that entirely disarranged for the rest of the day the set look that he creased into his features before his mirror every morning. Several clients took advantage of his blandness and renewed notes without paying the premium that Britt exacted when he loaned his own money as a private venture.

President Britt entered the door, but he did not go into the bank at once. He marched along the corridor and unlocked his office and toasted himself over the furnace register while he finished his cigar; Vaniman was a good fireman and was always down early. Mr. Britt kept his ear cocked; he knew well the tap of certain brisk boot heels that sounded in the corridor every morning and he timed his movements accordingly.

By being on the alert for sounds, he heard what did not comport with the comfort of his office. Prophet Elias was engaged in his regular morning tour of duty, picketing T. Britt's domains, giving an hour to deliverance of taunting texts before going abroad through the town on his mission to the people with texts of comfort; the Prophet carried plenty of penetrating, textual ammunition, but he carried poultices for the spirit as well.

Mr. Britt heard: "'Will he esteem thy riches? No, not gold, nor all the forces of strength.'"

The usurer commented under his breath with remarks that were not scriptured. He threw away his cigar and went to a case where he kept some law books which contained the statutes that were concerned with money and debts and dependence; he had been hunting through the legislative acts regarding vagrants and paupers and had been hoping to light on some legal twist that would serve him. The Prophet kept on proclaiming. But all at once he shifted from taunts about riches. His voice was mellow with sincere feeling.

Said the Prophet: "'Behold, thou art fair, my love; thou hast doves' eyes within thy locks. Thy teeth are like a flock of sheep which came up from the washing. Thy lips are like a thread of scarlet, and thy speech is comely. Thou art all fair, my love; there is no spot in thee.'"

Mr. Britt did not wait in his office for the completion of the panegyric. He knew well enough what arriving personage it heralded. He hurried out into the corridor and faced the radiant girl who came in from the sunshine. Even one who might question the Prophet's tact would not have blamed his enthusiasm.

"Vona, you swear out a warrant and I'll have him arrested," stammered the employer.

She checked a chirrup of laughter and her smile faded when she opened her eyes on Britt's sourness.

"There's a law about hectoring and insulting a female person on the street—some kind of a law—and we'll invoke it in this case," Britt insisted.

"Why, Mr. Britt, he's only a harmless old man with extremely poor judgment about most things, including a girl's looks," she protested.

"Don't you call that gabble an insult to you, walking along and minding your own business?" His heat was alarming; he shook his fist to indicate the Prophet.

She was unable to restrain her demure smile. "The specifications, sir, are overflattering; but I'm sure I don't feel insulted."

In the past Britt had purred paternally in her presence and had stared at her in a way that often disconcerted her. Now his expression alarmed her. His face grew red. At first she thought he was embarrassed by the reflection that he had been terming the Prophet's compliments an insult—intimating that she had no claim to such compliments. But Mr. Britt did not bother to deal with that phase of the matter. The flame was shifted from his face to his eyes; his cheeks grew pale. He tried to put his arm about her. She set her gloved hands against the arm and pushed it away, fright popping her eyelids wide apart.

"I want to protect you," Britt stuttered. "I don't want any harm or trouble to come to you."

He stepped back and gazed at her imploringly. His abashed obedience, his promptness in desisting, restored her self-possession immediately. She had the air of one who had misunderstood friendly interest. "Oh, Mr. Britt, I know you have a kind heart underneath your—I mean that folks don't realize how good you are unless they are near to you, as Frank and I are. We often speak of it." She hurried on. She opened the door admitting to the bank from the corridor and cheerily called her "Good morning!" to the cashier as she crossed the threshold.

Mr. Britt stood in his tracks in the corridor after she closed the door. He stared at the floor with eyes that saw nothing. He slowly raised his hand and set his right index finger upon the toupee and scratched meditatively through the mesh—scratched carefully, having accustomed himself to handling his boughten hair with cautious touch. He had not liked her intonation when she said "Frank and I." He muttered something about his feelings. He had never thought of Frank as belonging in Vona's calculations. He had never considered even the linking of their names, much less their interests.

But Mr. Britt, having made money his idol, could not understand worship directed to any other shrine. His face cleared while he pondered. A girl who frankly declared at all times that she would do 'most anything to help her family out of their troubles was not of a mind to hitch up with another pauper—a combination of choreman and cashier—even though she had linked their names casually in speech. And Mr. Britt mouthed mumblingly some of the sentiments he had put into words that morning when he arose. He smoothed down the top piece and looked more at ease. He smiled when he reflected on what he would have to say to her after Emissary Orne had returned with something in the line of fruits from the Promised Land. His self-assurance revived; nevertheless, he tiptoed along the corridor and listened at the door of the bank.

The reassuring swish of a broom and their casual chatter—he heard only those commonplace sounds!

She was asking Vaniman if he had mislaid her dustcloth.

Vaniman replied in a tone which indicated that the two were at some distance from each other. There was no subdued conference—no murmuring of mushiness such as a meeting in the morning might be expected to elicit in case there was any sort of an understanding between them. Mr. Britt tiptoed away from the door and braced back his shoulders and gave himself a shake of satisfied confidence, and went serenely into his office, plucking a cigar from his vest pocket. By permitting himself to smoke again he was breaking the habit of confining himself to one cigar after breakfast. But many men in moments of exaltation seek tobacco or alcohol.

Mr. Britt felt that he had broken the ice, at any rate. Mr. Britt decided that the girl was heart-free and entertained sensible ideas about the main chance—and she had had a good word to say about Britt's kind heart. Mr. Britt was sure that Frank Vaniman knew his place and was keeping it. Therefore, Mr. Britt lighted a fresh cigar and blew visible smoke rings and inflated invisible mental bubbles and did not pay any more attention to what Prophet Elias was saying outside. And as if the Prophet had received a psychological hint that his text shafts were no longer penetrating the money king's tough hide, the diminuendo of his orotund marked the progress of his departure.

Usually Mr. Britt went across into the bank and hung around after the girl arrived. On this morning he stayed in his office. According to his notion, his advances to her in the corridor, though he had not intended to be so precipitate in the matter, had given her something to think about—and he decided to keep away and let her think. If she saw him following the usual routine, her thoughts might drop back into routine channels.

Holman Day

He thrilled at the memory of her touch on his arm, even though the touch had been a thrusting of her hands in self-defense and her eyes had been big with fright.

He sat down at his desk and tore the leaf off his pad calendar, starting his business day as usual. He looked at the disclosed date and his eyes became humid. It was February 14th, the day of St. Valentine. An idea came to Mr. Britt. He had been wondering how to approach the question with Vona without blurting the thing and making a mess of it. He determined to do something that he had not attempted since he had beaued Hittie; he set himself to compose a few verses for a valentine—verses that would pave the way for a formal declaration of his love and his hopes.

The determination indicated that Mr. Britt was having a severe run of a second attack of the same malady, and he acknowledged that much to himself as he sat there and chewed the soggy end of an extinguished cigar and gazed aloft raptly, seeking rhymes.

He made slow progress; his pen trailed as sluggishly as a tracking snail—a word at a time. He lost all notion of how the hours were slipping past.

A man walked in. He was Stickney, a cattle buyer, and a minor stockholder in the bank. Mr. Britt, his eyes filmy with prolonged abstraction, hooked his chin over his shoulder and scowled on the intruder; a man bringing business into that office that day was an intruder, according to Mr. Britt's opinion.

Stickney walked close to the desk and displayed a flash of curiosity when Britt laid his forearm over his writing.

"Spring pome, or only a novel?" queried Stickney, genially,

figuring that such a question was the height of humor when put to a man of Tasper Britt's flinty, practical nature.

Mr. Britt, like a person touched smartly by a brad, twitched himself in his chair and asked in chilly tone what he could do for Stickney. The caller promptly became considerable of an icicle himself. He laid down a little sheaf of papers beside the shielding forearm.

"If you'll O. K. them notes for discount, I'll be much obliged, and won't take up valuable time."

"We're tightening up on discounts—calling in many loans, too," stated President Britt, with financial frigidity.

"I know all about your calling loans, Mr. Britt. Much obliged. It makes a crackerjack market for me in the cattle business. They've got to raise money, and I'm setting my own prices." Stickney thawed and beamed on Britt with a show of fraternal spirit, as if the banker were a co-conspirator in the job of shaking down the public. "However, my notes there are all good butchers' paper—sound as a pennyroyal hymn! I've got to have the cash so as to steal more cattle while the market is as it is."

Britt pushed away the notes and seized the opportunity to turn his own papers upside down on the desk. "We can't accommodate you at present, Stickney."

The customer stepped back and propped his palms on his hips. "I reckon I've got to call for an explanation."

"We're not in the habit of explaining the details of our business to individuals."

Stickney slipped the leash on his indignation. "'We,' say you?

Holman Day

All right! 'We' it is. I'm in on that 'we.' I'm a stockholder in the bank. What sort of investments are 'we' making that have caused money to be so tight here that a regular customer is turned down—and after enough loans have been called to make the vault bulge?"

"The report will show," returned Britt, coldly. "I am not called on to issue that report in installments every time a stockholder turns in here."

The especial stockholder stepped forward and tapped his finger on the desk. "I don't say that you are. But now that this subject is opened up—"

"The subject is closed, Stickney."

"Now that the subject is opened up," insisted the other man, "I'll make mention of what you probably know—that I have regular business 'most every day down in Levant at the railroad terminus. And I'm knowing to it that regular shipments of specie have been coming to the bank. If that specie is in our vaults it ain't sweating off more gold and silver, is it, or drawing interest? I know you're a shrewd operator, Britt. I ain't doubting but what your plans may be good."

"They are!" President Britt's retort was crisp.

"But when those plans put a crimp into *my* plans—and me a steady customer—I'm opening my mouth to ask questions."

"You—and all other stockholders—will be fully informed by the annual report—and will be pleased." Britt's air was one of finality.

"Let me tell you that the mouth I have opened to ask

questions will stay open in regard to hoarding that specie where it ain't drawing interest."

Britt jumped up and shook his fist under Stickney's snub nose. "Don't you dare to go blabbing around the country! You might as well set off a bomb under our bank as to circulate news that will attract robbers."

"Bomb? Britt, I'm safe when I'm handled right, but if I'm handled wrong—" Stickney did not finish his sentence; but his truculent air was pregnant with suggestion.

"Do you think you can blackmail me or this bank into making an exception in your case against our present policy? Go ahead and talk, Stickney, and I'll post the people of this town on your selfish tactics—and you'll see where you get off!"

Stickney did not argue the matter further. He looked like a man who was disgusted because he had wasted so much time trying to get around a Tasper Britt stony "No!" He picked up his papers, stamped out, and slammed the door.

Britt shook himself, like a spiritualist medium trying to induce the trance state, and went back to his writing.

After a time a dull, thrumming sound attracted his attention. It was something like Files's dinner gong, whose summons Mr. Britt was wont to obey on the instant.

Mr. Britt was certain that it was not the gong; however, he glanced up at the clock on the wall, then he leaped out of his chair. In his amazement he rapped out, "Well, I'll be—"

That clock was reliable; it marked the hour of twelve.

Holman Day

Mr. Britt had received convincing evidence that the rhapsody of composition makes morsels of hours and gulps days in two bites.

But he had completed five stanzas. He concluded that they would do, though he had planned on five more. Glancing over his composition, he decided that it might be better to leave the matter a bit vague, just as the poem left it at the end of the fifth stanza. In the corridor that morning Vona had shown that too much precipitateness alarmed her; he might go too far in five more stanzas. The five he had completed would give her a hint—something to think of. He pondered on that point while he stuck the paper into an envelope and sealed it.

Mr. Britt hurried the rest of his movements; Files's kitchen conveniences were archaic, and the guest who was not on time got cold viands.

The lover who had begun to stir Miss Harnden's thoughts into rather unpleasant roiliness of doubts came hustling into the bank, hat and coat on.

The girl and young Vaniman were spreading their respective lunches on the center table inside the grille.

Britt called Vona to the wicket. He slipped the envelope through to her. "There's no hurry, you understand! Take your time. Read it in a slack moment—later! And"—he hesitated and gulped—"I want to see you after bank hours. If you'll step in—I'll be much obliged."

She did not assent orally, nor show especial willingness to respond to his invitation. She took the envelope and turned toward the table after Britt had left the wicket.

She walked to the window and gazed at the retreating back of Mr. Britt, and put the envelope into a velvet bag that was attached by slender chains to her girdle.

When she faced Vaniman, the young cashier was regarding her archly.

"I wonder if congratulations are in order," he suggested.

Her quick flush was followed by a pallor that gave her an appearance of anger. "I don't relish that sort of humor."

"My gracious, Vona, I wasn't trying to be especially humorous," he protested, staring at her so ingenuously that his candor could not be questioned. "I reckoned that the boss was raising your pay, and was being a bit sly about it! What else can it be?"

Then she was truly disconcerted; at a loss for a reply; ashamed of her display of emotion.

He stared hard at her. His face began to show that he was struggling with an emotion of his own. "Vona," he faltered, after a time, "I haven't any right to ask you—but do you have any—is that paper—"

He was unable to go on under the straight and strange gaze she leveled at him. She was plainly one who was taking counsel with herself. She came to a sudden decision, and drew forth the envelope and tore it open, unfolded the paper, and began to read.

When her eyes were not on him Vaniman revealed much of what a discerning person would have known to be love; love that had been pursuing its way quietly, but was now alarmed and up in arms. He narrowed his eyes and studied her face

Holman Day

while she read. But she did not reveal what she thought and he became more perturbed. She finished and looked across at him and then she narrowed her eyes to match his expression. Suddenly she leaned forward and gave him the paper. He read it, amazement lifting his eyebrows.

When he met her stare again they were moved by a common impulse—mirth; mirth that was born out of their mutual amazement and was baptized by the tears that their merriment squeezed from their eyes.

"I am not laughing at Tasper Britt," he gasped, checking his hilarity. "I would not laugh at any man who falls in love with you, Vona. I am laughing at the idea of Tasper Britt writing poetry. Let me look out of the window! Has Burkett Hill tipped over? Has the sun turned in the heavens at high noon and started back to the east?"

"What does it mean?" she asked. Her expression excused the banality of her query; her eyes told him that she knew, but her ears awaited his indorsement of her woman's conviction.

He pointed to the big calendar on the wall. "It's a valentine," he said, gravely. But the twinkle reappeared in his eyes when he added, "And valentines have always been used for prefaces in the volume of Love."

She did not reflect any of his amusement. She clasped her hands and gazed down on them, and her forehead was wrinkled with honest distress.

"Of course, you have sort of been guessing," he ventured. "All the renovating process—the way he has been tiptoeing around and squinting at you!"

She looked up suddenly and caught his gaze; his tone had

been hard, but his eyes were tender.

Then it happened!

They had been hiding their deeper feelings under the thin coating of comradeship for a long time. As in the instance of other pent-up explosives, only the right kind of a jar was needed to "trip" the mass.

The threat of a rival—even of such a preposterous rival as Tasper Britt—served as detonator in the case of Frank Vaniman, and the explosion of his emotions produced sympathetic results in the girl across the table from him. He leaped up, strode around to her and put out his arms, and she rushed into the embrace he offered.

But their mutual consolations were denied them—he was obliged to dam back his choking speech and she her blessed tears.

A depositor came stamping in.

They were calm, with their customary check on emotions, when they were free to talk after the man had gone away.

"Vona, I did not mean to speak out to you so soon," he told her. "Not but what it was in here"—he patted his breast—"and fairly boiling all the time!"

She assured him, with a timid look, that her own emotions had not been different from his.

"But I have respected your obligations," he went on, with earnest candor. "And this is the first real job I've ever had. It's best to be honest with each other."

Holman Day

She agreed fervently.

"I wish we could be just as honest with Britt. But we both know what kind of a man he is. The sentiment of 'Love, and the world well lost' is better in a book than it is in this bank just now, as matters stand with us. I have had so many hard knocks in life that I know what they mean, and I want to save you from them. Isn't it best to go along as we are for a little while, till I can see my way to get my feet placed somewhere else?"

"We must do so, Frank—for the time being." Her candor matched his. "I do need this employment for the sake of my folks. Both of us must be fair to ourselves—not silly. Only—"

Her forehead wrinkled again.

"I know, Vona! Britt's attentions! I'll take it on myself—"

"No," she broke in, with dignity. "I must make that my own affair. It can be easily settled. It's pure folly on his part. I'll make him understand it when I talk with him this afternoon."

"But I'll feel like a coward," he protested, passionately.

She put up her hand and smiled. "You're not a coward, dear! Nor am I a hypocrite. We're just two poor toilers who must do the best we can till the clouds clear away."

She went to him, and when her hands caressed his cheeks he bent down and kissed her.

Then they applied themselves to their tasks in Mr. Britt's bank.

CHAPTER IV

THE ACHE OF RAPPED KNUCKLES

Landlord Files set forth a boiled dinner that day; he skinched on corned beef and made up on cabbage; but he economized on fuel, and the cabbage was underdone.

Mr. Britt, back in his office, allowing his various affairs to be digested—his dinner, his political project, the valentine—his hopes in general—found that soggy cabbage to be a particularly tough proposition. He was not sufficiently imaginative to view his punishment by the intractable cabbage as a premonitory hint that he was destined to suffer as much in his pride as he did in his stomach. His pangs took his mind off the other affairs. He was pallid and his lips were blue when Emissary Orne came waddling into the office.

Mr. Orne, in addition to other characteristics that suggested a fowl, had a sagging dewlap, and the February nip had colored it into resemblance to a rooster's wattles. When he came in Mr. Orne's face was sagging, in general. It was a countenance that was already ridged into an expression of sympathy. When he set eyes on Britt the expression of woe was touched up with alarm. But that the alarm had to do with the personal affairs of Mr. Orne was shown when he inquired apprehensively whether Mr. Britt would settle then and there for the day's work.

The candidate looked up at the office timepiece. "It ain't three o'clock. I don't call it a day."

"You call it a day in banking. I've got the same right to call it a day in politics."

"What infernal notion is afoul of you, Orne, grabbing for my money before you report?"

"I do business with a man according to his own rules—and then he's suited, or ought to be. You collect sharp on the dot after service has been rendered. So do I." Mr. Orne was displaying more acute nervous apprehension. "And the understanding was that you'd leave it to me as your manager, and wouldn't go banging around, yourself."

Britt found the agent's manner puzzling. "I haven't been out of this office, except to go to my dinner. I haven't talked politics with anybody."

"Oh!" remarked Orne, showing relief. "Perhaps, then, it was the way the light fell on your face." He peered closely at his client. Mr. Britt's color was coming back. Orne's cryptic speeches and his haste to collect had warmed the banker's wrath. "It'll be ten dollars, as we agreed."

Britt yanked a big wallet from his breast pocket, plucked out a bill, and shoved it at Orne. The latter set the bill carefully into a big wallet of his own, "sunk" the calfskin, and buttoned up his buffalo coat.

"It does beat blazes," stated "Sniffer" Orne, "what a messed up state all politics is in since this prim'ry business has put the blinko onto caucuses and conventions. Caucuses was sensible, Mr. Britt. Needn't tell me! Voters liked to have the wear and tear off 'em. Now a voter gets into that booth and has to caucus by himself, and he's either so puffed up by importance that he thinks he's the whole party or else—"

Mr. Britt's patience was ground between the millstones of anger and indigestion. He smacked the flat of his hand on his desk. "When I want a stump speech out of you, Orne, I'll drop you a postcard and give you thirty days' notice so that you can get up a good one. You have made a short day of it, as I said, but you needn't feel called on to fill it up with a lecture." Mr. Britt continued on pompously and revealed that he placed his own favorable construction on the emissary's early return from the field. "You didn't have to go very far, hey, to find out how I stand for that nomination?"

"I went far enough so that you can depend on what I tell you."

"Go ahead and tell, then."

Mr. Orne slowly fished a quill toothpick from the pocket of his overcoat, set the end of the quill in his mouth, and "sipped" the air sibilantly, gazing over Britt's head with professional gravity. "Of course, you're the doctor in this case and are paying the money, and if you don't want any soothing facts, like I was intending to throw in free of charge and for good measure, showing how the best of politicians—"

There were ominous sounds from the direction of Britt. Orne checked his discourse, but he did not look at the candidate. "But no matter," said the agent. "That may be neither here nor there. You're the doctor, I say! When I first came in here I thought you had been disobeying my orders and had dabbled into the thing. Your face looked like you was posted."

Holman Day

"I'm paying for the goods, not for gobbling, you infernal old turkey! Come out with the facts!"

"Facts is that the whole thing is completely gooly-washed up," stated Mr. Orne, with an oracle's decisiveness.

But that declaration in Mr. Orne's political terminology did not convey much information to the candidate. Britt, thoroughly incensed by what seemed to be evasion, leaped up, twitched the toothpick from Orne's lips, and flung it away. "I've paid for the English language, and I want it straight and in short words, and not trigged by a toothpick."

"All right! You're licked before you start."

It was a bit too straight from the shoulder—that piece of news! Britt blinked as if he had received a blow between the eyes. He sat down and stared at Orne, elbows on the arms of the chair, hands limply hanging from lax wrists.

"It's this way!" Mr. Orne started, briskly, with upraised forefinger; but he shook his head and put down his hand. He turned away. "I forgot. You ordered plain facts."

"You hold on!" Britt thundered. "How do you dare to tell me that you can go out and in fifteen minutes come back with information of that sort?"

Mr. Orne glanced reproachfully from his detractor to the clock; he had not the same reasons as Mr. Britt had for finding the hours of the day fleeting. "Mr. Britt, a man doesn't need to make a hoss of himself and eat a whole head of cabbage by way of sampling it." Britt winced at the random simile. "It's the same way with me in sampling politics, being an expert. Your case, to start with, had me gy-poogled and—"

"English language, I tell you!" Britt emphasized his stand as a stickler by a tremendous thump of his fist on the desk.

Orne jabbed his finger back and forth from his breast to the direction of Britt, with the motions of the "eeny, meeny" game. "I was mistook. You was mistook. I figgered on your money. So did you. I figgered you'd go strong in politics like you had in *finance*. So did you." Mr. Orne put his hand up sidewise and sliced the air. "Nothing doing in politics, Mr. Britt! You can cash in on straight capital, but there ain't a cent in the dollar for you when you try to collect in what you 'ain't ever invested. A man don't have to be so blamed popular after he is well settled in politics; but you've got to have some real human-nature assets to get a start with. You've got to depend on given votes—not the boughten ones."

"Orne, you're rasping me mighty hard."

"You demanded facts—not hair-oil talk."

"Then the facts are—" Britt hesitated.

"Facts is that, by the usual arrangement in the legislative class of towns, Egypt had the choice this year. You won't get a vote in Egypt."

"But the men who come in here—" Again Britt halted in a sentence.

"The men who come in here and sit down at that desk and pick up a pen to sign a note have fixed on their grins before they open your door. But the men who get into a voting booth alone with God and a lead pencil, they'll jab down on to that ballot a cross for t'other candidate that'll look like a dent in a tin dipper. Somebody else might lie to you about the situation, Mr. Britt. I've done consid'able lying in politics, too. But when I'm hired by a man to deliver goods—and same has been paid for—my word can be depended on."

Britt turned around and looked into the depths of his desk, staring vacantly. His rounded shoulders suggested grief. Orne settled his wallet more firmly, pressing on the outside of the buffalo coat. His face again sagged with sympathy. "Mr. Britt, it's only like what most of us do in this life—take smiles without testing 'em with acid—take words-current for what they seem to be worth, and then we do test 'em out and—"

Britt whirled and broke on this fatuous preachment with an oath. Mr. Orne thriftily withheld further sympathy; it was plainly wasted.

"Orne, I hope it's about due to revise the New Testament again. I want to send in some footnotes for that page where Judas Iscariot is mentioned. I want a full roster of his descendants to appear; I'll furnish the voting list of this town. Get out of here and pass that word."

But a yelp from the candidate halted the departing Orne at the door. "Seeing that you have my ten dollars and are full of political information, perhaps you'll throw in free of charge who it is this town is going to send to the legislature!"

"Only one thing has been decided on so far," returned the politician. "And, having no desire to rub it in, I'll let you draw your own conclusions." Mr. Orne had the door open; he dodged out and slammed the door shut.

It was promptly opened—so promptly that Mr. Britt was fairly caught at what he was about. He was standing up, shaking both fists at the door and cursing roundly. Vona was gazing at him in alarm.

"I was waiting in the corridor, sir, till you—till your business—till Mr. Orne went away," she stammered.

"Come in!" muttered Britt, even more disconcerted than the girl.

Then he wished that he had told her to go away. He realized that he was in no mood or condition to woo; the cabbage had tortured him, but this new sort of indigestion in the very soul of him had left him without poise or courage.

He slumped down in his chair and waved a limp hand in invitation for her to take a seat near him. But she merely came and stood in the middle of the room and surveyed him with an uncompromising air of business. From the velvet toque, with just a suggestion of a coquettish cant on her brown curls, down her healthily round cheeks, a bit flushed, above the fur neckpiece that clasped her throat, Britt's fervent eyes strayed. And some of the words of the Prophet's singsong monotone echoed in the empty chambers of Britt's consciousness, "'Thou hast dove's eyes within thy locks—thy lips are like a thread of scarlet.'"

But she was aloof. She held herself rigidly erect. Her eyes were coldly inquiring. Those lips were set tightly. Mr. Britt had just been reaching out for honors, and his knuckles had been rapped cruelly. He wanted to reach out for love—and he dared not. The girl, as she stood there, was so patently among the things he was not able to possess!

She had come into his presence with expectation keenly alert, with her fears putting her into a mental posture of defense. She felt that she knew just what was going to happen, and she was assuring herself that she would be able

Holman Day

to meet the situation. But she was not prepared for what did happen. She did not understand Britt's mental state of that moment. Mr. Britt, himself, did not understand. He had never been up against conditions of that sort. He had not had time to fix his face and his mood, as he did daily before the mirror in his bedroom. He did what nobody had ever seen him do—what neither he nor the girl would have predicted one minute before as among human probabilities—he broke down and blubbered like a whipped urchin.

And after he had recovered some of his composure and was gazing up at her again, sniffling and scrubbing his reddened eyes with the bulge at the base of his thumb, knowing that he must say something by way of legitimate excuse, dreading the ridicule that a girl's gossip might bring upon him, a notion that was characteristic of Mr. Britt came to him: he grimly weighed the idea of telling her that Files's boiled dinner was the cause of his breakdown. However, in his weakness, his love flamed more hotly than ever before.

"Vona, I'm so lonesome!" he gulped.

Miss Harnden had entered behind her shield, nerved like a battling Amazon. She promptly lowered that shield and became all woman, with a woman's instinctive sympathetic understanding, but womanlike, she took the opportunity to introduce for her own defense a bit of guile with her sympathy. "I quite understand how you feel about the loss of Mrs. Britt, sir. And I'm glad because you remain so loyal to her memory."

Mr. Britt, like a man who had received a dipperful of cold water in the face, backed away from anything like a proposal at that unpropitious moment. But in all his arid nature he felt the need of some sort of consolation from a feminine source. "Vona, I've just had a terrible setback," he mourned. "There's only one other disappointment that could be any worse—and I don't dare to think of that right now."

Miss Harnden apprehensively proceeded to keep him away from the prospective disappointment, dwelling on the present, asking him solicitously what had happened.

He told her of his ambition and of what Ossian Orne had reported.

"But why should that be so very important for a man like you—to go to the legislature—Mr. Britt?"

He opened his mouth, hankering to blurt out what he had been treasuring as dreams whose realization would serve as an inducement to her. He had been picturing to himself their honeymoon at the state capital, away from the captious tongues of Egypt—how he would stalk with his handsome bride into the dining room of the capital's biggest hotel; how she would attract the eyes of jealous men, in her finery and with her jewels; how she would sit in the gallery at the State House and survey him making his bigness among the lawmakers; for some weeks he had been laboring on the composition of a speech that he intended to deliver. But her second dash of cold water kept him from the disclosure of his feelings. He went on so far as to ask her if she did not think a session at the state capital would be interesting.

"I have never thought anything about such a matter, of course, Mr. Britt, being only a girl and not a politician."

"But women who are there get into high society and wear fine clothes and have a grand time, Vona."

"It must be a tedious life," she replied, indifferently.

"Wouldn't you like to try it?" Now that he could not offer her the grand inducement he had planned as an essential part of his campaign of love he sought consolation in her assurance that the prospect did not tempt her. His hopes revived. He was reflecting that his money could buy railroad tickets, even if he had not the popularity with which to win votes. She shook her head promptly when he asked the question, and he went on with his new idea. "I suppose what a girl really enjoys is to see the world, after she has been penned up all her life in a town like this."

"I don't waste my time in foolish longings, Mr. Britt. In fact, I have no time to waste on anything." She gave him a bit of a smile. "In that connection I'll confess that I must hurry home and help mother with some sewing. Did you want anything especial of me?" Her smile had vanished, and in her tone there was a clink of the metallic that was as subtly suggestive of "On guard" as the click of a trigger.

Mr. Britt had planned upon a radiant disclosing of his projects—expecting to be spurred in his advances by the assurance of what he could offer her as the consort of a legislator—as high an honor as his narrow vision could compass. She had found him cursing, had kept him at bay, and he had already had evidence of the danger of precipitateness in her case. And his tears made him feel foolish. His ardor had been wet down; it took a back seat. His natural good judgment was again boss of the situation.

"I had something on my mind—but it can wait till you're in less of a hurry, Vona. Never neglect a mother. That's my attitude toward women. I'm always considerate where they're concerned. It's my nature. I hope you'll hold that in mind."

"Yes, Mr. Britt." She turned and hurried to the door, getting away from a fire that was showing signs of breaking out of its smoldering brands once more.

Britt recovered some of his courage when her back was turned. "You haven't said anything about those verses," he stammered.

"I think it's a beautiful way of putting aside your business cares for a time. I'm taking them home to read to mother."

He marched to the window and watched her as long as she was in sight.

Then he glowered on such of the Egyptians as passed to and fro along the street on their affairs. He muttered, spicing his comments with profanity. The girl's disclaimer of personal interest in Britt's ambitions did not soften his rancorous determination to make the voters of Egypt suffer for the stand they had taken—suffer to the bitter limit to which unrelenting persecution could drive them. He gritted his teeth and raved aloud. "From now on! From now on! Anything short of murder to show 'em! And as for that girl—if there's somebody—"

Britt stopped short of what that rival might expect, but his expression indicated that the matter was of even more moment than his affair with the voters of the town.

Holman Day

CHAPTER V

"AND PHARAOH'S HEART WAS HARDENED"

When Vona left him that afternoon, Vaniman paced the floor.

She had gone bravely to her meeting with Britt, bearing Frank's kiss on her cheek—a caress of encouragement when he had walked with her to the door in order to lock it after her.

It was not worry that caused him to tramp to and fro, frowning. Vona's demeanor of self-reliance had helped his feelings a great deal. But the corollary of devoted love is chivalry, and he felt that he was allowing her to do something that belonged to him to so, somehow. The policy which they had so sanely discussed did not seem to be such a comfortable course when he was alone, wondering what was going on across the corridor.

At last the sound of a door and the click of her heels signaled the end of the interview. He hoped that she would come back into the bank, making an excuse of something forgotten, in order to give him a soothing bulletin. He ran to the door and opened it. But the slam of the outside door informed him that she had gone on her way. Her prompt departure indicated that she was consistently pursuing the level-headed policy they had adopted; but the young man, impatient and wondering, was wishing she had taken a change, for once, even to the prejudice of policy. He shut his door and hurried to the window.

Though two men were watching her going-away, and though she must have been conscious of the fact, she did not turn her head to glance behind her.

At any rate, the thing was over, whatever had happened, the cashier reflected with relief. Nevertheless, curiosity was nagging at him; he felt an impulse to go in and inspect the condition of Tasper Britt by way of securing a hint.

Vaniman, however, shook his head and dropped into the routine of his duties. The ruts of life in Egypt, especially in the winter, were deep ones. The cashier had become contented with his little circle of occupation and recreation.

He carried the books into the vault. He wound the clock that controlled the mechanism of bolts and bars, and pushed the big outer door shut and made certain that it was secure.

Having finished as cashier, he became janitor.

Egypt had no electric lights. Vaniman trimmed the kerosene reflector lamp and set it on the table so that the front of the safe would be illuminated for the benefit of the village's night watchman.

Then he put on his cap and overcoat and locked the grille door and the bank door after he had passed each portal. His last chore of the day was always a trip into the basement to make sure that the dying fire in the wood furnace was carefully closed in for the night.

The basement stairs led from the rear of the corridor. When Vaniman returned up the stairs he had settled on a small matter of business which would serve as a valid excuse for entering the presence of President Britt. But he did not need to employ the excuse. Britt stood in his open door and called to the cashier and walked back to his chair, leaving Vaniman to follow, and the employee obeyed the summons with alacrity; he was consumed with desire to get a line on the situation that had been troubling him.

An observer would have called the contest of mutual inspection a fifty-fifty break—perhaps with a shade in favor of Britt, for the usurer's face was like leather and his goggling marbles of eyes under the lids that resembled little tents did not flicker.

"What can I do for you?" Britt demanded, and the query made for the young man's discomposure.

"Why, you called me in, sir!"

"Uh-huh!" the president admitted, "but somehow I had the impression that you said you wanted to see me after the bank closed." He was taking account of stock of Vaniman's personality, his eyes going up and down the stalwart figure and dwelling finally and persistently on the young man's hair; it was copper-bronze in hue, it had an attractive wave, there was plenty of it, and it seemed to be very firmly rooted.

"I don't remember that I mentioned it, Mr. Britt, but I do have an errand with you."

"All right! What is it?" Mr. Britt was not revealing any emotions that Vaniman found illuminating in regard to his particular quest.

"I am being tongue-lashed terribly through the wicket. Men won't believe that I'm obeying the orders of you and the board when accommodation is refused. Won't you take the matter off my hands—let me refer all to you?"

"I don't keep a dog and do my own barking," rasped the president. He brought his eyes down from the young man's hair and noted that Vaniman stiffened and was displaying resentment.

"That's only a Yankee motto—you needn't take it as personal, Vaniman. I have turned over to you the running of the bank. I say to all that you're running it. You ought to feel pretty well set up!"

"I obey your orders, sir," returned the cashier, not warming.

"That's all right for an understanding between us two. But I let the public think you're the whole thing. I tell 'em I've got full confidence in you. You don't want the public to think you're only a rubber stamp, do you?"

"The general opinion right now seems to be that I'm either a first-class liar or Shylock sentenced to a second term on earth," retorted Vaniman, with bitterness.

There was a long silence in the room, where the early dusk was deepening. The two men regarded each other with expressions that did not soften.

After a time Britt turned to his desk, unlocked a compartment, and produced a letter, which he unfolded slowly, again staring hard at the cashier.

"Speaking of being sentenced!" There was something ominous in his drawl. "You told me a whole lot about yourself, Vaniman, when I was talking of hiring you. But there was one important thing you didn't mention—mighty important, seeing that you wanted a job as boss of a bank." He tapped the open letter. "I've had this letter for a good many weeks, not saying anything about it to you or anybody else. I'm not sure just why I'm saying anything now."

Vaniman flushed. His face worked with emotion. He put up his hand and started to speak, but Britt put up a more compelling hand and went on. "I reckon I'm bringing this matter up so that you'll know just where you stand—so that you'll mind your eye and look out for my interests in every way from now on—so that—" He hesitated a moment. His eyes flamed. "So that you'll know your place! That's it! Know your place—and be mighty careful how you go against me in anything—anything where I'm interested." Britt had whipped himself into anger. That anger, fanned by a flame of jealousy after it had been touched off by his inspection of youth and good looks, had carried Mr. Britt far. He shook the letter at the young man. "There's a reliable name signed to this letter; he is a friend of mine, one of the big financiers in the city, and this was in the way of friendly warning."

"I understand, Mr. Britt." The cashier had recovered his self-possession. "You are warned that my father was sentenced to the penitentiary for embezzlement. No, I did not mention that to you. It concerned a man who is dead. It has nothing to do with my honesty."

"Well, there's another motto about 'blood will tell,'" sneered Britt.

Vaniman stepped forward, honestly indignant, manfully resolute. "Let me tell you, sir, that the letter you hold there— no matter who wrote it—concerns a *good* man who is dead.

He was the scapegoat of one of those big financiers." Vaniman's lip curled. "My father was railroaded to jail on a track greased with lies—and died because the heart had been ripped out of him and—"

"Hold on! It won't get us anywhere to try that case all over, Vaniman. Let the letter stand as it is—it was probably meant in the right spirit. But I didn't write it. You and I better not fight over it. I've shown, by laying it away and saying nothing, that I have a decent nature in me. I hope I'll never have any need to take it out of this desk again." He turned and shoved the paper back and locked the compartment.

"I think it is best for me to resign, Mr. Britt."

"Don't be a fool, young man. Now that this thing is off our minds there's a better understanding between us than ever. I don't think—I hope"—he surveyed Vaniman with leisure in which there was the suggestion of a threat—"I'll never have any occasion to take that letter out again. Er—ah—" Britt joggled a watch charm and inquired, casually, "Would you plan on getting married if I boost your wages a little?"

In spite of an effort to control himself under Britt's basilisk stare, Vaniman showed how much the query had jumped him.

"Of course, a chap like you has had his sweetheart down in the city," pursued the inquisitor when the young man failed to answer. "Must be one there now."

"I have no sweetheart in the city, Mr. Britt."

Then there was a longer silence in the room. The cashier was not enduring inspection with an air that did credit to his promise to keep a secret. Britt had made a breach in the wall

Holman Day

of Vaniman's mental defense by the means of that letter and its implied accusation; Britt was taking advantage of that breach. Right then the young man was in a mood that would have prompted him to fling the truth and his defiance at Britt if the latter had kept on to the logical conclusion of his interrogation and had asked whether there was a sweetheart elsewhere; Vaniman had the feeling that by denying his love at that moment—to that man of all others—he would be dealing insult to Vona Harnden, as well as taking from her the protection that his affection gave her.

The attention of Britt was diverted from the quarry he was pursuing.

Outside Britt Block, Prophet Elias raised his voice in his regular "vesper service." It was his practice, on his way to Usial Britt's cottage from his daily domiciliary visits, to halt in front of the bank and deliver a few texts. The first one— and the two men in the office listened—was of the general tenor of those addressed to "Pharaoh." Said the Prophet, in resounding tones, "'As a roaring lion and a ranging bear, so is a wicked ruler over the poor people.'"

"Vaniman, go out and tell that old hoot owl to move on! I'm in a dangerous frame of mind to-day." Britt's lips were pulled tightly against his yellow teeth.

The Prophet's next deliverance was more concretely to the point—indicating that the exhorter was not so much wrapped up in religion that he had no ear out for the political news current in Egypt that day, "'Pride goeth before destruction, and an haughty spirit before a fall.'"

There was a fireplace in the office and Britt leaped to it and grabbed a poker. The cashier was moved to interfere, urged by two compelling motives. He wanted to get away from his own dangerous situation of the moment in that office—and he wanted to protect the old man outside from assault. "I'll attend to him, sir!" But he halted at the door and turned. "Mr. Britt, our talk has driven an important matter from my mind. The men who bellow at me through the wicket have considerable to say about our hoarding specie. It makes me uneasy to have that sort of gossip going the rounds."

"We'll have the money out of here in a short time, Vaniman, as I have told you. That broker says that foreign money is going lower yet—and seeing that we've taken all this trouble to get the hard cash ready for the deal, we may as well make the clean-up as big as we can."

"Don't you think we'd better hire a couple of good men with rifles and put 'em in the bank nights, sir?"

President Britt declared with scorn that the expense was not necessary, that putting guards in the bank would only start more talk, and that it also would be essential to hire old Ike Jones to sit in front of the vault and play all night on his trombone to keep awake any two men picked from Egypt. While Britt was expressing his opinion of inefficiency and expense, the Prophet was furnishing this obbligato outside, "'He that by usury and unjust gain increaseth his substance, he shall gather it for him that will pity the poor.'"

Vaniman closed the door on Britt's objurgations.

The young man did not find it necessary to prevail upon the Prophet to give over his discourse. As soon as the emissary appeared Elias folded his ample umbrella, tucked it under his arm, gave Vaniman a friendly greeting, and winked at him. The twilight dimmed the seamed face and the young man wondered whether he had been mistaken about the sly suggestiveness of that wink.

"Joseph, how doth Pharaoh rest on his throne? Doth he sit easy?"

Always in their brief but good-natured interviews the evangelist called the young man "Joseph." Elias took Vaniman's arm and walked along with him.

"I'm afraid, Prophet Elias, that you'll provoke Mr. Britt too far. Take my advice. Keep away from him for a time."

"'There be three things which are too wonderful for me, yeah, four which I know not: the way of an eagle in the air, the way of a serpent upon a rock, the way of a ship in the midst of the sea, and the way of a man with a maid,'" said the Prophet, placidly. "Furthermore, 'The proud have digged pits for me.' Joseph, the pitfalls encompass thee."

Vaniman refrained from making a reply; the Prophet was displaying an embarrassing amount of sapience as to conditions.

In front of Usial Britt's cot they halted and the eccentric leaned close to Vaniman's ear. "Joseph, my son, keep thine eye peeled." He released the cashier's arm and strode to the door of Usial's house.

Vaniman, delaying his departure, noted that the door did not give way when the Prophet wrenched at the knob. The guest banged his fist against a panel. "Let it be opened unto me!" he shouted.

His voice served as his guaranty; Usial Britt opened the door and slammed it shut so suddenly after the Prophet had entered that it was necessary to reopen the portal and release the tail of Elias's robe.

CHAPTER VI

"THE HORNET" GOES TO PRESS

Vaniman did not go on his way at once, though, by his daily routine, he was headed toward his bit of recreation which cheered the end of his day of occupation. Every afternoon he dropped in at the office of Notary Amos Hexter—"Squire" Hexter, the folks of Egypt called him—and played euchre with the amiable old chap. After the euchre, the Squire and Frank trudged over to the Hexter home; the cashier boarded with the Squire and his wife, Xoa.

In his general uneasiness, in his hankering for any sort of information that would help his affairs, the young man was tempted to follow the provocative Elias and pin him down to something definite; the flashes of shrewd sanity in the fanatic's mouthings had encouraged Frank to believe that the Prophet was not quite as much of an ingenuous lunatic as his gab and garb suggested.

Right away, curiosity of another sort added its impulse.

Usial's windows were uncurtained, though the grime on them helped to conceal activities within by a sort of ground-glass effect. But Vaniman could see well enough to understand what was going on. Every once in a while a canvas flap came over in a half circle across Vaniman's line of vision through one of the windows. Then a hairy arm turned a crank briskly; a moment later the arm pulled at a horizontal bar with vigor.

It was plain that Usial Britt was printing.

Vaniman had seen the shoemaker's printing equipment in common with everybody else who dropped into the shop. There were a few cases of worn type; there was a venerable Washington hand press. Vaniman had even been down on his knees, by Usial's invitation, and had peered up at the under surface of the imposing stone.

When Tasper Britt wanted a burial lot in the Egypt cemetery of a size sufficient to set off his statue in good shape, he secured a hillock in which some of the patriarchs of the pioneers had been interred. There was no known descendants to say him nay. A fallen slate slab that had been long concealed in the tangled grass was tossed over the cemetery fence by the men who cleared up the hillock. Usial Britt considered the slab a legitimate find and with it replaced a marble imposing stone that had become gouged and cracked. Vaniman had found the inscription interesting when he knelt and peered up:

Here Lies the Body of THOSPIT WAGG,
In Politics a Whig.
By Occupation a Cooper in a Hoop-pole Town.
Now Food for Worms.
Here I Lie, Like an Old Rum Puncheon,
Marked, Numbered and Shooked,
To be Raised at Last and Finished by the Hand of My Maker.

As Egypt knew, Usial Britt did not print for profit. He accepted no pay of any sort for the product of his press.

When the spirit moved, or he felt that the occasion demanded comment in print, he "stuck" the worn type, composing directly from the case without first putting his thoughts on paper, and printed and issued a sheet which he titled *The Hornet*. Sometimes *The Hornet* buzzed blandly—more often it stung savagely.

Vaniman obeyed his impulse; he went to the door and knocked. He had always found Usial Britt in a sociable mood.

"Who is it?" inquired the shoemaker.

"Vaniman of the bank."

"Leave your job, whatever it is, on the threshold, sir."

"I am not bringing you any work, Mr. Britt."

"Then kindly pass on; I'm in executive session, sir."

The grumble of the cogs and the squeak of the press went on.

So did Vaniman, after he had waited at the door for a few moments.

Squire Hexter had a corner of his table cleaned of paper litter, in readiness for the euchre game.

He was tilted back in his chair, smoking his blackened T. D. pipe, and a swinging boot was scraping to and fro along the spine of a fuzzy old dog whose head was meditatively lowered while he enjoyed the scratching. The Squire called the old dog "Eli"; that name gave Hexter a frequent opportunity to turn his little joke about having owned another dog that he called "Uli" and presented to a brother

Holman Day

lawyer as an appropriate gift.

The Squire had little dabs of whiskers on his cheeks like fluffs of cotton batting, and his wide mouth linked those dabs when he smiled.

He came forward promptly in his chair, slapped his palm on the waiting pack of cards, and cut for the deal while Vaniman was throwing off his coat.

"Judging by signs, as I came past Britt's shop, *The Hornet* is getting ready to buzz again," said the cashier.

"Aye! I reckoned as much. I have looked across there from time to time to-day and have seen customers knocking in vain on the door. It's your deal, boy!"

Vaniman shuffled obediently.

"And there was a run-in this morning between your boss and his brother," observed the Squire, scratching a match. "And Eli, here, called my attention to the fact that two sun dogs, strangers to him, were chasing along with the sun all the forenoon. Signs of trouble, boy—sure signs!" He sorted his cards. It was more of the Squire's regular line of humor to ascribe to Eli various sorts of comment and counsel.

"How crazy do you think Prophet Elias is?" inquired the young man, avoiding further reference to his employer.

"After listening many times to the testimony of expert alienists in court trials I have come to the conclusion that all the folks in the world are crazy, son, or else nobody is ever crazy. I don't think I'll express any opinion on the Prophet. I might find myself qualifying as an alienist expert. I'd hate to!"

After that mild rebuff Vaniman gave all his mind to the game—for when the Squire played euchre he wanted to attend strictly to the business in hand. And in the span of time between dusk and supper the two were rarely interrupted.

But on this afternoon they were out of luck.

Men came tramping up the screaking outside stairs that conducted to the office; the Squire had a room over Ward's general store.

The men were led into the office by Isaac Jones—"Gid-dap Ike," he was named—the driver of the mail stage between Egypt and the railroad at Levant.

For a moment Squire Hexter looked really alarmed. There were half a dozen men in the party and he was not accustomed to irruptions of numbers. Then his greeting smile linked his whisker tufts. Mr. Jones and his party pulled off their hats and by their demeanor of awkward dignity stood convicted as being members of a delegation formally presenting themselves.

"Hullo, boys! Have chairs. Excuse the momentary hesitation. I was afraid you had come after me with a soaped rope."

"I reckon we won't set," stated Mr. Jones. "And we'll be straight and to the point, seeing that a game is on. Squire Hexter, me and these gents represent the voters of Egypt. We ask you to accept the nomination to the legislature from this town for next session. So say I."

"So say we all!" chorused the other men.

The Squire set the thumb and forefinger of each hand into a

whisker fluff and twisted a couple of spills, squinting at them. "The compliment is esteemed, boys. But the previousness is perplexing. This is February, and the primaries are not till June."

"Squire Hexter, it ain't too early to show a man in this town where he gets off. That man is Tasper Britt. He has had ten dollars' worth of telling to-day by 'Sniffer' Orne. But telling ain't showing. What do you say?"

The Squire gave Jones a whimsical wink and indicated the attentive Vaniman with a jab of the thumb. "S-s-sh! Look out, or the rate of interest will go up."

Jones and his associates scowled at the cashier, and Vaniman understood with added bitterness the extent of his vicarious atonement as Britt's mouthpiece at the wicket of the bank.

"The interest-payers of this town have been well dreened. But the voters—the *voters*, understand, still have assets. The voters have got to the point where they ain't afraid of Tasper Britt. The cashier of his bank can so report to him, if the said cashier so chooses—and, as cashier, probably will."

"The cashier will attend strictly and exclusively to his bank duties, and to nothing else," declared Vaniman, with heat.

"Hope you're enjoying 'em, such as they are of late," Jones retorted. "But once again, what say, Squire Hexter?"

"Boys, you'd better get somebody else to sandpaper Tasper Britt with. I'm not gritty enough."

"I'll come across with our full idea, Squire. It ain't simply to sandpaper Britt with that we want you to go. But we need some kind of legislation to help this town out of the hole. We don't know where we are. We can't raise money to pay state taxes, and we ain't getting our school money from the state, nor any share of the roads appropriation, nor—"

"I know, Ike," broke in the Squire, not requiring any legal posting from a layman. "But it's the lobbyist, instead of the legislator, who really counts at the state capital. I've been planning to do a little lobbying at the next session. I'll tell you now that I'll go, and, by hooking a clean collar around each ankle under my socks, I'll be prepared for a two weeks' stay. Send somebody else to work for the state and I'll go and work for Egypt."

"The voters want you," Jones insisted.

The Squire rapped his toe against the old dog at his feet. "What say, Eli?"

"Wuff!" the dog replied, emphatically.

"Can't go as a legislator, boys! Eli says 'No.'"

"This ain't no time for joking," growled the spokesman.

"Certainly not!" The Squire snapped back his retort briskly. He was serious. "I agree with you that this poor old town needs help and a hearing. But when I go to the State House I propose to wear out shoe leather instead of pants cloth. If you must rasp Britt, go get a real file!"

"Who in the blazes can we get?" demanded Jones, helplessly.

The Squire laid down the hand of cards which he had just picked up, thus signaling the end of the interview, impatiently motioning to Vaniman to play; then the notary narrowed his eyes and pondered.

The silence was broken by more screaking of the outside stairs.

Prophet Elias stalked into the office. He carried limp, damp sheets across a forearm—papers that had been well wet down in order to take impressions from the Washington press. The men in the room waited for one of his sonorous promulgations of biblical truth. But he said no word, and his silence was more impressive because it was unwonted. He marched straight to the Squire and gave him one of the sheets. Then the Prophet turned and strode toward the door. Jones put out his hand, asking for one of the papers. Elias shook his head. "Yon scribe has a voice. Let him read aloud. I have but few papers—they must be spent thriftily." He passed on and went out.

"One of the city newspapers ought to hire him for a newsboy," remarked Mr. Jones, acridly. "He could scare up a big circulation."

The only light in the dim room was afforded by the big lamp at the Squire's elbow. He spread the sheet on the table in the lamp's circle of radiance. "Boys, *The Hornet* is out and it looks as if it has a barb in its stinger," he stated, and then paused while he fixed his spectacles upon his nose.

Vaniman, sitting close by, felt that a glance at a public sheet was not invading privacy.

A smutted heading in wood type was smeared across the top of the page. It counseled:

VOTE FOR BRITT. GIVE PHARAOH HIS KINGLY CROWN

There was a broad, blank space in one of the upper corners

of the sheet. Under the space was this explanation:

Portrait of Tasper Britt, with his latest improvements. But, on second thought, out of regard for the feelings of our readers, we omit the portrait.

The Squire, getting control of emotions which the observing Jones and his associates noted with rising interest, demurely explained to them the layout of the page after he had carefully inspected the sheet.

Then Squire Hexter began to read aloud, in a tone whose twist of satire gave the text its full flavor:

"We hasten to proclaim in the land of Egypt that Pharaoh Britt has reached for the scepter, though he had not loosed his grip on the gouge. You will know him here and hereafter by his everlasting grip on the gouge. He will take that gouge to Tophet with him. Then it will be heated red-hot and he will prance around hell astraddle of it. But in the meantime he is hot after the honors of this world. Give him his crown, say we. He has prepared a nice, new hair mattress on his brow where the diadem will rest easy. Under his coat of arms—to wit, a yellow he-goat rampant in a field of purple thistles—let him write the word 'Victory.'"

The men in that room were Yankees, with a sense of humor as keen as a new bush scythe.

The Squire sat back and wiped his spectacles and beamed on their laughter. Then he read on down the column, through the biting satire to the bitter end, having an audience whose hilarity would have delighted a vaudeville performer's soul.

Therefore, it was with inspired unction that the reader delivered the "tag lines" of the screed.

Holman Day

"We confess that we have a selfish purpose in paying this affectionate, brotherly tribute to Pharaoh. When he has deigned to refer to us in the past he has called us 'Useless' Britt. Now, if this tribute has the effect that we devoutly hope for, Pharaoh may be of a mind to give us back our right name. We ask nothing else in the way of recompense."

The Squire folded the paper carefully and put it away in his breast pocket with the manner of one caching a treasure. "Boys, what are you waiting for?" he inquired, with an affectation of surprise.

Their wide grins narrowed into the creases of wonderment of their own.

Hexter patted his breast where he had stowed away the paper. "Egypt has a literary light, a journalist who wields a pen of power, a shoemaker philosopher. And modest—not grasping! See how little he asks for himself. Why not give him a real present? Why not—"

Spokesman Jones perceived what the counsel was aiming at and ecstatically shouted, "Gid-dap!"

"Why not use real sandpaper?" urged the squire, with innocent mildness.

Jones whirled and drove his delegation ahead of him from the room, both hands upraised, fingers and thumbs snapping loud cracks as if he were urging his horses up Burkett Hill with snapping whip. The men went tramping down the outside stairs, bellowing the first honest-to-goodness laughter that Egypt had heard for many a day.

Squire Hexter leaped up and grabbed his hat and coat from their hooks. "Come on, boy! It looks as if there's going to be a nominating bee at *The Hornet* office—and we mustn't miss any of the buzzing."

The two followed close on the heels of the noisy delegation.

Usial Britt opened his door and stood in the frame of light after Jones had halted his clamorous crowd. The amateur publicist rolled his inky hands in his apron and showed doubt that was growing into alarm.

"Hold your nippety pucket, Usial," counseled Hexter, calling over the heads of the men. "The boys had me guessing, too, a few minutes ago. But this isn't a lynching bee."

However, while the crowd laughed and others came hastening to the scene, and while Spokesman Jones was trying to make himself heard above the uproar, an element was added which seemed to discount the Squire's reassuring words.

Tasper Britt rushed out from Files's tavern and stood on the porch. He had one of the papers in his hand. He ripped the paper to tatters and strewed about him the bits and stamped on the litter. He shrieked profanity. Then he leaped off the porch.

In the tavern yard was "Gid-dap" Jones's stage pung. Britt yanked the big whip from its socket and bounced across the street, untangling the lash.

"No, you don't!" bellowed Jones, getting in the way and making grabs at the whip. "Not with my own private persuader! Get aholt of him, men! Down him. Don't let him whale the representative we're going to send from the town of Egypt!"

That declared hint of what was afoot put the last touch on

Tasper Britt's fury. He fought savagely to force his way through the men.

The voice of Usial checked the melee. He shouted with a compelling quality in his tone. As the man on whom they proposed to bestow the town's highest honor, he had already acquired new authority. The men loosed Tasper Britt.

"This is between brothers," said Usial. He had stepped from his doorway. He stood alone. "What outsider dares to interfere?"

Tasper Britt employed his freedom promptly and brutally; he leaped along the avenue the men left for him and began to lash Usial with the whip. The stolid townsfolk of Egypt stood in their tracks.

"That's the best way—let 'em fight it out," counseled Spokesman Jones. "Tasp Britt will get his, and it'll be in the family!"

But Usial merely tossed his big apron over his head and crouched and took the lashing.

"Isn't somebody going to stop that?" Vaniman demanded.

Nobody moved. Egypt had its own ideas about interference in family matters, it seemed, and had been tartly reminded of those ideas by Usial Britt himself.

But Vaniman was an outlander. He saw his employer disgracing himself; he beheld an unresisting victim cruelly maltreated.

The young man jumped on Tasper Britt and tried to hold his arms. When Britt whirled and broke loose by the twist of his quick turn and struck the cashier with the whip, Vaniman wrested away the weapon, using all his vigorous strength, and threw it far. Then he seized the frothing assailant and forced him back toward the tavern. "Mr. Britt, remember what you are—the president of our bank—a prominent man—" Vaniman gasped, protesting. "When you're yourself you'll thank me!"

But there was no sign of gratitude in Britt's countenance just then. His crazed rage was shifted to this presumptuous person who had interfered and was manhandling him; at that moment the liveliest emotion in Britt was the mordant jealousy that he had been trying to stifle. It awoke and raged, finding real excuse for the venting of its rancor on the man who had made him jealous.

"You damnation spawn of a jailbird—"

The young man had a rancor of his own that he had been holding in leash ever since he had sent Vona to fight her own battle, with his kiss on her cheek. He broke off that vitriolic taunt by dealing Britt an open-handed slap across the mouth, a blow of such force that the man went reeling backward. And when Britt beheld Vaniman's face, as the young man came resolutely along, the magnate of Egypt kept going backward of his own accord, flapping hands of protest. "Vaniman, here and now I discharge you from the bank."

"Mr. Britt, that's a matter for the vote of the directors—and I'll wait to hear from them."

Vaniman whirled from Britt, for the impulse was in him to smash his doubled fist into that hateful visage; his palm still itched; the open-handed buffet had not satisfied the tingling nerves of that hand.

Usial Britt had not hurried about raising himself from his crouching position. He was standing with his apron over his head and faced the citizens. He was smiling—an irradiating, genial, triumphant sort of smile! One might readily have taken him for the victor in a contest!

Spokesman Jones gulped. "We came—we was intending—but this hoop-te-doo—"

Usial beamed blandly and helped out Mr. Jones's efforts to express his intentions. "Yes, Brother Jones, it was quite a shower while it lasted. What were you intending to do?"

"Ask you to take the nomination for the legislature."

The crowd indorsed the request with *viva-voce* enthusiasm.

"I certainly will. I am pleased and proud," declared Usial.

Through the circle of men came Prophet Elias, his robe trailing on his heels. He stood beside Usial and faced the bystanders. He proclaimed, "'Nay, in all these things we are more than conquerors, through Him that loved us.'"

Somebody handed to Mr. Jones his whip and he inspected it carefully. "Of course, there's more than one way of fighting a man—and I have my own notions—but maybe I'm wrong."

"Eli has observed many a dog-fight," Squire Hexter remarked; "and, so far as he sees, the attacking dog doesn't get much out of the fracas except a ripped ear and a raw reputation in the neighborhood." He marched to Vaniman, took that perturbed young man by the arm, and said that Xoa would be waiting supper.

CHAPTER VII

SQUARED OFF AND ALL SET

As Squire Hexter and Vaniman walked on together the notary deferred comment on the recent happenings, as if he hoped that the cashier would open up on the topic. But Frank was grimly silent.

Therefore the Squire broke the ice. "What kind of a partner does Tasp Britt make in a polka, son? I saw you and him going at it pretty briskly."

"I stopped him from making a fool of himself."

"Quite a contract, boy! Quite a contract! And when you got to the matter of his purple whiskers and his lamp-mat hair—"

"I said nothing to Mr. Britt on such a ridiculous topic—certainly not, sir!"

"And yet you brag that you have stopped him from making a fool of himself," purred the Squire. "Tut! Tut! He's worse than ever. I heard him tell you that you're discharged from the bank."

"Yes, I heard him, too!"

"I didn't catch what you answered back."

"I told him I should ask the directors to decide that matter."

"Quite right! You're sure of one vote for your side—that's mine! And I think that when President Britt considers that he has no other charge against you except that you took away a horsewhip that he was using not wisely but too well—"

"I struck him across the mouth."

"Oh, I missed that," said the Squire, regretfully. "Why the pat?"

"I could not express my feelings in any other way. As to what those feelings were and why he stirred them, I'll have to ask you to excuse me, Squire Hexter. If I were going to stay in the bank I would explain the matter to you and to the directors. But I'm going to resign. Under these conditions, nobody has the right to tear the heart out of me and stick it up for a topic of conversation."

The Squire glanced sideways at the convulsed face of the cashier and opened his eyes wide; but he promptly hid his wonderment and checked an exclamation that sounded like a question. "I reckon all of us better wait till morning, son— Tasper and you and I and all the rest." He looked up at the bright stars in a hard sky. "A snappy night like this will cool things off considerable."

"I'll wait till morning, sir! Then I propose to resign," Frank insisted.

"Don't say anything like that in front of Xoa," pleaded Squire Hexter. "I don't ever want to see again on her face the look she wore when she followed our own Frank to the cemetery;

now that she has sort of adopted you, boy, I'm afraid she'll have the same look if she had to follow you to Ike Jones's stage."

The supper was waiting, as the Squire had predicted; but he took no chances on sitting at table at once and having her keen woman's eyes survey Vaniman's somber face; he feared that her solicitude would open up a dangerous topic.

"Leave your biscuits in for a few minutes, Mother," the Squire urged. "Let's have some literature for an appetizer."

So he sat down and read the brotherly tribute in the new issue of *The Hornet*, and Xoa's eyes glistened behind her spectacles, though she decorously deplored the heat of the sting dealt by Usial. Frank, watching her efforts to hide mirth and display womanly concern at this distressing affair between brothers, forgot some of his own troubles in his amusement. Therefore the Squire's tactics were successful, and the talk at the supper table over the hot biscuits and the cold chicken and the damson preserves was concerned merely with the characters of the brothers Britt. Squire Hexter did mention, casually, that Frank had succeeded in inducing Tasper to stop whipping Usial. Xoa reached and patted the young man's arm and blessed him with her eyes.

Frank, as usual, helped Xoa to clear away the supper things. Early in his stay he had been obliged to beg for permission to do it, and she had consented at last when he pleaded that it made him feel less like a boarder in the Hexter home.

While she finished her work in the kitchen Vaniman sat with the Squire in front of the fireplace and smoked his pipe, but not with his customary comfort; the tobacco seemed to be as bitter as his ponderings; he was trying to stiffen his resolution to go away from Egypt.

Squire Hexter chatted. It was hard to keep off the Britt affair, but the notary tactfully kept away from the sore center of it.

"It has been going on a long time—the trouble between 'em, son. For two men who look alike outside, they're about as different inside as any two I've ever known. Tasper has been all for grab! He grabbed away Usial's share of the home place and then he grabbed Mehitable Dole while she was keeping company with Usial. I suppose Hittie reckoned there was no choice in outside looks, but saw considerable inducement in the home place. Plenty of other women for Usial! Yes! But I can't help thinking that I might be keeping bach hall in my law office if I hadn't got hold of Xoa in my young days. So there's Usial! Right in his rut because he's the kind that stays in a rut. Pegs shoes days and reads books nights. No telling how the legislature may develop him. Glad he's going."

The Squire rapped out his pipe ashes against an andiron. His posture gave him an opportunity to say what he said next without meeting Vaniman's gaze. "Vona Harnden was a mighty smart girl when she was teaching school. I was superintendent and had a chance to know. Does she take hold well in the bank?"

Vaniman had hard work to make his affirmative sound casual.

"Have you met Joe, her father, since you've been in town?"

"No, sir."

"Not surprising, and no great loss. Joe is on the jump a lot—geniusing around the country. Joe's a real genius."

The young man looked straight into the fire and returned no

comment. He knew well the dry quality of Hexter's satirical humor and perceived that the notary was indulging in that humor.

"Yes, Joe Harnden is quite an operator, son. Jumps, as I have said. A good optimist. Jumps up so high every day that he can see over all the bothersome hills into the Promised Land of Plenty. Only trouble is that Joe's jumping apparatus is so geared that he only jumps straight up and lands back in the same place. Now, if only he could jump ahead."

Xoa had come in from the kitchen and was setting out a small table on which the pachisi board was ready for the evening's regular recreation. She broke in with protest. "Amos, you shouldn't make fun of the neighbors!"

"I'm complimenting Joe Harnden," the Squire went on, with serenity. "I'm saying that when he uses that inventive genius of his on his own jumping gear he'll leap ahead and make good. For instance, son, here's an example. Joe invented an anti-stagger shoe—a star-shaped shoe—to be let out at saloons and city clubs like they lend umbrellas for a fee— and then the reformers went and passed that prohibition law. Always a little behind with a grand notion—that's the trouble with Joe!"

"Amos, you're making up that yarn about a shoe!" declared Xoa.

"Well, if it wasn't an anti-stagger shoe, it was—oh— something," insisted the Squire. "At any rate, Joe was in my office to-day. He's home again. He's all cheered up. He is taking town gossip for face value." The notary looked away from Vaniman and gave his wife an ingenuous glance. "Of course, I don't need to remind you, Xoa, speaking of gossip, that the folks will have it that Tasp Britt has put on that war paint so as to go on the trail of a Number Two. And Joe says that, in picking Vona, Britt has picked right. Joe's a genius in inventing. I'm expecting that he'll now invent a lie about himself or Britt or somebody else to make that girl either sorry enough or mad enough to carry out what gossip is predicting."

Xoa had seated herself at the small table and was vigorously rattling the dice in one of the boxes by way of a hint to the laggard menfolks. "Women have a soft side, and men come up on that side and take advantage—and Joe Harnden's mealy mouth has always served him well with his womenfolks—but I do hope Vona Harnden has got done being fool enough to galley-slave and sacrifice for the rest of her life," sputtered the dame. "Britt for her? Fs-s-sh!" Her hiss of disgust was prolonged. Then she rattled the dice more vigorously.

"It's a mighty good imitation of a—diamond-backed rattler, mother! But come on over to the table, son! She isn't as dangerous as she sounds!" The Squire dragged along his chair.

Vaniman leaped from his seat with a suddenness that was startling in that interior where peace prevailed and composure marked all acts. For the first time in his stay in the Hexter home his mood fought with the serenity of the place. The prospect of that bland contest with disks and dice was hateful, all of a sudden. His rioting feelings needed room—air—somehow there seemed to be something outside that he ought to attend to.

"Dear folks, let me off for to-night," he pleaded. "It's been a hard day for me—in the bank—I'm nervous—I think a walk will do me good."

He rushed into the hallway without waiting for any reply. He put on his cap and finished pulling on his overcoat when he was outside the house. His first impulse was to stride away from the village—go out along the country road to avoid the men who scowled at him as Britt's right-hand servitor.

But he noted that some kind of tumult seemed to be going on in the village—and any kind of tumult fitted the state of his emotions right then. He hurried toward the tavern.

Up and down the street men were marching, to and fro before Usial's shop. Vaniman saw tossing torches and the light revealed that some of the marchers wore oilcloth capes, evidently relics of some past and gone political campaign when parades were popular.

There was music, of a sort. A trombone blatted—there was the staccato tuck of a snare drum, and the boom of a bass drum came in with isochronal beats.

Vaniman went to the tavern porch and stood there with other onlookers.

"Give Ike Jones half a chance with that old tramboon of his and he ain't no slouch as a musicianer," remarked Landlord Files to the young man. "I hope Egypt is waking up to stay so."

"If we keep on, the town will get to be lively enough to suit even a city chap like you are," said another citizen. "Hope you're going to stay with us!" But there was no cordiality in that implied invitation; that there was malice which hoped to start something was promptly revealed. "In spite of what is reported about Tasp Britt firing you out of your job!" sneered the man.

Holman Day

The morrow held no promise for Vaniman, no matter what the Squire had said in the way of reassurance. To stay with Britt in that bank would be intolerable punishment. He decided that he might as well talk back to Egypt as Egypt deserved to be talked to, considering what line of contumely had been passed in through that bank wicket. He was obliged to speak loudly in order to be heard over the trombone and the drums. Therefore, everybody in the crowd got what he said; he was young, deeply stirred, and he had held back his feelings for a long time. "I'm going to leave this God-forsaken, cat-fight dump just as soon as I can make my arrangements to get away. Good night!"

He was ashamed of himself the moment that speech was out of his mouth. He was so much ashamed that he immediately became afraid he would be moved to apologize; and he was also ashamed to apologize. He was, therefore, suffering from a peculiar mixture of emotions, and realized that fact, and hurried off before his tongue could get him into any worse scrape.

He suddenly felt an impulse to get back to sanity by a talk with Vona. He had never called at her home. He knew his Egypt all too well—short as his stay had been! A call on a young woman by a young man was always construed by gossip as a process of courtship—and until that day Frank had been keeping his feelings hidden even from Vona herself.

But, having definitely decided to leave the town, he was in a mood to put aside considerations of caution in regard to their mutual affairs, for one evening, at any rate. He was moved also by the reflection that her father was at home—and the Squire and Xoa had dropped broad hints as to that gentleman's methods of operation with his womenkind. Vaniman possessed youth's confidence in his ability to make good in the world. He wondered if it would not be well to have a general show-down in the Harnden family, in order that when he went away from Egypt he might go with the consolation of knowing that Vona was waiting for him, her love sanctioned.

Pondering, he arrived in front of Egypt's humble town hall. Young folks were coming out of the door. He remembered then! For some weeks they had been rehearsing a drama to be presented on the eve of Washington's Birthday, and Vona had the leading role; she had employed him at slack times in the bank to hold the script and prompt her in her lines.

He saw her and stopped, and she hastened to him. "I suppose a political parade on Broadway wouldn't break up a rehearsal, Frank. But that's what has happened in this case. Not one of us could keep our minds on what we were saying."

"I'm not surprised. Any noise of an evening in this place, except an owl hooting, is a cause for hysterics."

She walked on at his side. "You're disgusted with our poor old town," she said, plaintively.

"I'm going to leave. Do you blame me?"

"I've heard about the—whatever it was!"

"That's right! Leave it unnamed—whatever it was!"

She touched his arm timidly. "Please be kind—to me—no matter how much cause you have to dislike others here."

He stopped, put his arms about her, and drew her into a close embrace. There were shadows of buildings where they stood; no one was near.

"I can't do my best here, Vona. You understand it. But I can't go away and do the best that's in me unless I go with your pledge to me."

"You have it, Frank! The pledge of all my love."

"But your folks! They tell me your father is at home."

"I have said nothing to father and mother—naturally." She smiled up at him. "I have never had any occasion to say anything to them about my loving anybody, because that matter has never come up till now."

"I am going home with you," he said, grimly, and drew her along, his arm linked in hers.

"If you think it is advisable for me to talk with father and mother, I'll do it—I'll do it to-night," she volunteered, courageously.

"Vona, I never want to feel again as I did this afternoon when I allowed you to go alone on an errand that concerned us both. After this, I'm going to stand up, man fashion, and do the talking for the two of us."

CHAPTER VIII

TWO AGAINST THE FIELD

Mr. Harnden had not had a bit of trouble late that afternoon in securing a promise from Tasper Britt to give him audience and view the plans and specifications of Mr. Harnden's latest invention. In fact, the consent had been secured so easily that Mr. Harnden, freshly arrived in town on Ike Jones's stage, and having heard no Egypt gossip during a prolonged absence from home, had blinked at Britt with the air of a man who had expected to find a door held against him, had pushed hard, and had tumbled head over heels when nothing opposed him.

Mr. Harnden went out on the street and put himself in the way of hearing some gossip. Then he went directly back into Britt's office and shook hands with the money king, giving Mr. Britt an arch look which suggested that Mr. Harnden knew a whole lot that he was not going to talk about right then. He said, ascribing the idea to second thought, that it might be cozier and handier to view the plans at the Harnden home. Mr. Britt agreed with a heartiness that clinched the hopes which gossip had given Mr. Harnden. The father causally said he supposed, of course, that Vona had gone home long before from the bank, and he watched Mr. Britt's expression when the banker replied to a question as to how she was getting on with her work.

"Yes, siree, she's a smart girl," corroborated the father, "and I have always impressed on her mind that some day she was bound to rise high and get what she deserves to have. Come early, Tasper, and we'll make a pleasant evening of it."

Mr. Britt went early, but not early enough to catch Vona before she left for the rehearsal.

Although it had been particularly easy to get Mr. Britt to come to the house, Mr. Harnden was not finding it easy to hold his prospective backer's attention. The patent project under consideration was what the inventor called "a duplex door," designed to keep kitchen odors from dining rooms. Mr. Harnden had a model of the apparatus. With his forefinger he kept tripping the doors, showing how a person's weight operated the contrivance, shutting the doors behind and simultaneously opening the doors in front; but Mr. Harnden did not draw attention to the palpable fact that a waiter would need to have the agility of a flea to escape being swatted in the rear or banged in the face.

Mr. Britt watched the model's operations with lackluster eyes; he seemed to be looking through the little doors and at something else that was not visible to the inventor.

Mr. Harnden was short and roly-poly, with a little round mouth and big round eyes, and a curlicue of topknot that he wagged in emphasis as a unicorn might brandish his horn. Mr. Harnden considered that he was a good talker. He was considerably piqued by Britt's apparent failure to get interested, although the banker was making considerable of an effort to return suitable replies when the inventor pinned him to answers.

"Suppose I go over the whole plan again, from the start," suggested Harnden.

"Joe, Mr. Britt looks real tired," protested Mrs. Harnden from the chimney corner. Her querulous tone fitted her lackadaisical looks; her house dress had too many flounces on it; she had a paper-covered novel in her hand.

"Yes, I *am* tired," declared Britt, mournfully. "Sort of worn out and all discouraged. I feel terribly alone in this world."

"Too bad!" Mrs. Harnden cooed her sympathy, affectedly.

"And I've been through hell's torments in the last few hours," declared Britt; ire succeeded his dolor.

"You must try and forget how those ingrates have abused you, Mr. Britt. This is a beautiful story I have just finished. You must take it with you and read it. The love sentiment is simply elegant. And it speaks of the sheltering walls of the home making a haven for the wounded heart. I hope you have found this home a haven to-night." She rose and crossed to him and laid the novel in his hands.

Mr. Harnden shoved his own hands into his trousers pockets, throwing back his coat from his comfortable frontal convexity. He presented a sort of full-rigged effect—giving the appearance of one of those handy-Jack "Emergency Eddies" who make personal equipment a fad: the upper pockets of his waistcoat bristled with pencils and showed the end of a folded rule and some calipers. He had all sorts of chains disappearing into various pockets—chains for keys and knife and cigar cutter and patent light. "Tasper," he advised, briskly, "seeing that you're now in a happy haven, as the wife says, why waste time and temper on this town? The only reason why I have kept my home here is because the town is solid rock and makes a good jumping-off place for me; I can get a firm toe hold. Why do you bother with a dinky office like the one you started out for? With your money and general eminence you can be the Governor of our state. Sure! I know all the men in this state. I've made it my business to know 'em. Let me be your manager and I'll make you Governor like"—Mr. Harnden yanked out one hand and tripped the doors of the model with a loud snap—"like that! Open goes the door to honors—bang goes the door against enemies!"

Mr. Britt glanced at the title of the story in his hands—*The Flowers Along Life's Pathway*—and perked up a bit as if he saw an opportunity to pluck some of those flowers. But when Mr. Harnden went on to say that politics was not as expensive—with the right manager—as some folks supposed, Mr. Britt exhibited gloomy doubt. "A home is about all I have in mind right now," he declared. "A man has got to have a happy home before his mind is free for big plans."

"My experience exactly!" stated Mr. Harnden, graciously indicating with a wave of the hand the happy home which he rarely graced. "And knowing what I do about the help a good home gives an enterprising man, you've got my full co-operation in your efforts, Tasper."

They heard the hall door open.

"It's Vona," announced Mrs. Harnden. She beamed on Britt. "I wonder why the dear girl is coming home so early."

The caller's face lighted up with the effect of an arc lamp going into action.

But when the sitting-room door opened and Vona escorted

Vaniman in ahead of her, Britt's illuminated expression instantly became the red glare of rage instead of the white light of hope. He leaped to his feet.

The situation made for embarrassment of overwhelming intensity; there was no detail of the affair in front of Usial's cot that had not been canvassed by every mouth in Egypt, including the mouths of the Harnden home.

Vaniman made the first move. He bowed to Mrs. Harnden; he knew the mother; she had called on Vona in the bank. "May I meet your father?" he asked the girl.

Vona presented him, recovering her composure by the aid of Frank's steadiness.

"How-de-do!" said Mr. Harnden, stiffly. He did not ask the caller to be seated. Vona gave the invitation. While Vaniman hesitated, the master of the household had a word to say, putting on his best business air. "Ordinarily, young man, the latchstring of my home is out and the boys and the girls are welcome here to make merry in a sociable way." Mr. Harnden was distinctly patronizing, with an air that put Frank into the intruding-urchin class. "But it so happens that this evening Banker Britt has seized the opportunity of my being in town and he and I are in close conference regarding an important matter in the investment line. You'll excuse us, I'm sure."

It was certainly no moment to go tilting in the field of Love, and Frank, though undaunted, was deferential; and he was compelled to recognize the father's rights as master of the household. He bowed and turned to leave, carefully keeping his eyes off Britt.

But Vona had her word to say then; her foot was on the

hearth of home; she had that advantage over Frank. Moreover, she was moved by the instinct of self-protection; she did not relish the notion of being left alone with that trio.

"We can kindle a fire in the front room, father!"

"There hasn't been a fire in that room all winter, dear girl." Mrs. Harnden's protest was sweetly firm. "No one shall run the chance of catching a cold."

"Exactly! It's tricky weather, and we must be careful of our guests," agreed Mr. Harnden. "Call again, young sir!"

"I will," stated Vaniman. He turned and addressed Vona. "The little matter will take no harm if it's postponed till to-morrow," he told her. His gaze was tender—and the girl looked up at him with an expression which even a careless observer would have found telltale. Britt's vision was sharpened by such jealous venom that he would have misconstrued even innocent familiarity. He had been struggling with his passion ever since Vaniman had appeared, escorting the girl in from the night where the two had been alone together. Age's ugly resentment at being supplanted by youth was sufficiently provocative in this case where Britt ardently longed, and had promised himself what he desired; but to that provocation was added the stinging memory of the blow dealt that day by Youth's hand across Age's withered mouth; he licked the swollen lips with a rabid tongue. He beheld the two young folks exchanging looks that gave to their simple words an import which roused all his fury. Britt shook himself free from all restraint. He had been assured by the Harndens that their home was his haven; he took advantage of that assurance and of the young man's more dubious standing in the household.

Britt was holding to the paper-covered novel—it was

doubled in his ireful grip and its title showed plainly above his ridged hand—a particularly infelicitous title it seemed to be under the circumstances, because Britt was shaking the book like a cudgel and his demeanor was that of a man who was clutching thorns instead of flowers. He advanced on Frank and his voice made harsh clamor in the little room. "You'd better not take on any more engagements for to-morrow, Vaniman. You'll be mighty busy with me, winding up our business together."

"Very well, sir. And suppose we leave off all matters between us until then!"

But Britt had started to run wild and was galloping under the whip of fury. He had been doing some amazing things that day—he had written verse, he had blubbered foolishly with a girl looking on, and he had horsewhipped his twin brother before the eyes of the populace—but what he did next was more amazing than all the rest. Having sourly admitted to himself that he was a coward when he was alone with the girl, he took advantage of this moment when his choleric desperation gave him fictitious courage. He slashed into the situation with what weapons he had at hand—and he held a reserve weapon, so he thought, in the big wallet that thrust its bulk reassuringly against his breast. "This thing seems to have come to a climax; and it ain't through any fault of mine. I've never yet been afraid to talk for myself, in a climax, and I ain't afraid now. The time to do business is when you've got your interested parties assembled—and the five folks in this room—the whole five—may not be collected together again," he stated, with vengeful significance, looking hard at Vaniman. Then he whirled on the girl. "Vona, I want to marry you. You know it. Your folks know it. It's all understood, even if it hasn't been put into words. I'll give you everything that money will buy. When you get me you know what you're getting. I put the question to you right here and now, before your home folks, and that shows you what kind of a square man I am. I don't sneak in dark corners." He accused her escort with a glowering side-glance.

Mrs. Harnden simpered.

Vona had never found her mother an especially stable support in times of stress, but the girl did feel that the maternal spirit might arise and help in an emergency as vital as that one! Mrs. Harnden, however, was gazing into the arena and was blandly indicating by her demeanor, "Thumbs down!"

Then the girl appealed to her father, mutely eager; denied sympathy, she was asking for protection. But Mr. Harnden was distinctly not extending protection. He was looking at Mr. Britt. By avoiding what he knew the girl was asking for with all her soul in her eyes, Mr. Harnden was indulging his consistent selfishness; he hated to be worried by the troubles of others; others' woes placed brambles on the pathway of his optimism.

"Tasper, you have certainly jumped the Harnden family— jumped us complete! You can't expect a girl to get her voice back right away. But I suppose it's up to me to speak for the family."

Vaniman stepped into the center of the room. "I suppose so, too, Mr. Harnden. I'll confess that I came into your house this evening with that idea in my mind."

Now the girl had eyes only for the one whom she recognized as her real champion; those eyes would have inspired a knight to any sort of derring-do, Frank was telling himself.

"That being agreed, I'll speak," stated Mr. Harnden, throwing back his coat lapels and displaying all his pencil quills.

"Just one moment, sir, till I have shown that Mr. Britt has no monopoly on courage—seeing that he has put invasion of a quiet home on that plane. I love your daughter. I want her for my wife. I came here to tell you so; but I was putting politeness ahead of my anxiety after you told me that you were engaged."

"Harnden, that man hasn't a cent in the world," Britt declared. "He sends away every sou markee he can spare from his salary. He buys checks from me. I can show 'em." Out came Britt's big wallet; he threw down the paper-covered novel.

"I support my mother and I'm putting my young sister through school," admitted the cashier. "Mr. Britt is right. But every time I buy one of his checks I buy a lot of honest comfort for myself."

"I think, young man, that the Harnden family better not interfere with the comfort of the Vaniman family," averred the father, loftily. "I'd hate to think I was a party to taking bread from the mouths of a mother and a sister. I'm sure Vona feels the same way."

"Certainly!" supplemented Mrs. Harnden. "I understand a woman's feelings in such a matter."

"Furthermore, I have discharged Vaniman for good and sufficient reasons," said President Britt. "He stands there busted and without a job."

"That is quite true," Vaniman admitted. "I cannot remain with the Egypt Trust Company, but that's a matter quite of my own choice."

"Oh, it is, is it?" scoffed the president.

"Yes, sir! I've had quite enough of your society."

"Therefore, it seems to me that there isn't much more to be said—not here—in a home that we try to make peaceful and happy at all times," said Mr. Harnden, pompously.

"But there's something more I'm going to say!" Britt was proceeding with malice in tones and mien. He had been waving the canceled checks. He pulled another paper from the wallet. "You think the directors would keep you on in that job, do you, Vaniman, if you forced the issue?"

"I do! Jealousy and petty spite would not show up very strong in a board meeting, Mr. Britt."

Britt shook the paper. "How would this show up?"

Vaniman did not lose his composure. "Why don't you read it aloud? You have stirred curiosity in Mr. and Mrs. Harnden, I see."

"And I'll stir something else in a girl you're trying to fool! But I'm gong to save this letter for that board meeting; I'll have you fired by a regular vote—and I'll send the record of that vote to every bank in this part of the country. Then see how far you'll get with your lies about my jealousy!" Britt was plainly determined to allow guesswork to deal in the blackest construction regarding the letter.

Vaniman turned his back on the others. He talked directly to Vona. The agonized query in her eyes demanded a reply from him. "Mr. Britt has in his hand a letter from some banking friend of his. The letter says that my father was sentenced to the penitentiary, charged with embezzlement.

That is so. My father died there. But it was wicked injustice. You and your father and mother are entitled to know that an honest man was made a scapegoat."

"Excuse me!" broke in Harnden. "We are outsiders and will probably remain so, and have no hankering to pry into family matters."

"I did not intend to tell the story now, Mr. Harnden. It's too sacred a matter to be discussed in the presence of that man who stands there trying to make a club of the thing to ruin my hopes and my life. This is a hateful situation. I apologize. But he has forced me to speak out, as I have done, telling you and your wife of my love for Vona."

"I don't see how you dare to speak of it, seeing what the circumstances are," declared the father; there was a murmur of corroboration from the mother.

"It's a cheeky insult to all concerned," shouted Britt.

"No, it's my best attempt to be honest and open and a man," insisted Vaniman. "I have left no chance for gossip to bring tales to you, Mr. Harnden."

But Mr. Harnden sliced the air with a hand that sought to sever further conference. "Absolutely impossible, young man."

"Vona's prospects must not be ruined by anybody's selfishness," stated Mrs. Harnden.

In his eagerness, encouraged by this parental backing, Mr. Britt did not employ a happy metaphor. "It has been my rule, in the case of bitter medicine, to take it quick and have the agony over with." He put all the appeal he could muster into his gaze at Vona. "That's why I have sprung the thing this

Holman Day

evening, on the spur of the moment. I ain't either young or handsome, Vona. I know my shortcomings. But I've got everything to make you happy; all you've got to do is turn around and take me as your husband and make me and your folks happy, too."

Mr. Harnden's optimism bobbed up with its usual serenity. "We're making a whole lot out of a little, come to think it over!" He turned to Vona, feeling that he was fortified against any appeal he might find in her eyes.

In the silence that she had imposed on herself while her champion was battling she had been gathering courage, piling up the ammunition of resolution. Love lighted her eyes and flung out its signal banners of challenge on her cheeks.

"Why, our girl has never said that she is in love with anybody," prated the father.

"I'll say it now, when there's a good reason for saying it," cried the girl, her tones thrilling the listeners. "I'll say it in my own way to the one who is entitled to know, and you may listen, father and mother!"

She went to Frank, stretching her hands to him, and he took them in his grasp. "I understand! I can wait," she told him. "And when the time comes and you call to me, I'll say, as Ruth said, 'Entreat me not to leave thee, or to return from following after thee; for whither thou goest, I will go; and where thou lodgest, I will lodge; thy people shall be my people, and thy God my God.'" Impulsively, heeding only him, she threw her arms around his neck and kissed him. Then she ran from the room.

And finding the light gone out of the place, Frank groped to the door, like a blind man feeling his way, and departed.

CHAPTER IX

THE NIGHT BROUGHT COUNSEL

Mr. Britt, left with the father and mother, got his voice first because he had been pricked most deeply; furthermore, the girl's method of expression had touched him on the spot which had been abraded by Prophet Elias's daily rasping.

The suitor drove his fist down on the center table with a force that caused the model of Mr. Harnden's doors to jump and snap. "By the joo-dinged, hump-backed Hosea, I've just about got to my limit in this text business!"

"The dear girl is all wrought up. She don't realize what she's saying. I'll run up to her room and reason with her. Don't mind what a girl says in a tantrum, Mr. Britt," Mrs. Harnden pleaded.

Mr. Britt, left with the father, began to stride back and forth across the room. The title of the book jeered up at him from the carpet where he had tossed the volume; he kicked the book under the table.

"The wife said a whole lot just now," affirmed Mr. Harnden, soothingly. "Consider where the girl has been this evening, Tasper! Off elocuting dramatic stuff! Comes back full of high-flown nonsense. Gets off something that was running in her head. Torched on by that fly-by-night who'll be getting out of town and who'll be forgotten inside a week. Where's your optimism?" He reached up and slapped Britt's back when the banker passed him.

"She is in love with him," complained the suitor; his anger was succeeded by woe; his face "squizzled" as if he were about to weep a second time that day.

"Piffle! She's a queer girl if she didn't have the usual run of childish ailments, along with the whooping cough and the measles. I have always known how to manage my womenfolks, Tasper. Not by threats and by tumulting around as you have been doing! You've got a lot to learn. Listen to me!"

Mr. Britt paused and blinked and listened.

Mr. Harnden plucked out a pencil and made believe write a screed on the palm of his hand while he talked. "'By the twining tendrils of their affections you can sway 'em to and fro,' as the poet said, speaking of women. I am loved in my home. I have important prospects, now that you are backing me."

Mr. Britt blinked more energetically, but he did not dispute.

"Another poet has said that's it's all right to lie for love's sake—or words to that effect. I know the right line of talk to give Vona. And I won't have to lie such a great lot to make her know how bad off I am right now. She has always had a lot of sympathy for me," declared Mr. Harnden, complacently. "I may as well cash in on it. She won't ruin a loving father and a happy home when she wakes up after a good cry on the wife's shoulder and gets her second wind and understands where she's at in this thing. Tasper, you sit down there in a comfortable chair and let me rub on some optimism anodyne where you're smarting the worst."

When Mrs. Harnden came into the room a half hour later she looked promptly relieved to find Mr. Britt in such a calm mood; when she had hurried out he was acting as if he were intending to kick the furniture about the place.

"A good cry—and all at peace, eh?—and a new view of things in the morning?" purred the optimist in the way of query.

"She didn't cry," reported the mother, with a disconsolateness that did not agree with the cheering words of the reports.

"Oh, very well," remarked Mr. Harnden, optimism unspecked. "That shows she is taking a common-sense view and is using her head. What says she?"

"I may as well post you on how the matter stands, Mr. Britt. By being honest all 'round we can operate together better."

Britt agreed by an emphatic nod.

After an inhalation which suggested the charging of an air gun, Mrs. Harnden pulled the verbal trigger. "Vona says she is all through at the bank."

"Oh, I know my girl," said Mr. Harnden, airily. "I'll handle her when morning's light is bright, and forgotten is the night!"

"I thought I knew my girl, too," the mother declared, gloomily. "But I guess I don't. I never saw her stiffen up like this before. She sat and looked at me, and I felt like a cushion being jabbed by a couple of hatpins—if there's any such thing as a cushion having feelings." Mrs. Harnden, settling her flounces, a soft and sighing example of "a languishing Lydia," was as unfortunate in her metaphor as Britt had been when he mentioned a bitter medicine.

"Tell her that I'll pay her ten dollars more a week," said President Britt, looking desperate. "She mustn't leave me in the lurch."

"She'll do it! Nothing to worry about!" affirmed the father. "And I'll grab in as cashier till my bigger projects get started. I've got a natural knack for handling money, Tasper."

The banker winced.

"We can make it all snug, right in the family," insisted Harnden. He jumped up, opened the door into the hallway, and called. He kept calling, his tones growing more emphatic, till the girl replied from abovestairs.

"She's coming down," reported the general manager of the household, taking his stand in front of the fireplace. He pulled on a chain and dragged out a bunch of keys and whirled them like a David taking aim with a sling.

Vona came no farther than the doorway, and stood framed there.

"What's this last nonsense—that you won't go to your work in the morning?"

"Your pay is raised ten dollars a week, starting to-morrow," supplemented Britt, appealingly.

But there was no compromise in the girl's mien. "Mr. Britt, I realize perfectly well that I ought to give you due notice—

the usual two weeks. That would be the honorable business way. But you have set the example of disregarding business methods, in your treatment of Mr. Vaniman. You mustn't blame others for doing as you're doing. Therefore I positively will not come into the bank, as conditions are. As I feel to-night I shall feel to-morrow! If you, or my father and mother, think you can change my mind on the matter, you'll merely waste your arguments."

That time she did not run away. She surveyed them in turn, leisurely and perfectly self-possessed. Even the optimist recognized inflexibility when he was bumped against it hard enough! She stepped backward, challenging reply, but they were silent, and she went upstairs.

"Still, nobody knows what the morning may bring forth," persisted Harnden, after waiting for somebody else to speak. "As I have said, I have a knack—"

"Of blowing up paper bags and listening to 'em bust!" snarled the banker, permitting himself, at least, to express his real opinion of a man whom he had always held to be an impractical nincompoop. "If you count cash the way you count chickens before they're hatched, you'd make a paper bag out of my bank. I'll bid you good night!"

He wrenched away from Harnden's restraining hands and shook himself under the shower of the optimist's pattering words, as a dog would shake off rain. In the hall he pulled on his overcoat and turned up the collar, for the words still pattered. He went out into the night and slammed the door.

Britt began his program of general anathema by shaking his fist at the Harnden house after he had reached the street. He shook his fist at the other houses along the way as he went tramping in the middle of the road toward his home. He even brandished his fist at his own statue in the facade of Britt Block. The moonlight revealed the complacent features; the cocky pose of serene confidence presented by the effigy affected the disheartened original with as acute a sense of exasperation as he would have felt if the statue had set thumb to nose and had wriggled the stone fingers in impish derision.

"Gid-dap" Jones and a few citizens who could not make up their minds to go to bed till they had sucked all the sweetness out of an extraordinary evening in Egypt, were walking up and down the tavern porch, cooling off. Mr. Britt, tramping past, shook his fist at them, too.

"Hope you enjoyed the music!" suggested Jones, wrought up to a pitch where he would not be bull-dozed even by "Phay-ray-oh."

"Yes, and I hope we'll have some more to-morrow night," retorted the banker. "You still have the poorhouse, the cattle pound, and the lockup to serenade."

"All right! Which one of 'em do you expect to be in?" inquired Jones. "We wouldn't have you miss a tune for the world!"

When Britt arrived in the shadows of his own porch he stood and looked out over Egypt and cursed the people, in detail and in toto. He had become a monomaniac. He had set himself to accomplish one fell purpose.

In his office, earlier that day, he had resolved upon revenge; but his natural caution had served as a leash, and he had pondered on no definite plans that might prove dangerous. Now only one fear beset him—the fear that he would not be able to think up and put through a sufficiently devilish program.

He banged his door behind him and lighted a lamp which he kept on a stand in the hall. He creaked upstairs in the lonely house. His sense of loneliness was increased when he reflected that Vona would not be at her desk in the morning.

The village watchman noted that the reflector lamp shone all night on the door of the vault in the Egypt Trust Company; it was the watchman's business to keep track of that light. But he noted also, outside of his regular business, that there was a light for most of the night in Tasper Britt's bedroom.

Holman Day

CHAPTER X

THE MAN WHO WAS SORRY

It was a heavy dawn, next day; a thaw had set in and a drizzle of rain softened the snow; gray clouds trailed their draperies across the top of Burkett Hill.

Landlord Files had trouble in getting his kitchen fire started—in the sluggish air the draught was bad. Mr. Files's spirits were as heavy as the air. He knew it was up to him to be the first man in Egypt to come in contact with Tasper Britt that morning.

Stage-driver Jones had an early breakfast, for he had to be off with the mail. Mr. Jones had been up late, for him, and he was grouchy. In the matter of the warfare on Pharaoh his mood seemed to be less assertive than it had been the night before. Mr. Files detected that much after some conversation while the breakfast was served.

"All you have to do is 'gid-dap' and get away," said Files, sourly. "I have to stay here on my job and be the first to meet him and get the brunt of the whole thing. And I condoned, as you might say, and as he'll probably feel. I let my porch be used for meeting and mobbing, as you might say. And he ketched me grinning over his shoulder when I read them heading words after that old lunkhead of a Prophet passed him the paper."

"Shut up!" remarked Driver Jones, stabbing a potato.

"I owe him money—and I let my porch be used—"

"Figure out the wear and tear on the planks and pass me the bill. Now shut up and don't spoil my vittles any morn'n you have done in the way of cooking 'em."

Mr. Files, left alone to meet Britt, resolved to hand that tyrant a partial sop by having breakfast on the table the moment the regular boarder unfolded his napkin; food might stop Britt's mouth to some extent, the landlord reflected.

Result of this precautionary courtesy! The breakfast was a mess when Britt arrived, a half hour late. Mr. Files had depended on his boarder's invariable punctuality and had been obliged to keep "hotting up" the food, watching the clock with increasing despair.

Britt smiled on the landlord when they faced each other in the dining room. The smile made the landlord shiver. He was dreading the explosion. He set on the viands as timidly as a child holding out peanuts to an elephant. Mr. Britt beamed blandly and spoke of the change in the weather and said he was hoping that "Old Reliable Ike wouldn't be bothered too much by the soft footing on his way to Levant."

Mr. Files gasped when he heard this consideration expressed for the ringleader of the evening's demonstration. He recovered sufficiently to start in on an explanation of the condition of the food.

"It's all right, Files! It's my fault. I overslept."

Britt ate for a few minutes; then he suspended operations and looked Files hard in the face; that face, as to mouth, was as widely open as the countenance of the office alligator. "I did a whole lot of thinking last night, Files. I'm telling you first, like I propose to tell others in Egypt as I come in contact with 'em during the day—it has been my fault—how things have happened! The night brings counsel! Yes, sir, it surely does." He went on eating.

"Mr. Britt, I was afraid—"

Pharaoh waved his knife expostulatingly. "I know it, Files! Your face told me the whole story when I stepped in here. But I'm a changed man. I know when I'm down. However, it's my own fault, I repeat. I stubbed my toe over the trigs I had set in the way of my own operations. I deserve what I'm getting—and the lesson will make me a different man from now on."

Mr. Files staggered out into the kitchen in order to be alone with his thoughts.

Britt spent a longer time than usual in the tavern office after breakfast; he smoked two cigars, himself, and gave a cigar to each of the early citizens who dropped in through the front way after they had received certain information from Files, who excitedly had beckoned them to come to him at the ell door. Mr. Britt frankly exposed his new sentiments about living and doing. When he put on his overcoat and went forth, Prophet Elias popped out of the door of Usial's cot like the little gowned figure of a toy barometer. Britt waved his hand in cheerful greeting. "Prophet Elias, hand me that text about the way of the transgressor being a hard one to travel, and I'll take it in a meek and lowly spirit and be much obliged." There was no sarcasm in Britt's tone; on the contrary, his manner agreed with his profession regarding meekness. The Prophet swapped stares with Files, who stood in the tavern door; that Elias was greatly impressed was evident, because he withheld speech.

That situation had enough drawing power to bring the brother to the cottage door; he appeared, his spider in his hand.

"Good morning, Usial," called Tasper. "I own up that you're a convincing writer. According to your request, you see I'm giving you your right name. The voters are giving you honors. Who knows what another issue of *The Hornet* may get for you?" Britt's tone was one of bluff sincerity.

Egypt's Pharaoh did not seem to be a bit put out because no one replied to him in this astonishing levee. He descended from the porch and strolled off toward Britt Block, puffing his cigar.

He found the cashier alone in the bank. Vaniman hastened to put in the first word. "President Britt, I'm ready to wind up my affairs, and I hope you see the wisdom in holding our talk strictly to the business in hand."

The president walked in past the grille and sat down at the table; by the mere look he gave the young man Britt succeeded in climaxing the succession of the morning's surprises; Vaniman had more reason than the others to be amazed.

"Frank, I'm sorry!" There was wistful fervor in the declaration; for the first time in their association the president had called the cashier by his Christian name.

Vaniman had risen from his stool; he sat down again and goggled at Britt.

"If the two of us begin to apologize, we'll get all snarled up," went on the president. "Real men can get down to cases in a better way. I did a lot of thinking last night; probably you did, too. The hell fire I went through yesterday would upset any man. To-day I'm scorched and sensible. I went after something I couldn't get. Just now I don't ask you to stay here permanently. You can stay right along if you want to, I'll say that here and now! But if you're bound to go—later— go when you can leave on the square, after you have broken another man into the job, if you feel you don't want it. I'll send you away then with my best wishes and a clean bill! Please don't make me crawl any more'n I'm doing!"

It was an appeal to Youth's hale generosity—and generosity dominated all the other qualities in Vaniman's nature. "I'll stay, Mr. Britt," he blurted. "After what you have said I can't help staying."

The banker rose and stretched out his hand. "Men can put more into a grip of the fist than women can into an afternoon of gabble, Frank."

After the vigorous clasp of palm in palm, Britt had something more to say. "Vona was terribly stirred up last night, and nobody can blame her. She served notice on me that she was done in the bank. But she needs the money and you and I need her help. Go up and ask her to walk back in here as if nothing had happened. And tell her that what I said about the raise in her pay holds good."

"I think you ought to go and tell her, Mr. Britt," Vaniman demurred. "And my standing with Mr. and Mrs. Harnden—"

"I guess your standing will be better from now on," Britt broke in, twisting his face into a wry smile. "I left Harnden with a hot ear on him last night! Furthermore, you'll have to ask her. She declared that if her father or mother or I tried to change her mind about coming back here we'd be wasting breath. Go on! I'll tend bank."

When Frank returned with Vona a half hour later the president beamed on them through the wicket. He immediately left the bank office, giving the bookkeeper a paternal pat on the shoulder as he passed her, calling her a good girl. And then the business of the Egypt Trust Company settled back into its usual routine.

During the day customers came to the wicket with notes sanctioned by the president's O. K. and his sprawling initials; Mr. Britt did not trouble himself by consulting the directors in regard to ordinary loans. He was well settled in his autocracy by virtue of the voting proxies which he handled for stockholders, although he had only a modest amount of his own money invested in the stock of the bank. Mr. Britt could use his own money to better advantage. He was permitted to make a one-man bank of the Trust Company because nobody in Egypt ventured to dispute his sapience as a financier.

The customers who came that day were plainly having a hard time of it in controlling their desire to share some of their emotions with the cashier. But Vaniman's stolid countenance did not encourage any confidences.

Some of the repression he exercised in the case of customers extended to his communion with Vona during the slack times of the business day. There seemed to be a tacit agreement between them to keep off the topic of what had happened the night before. Words could not have added to their understanding of their mutual feelings. That understanding had established for them the policy of waiting. Though Frank said but little to the girl about his talk with the president, he imagined he could feel the tingle of Britt's handclasp as he remembered the look on Britt's face, and he pitied the old man. To go on, seizing every opportunity to make love, would seem like "rubbing it in," Frank told himself. He also said something of the sort to Vona, and she agreed with an amiable smile.

And the two of them agreed on one thing, more especially: Tasper Britt must have had a strange housecleaning of the heart during that vigil in his home on the hill.

Among other convincing evidences of Britt's transformation was his treatment of Prophet Elias at the end of that day.

The Prophet did not deliver his usual matutinal taunts in front of Britt Block. But when he came back from the field in the afternoon, he returned from conferences with Egyptian skeptics who had not seen Tasper Britt in his new form, and therefore, perhaps, their assertions had caused Elias to doubt the evidences of his own senses. At any rate, the Prophet resolved to put the reform of Pharaoh to the test of texts, and he raised his voice and declaimed.

Britt came to the front door and mildly entreated the Prophet to walk in. "I'll be glad to listen to you. Isn't it a good idea to tell me, man to man, in my office what's wrong with me, instead of standing out there in the snow, telling the neighborhood?"

The Prophet went in, having first slapped his hand on his breast, urging action, "'Go in, speak unto Pharaoh, king of Egypt, that he let the children of Israel go out of his hand.'"

He trudged forth, after a time, and walked along slowly toward Usial's house, clawing his hand above his ear with the air of a man trying to solve a perplexing puzzle.

CHAPTER XI

SACKS AND MOUTHS—ALL SEALED

Every now and then the fad of a new trick puzzle—a few bits of twisted wire, or a stick and a string—will as effectually occupy the time of an entire community as a cowbell will take up the undivided attention of a cur, if the bell is hitched to the cur's tail.

The folks of Egypt had a couple of brain-twisters to solve.

What had happened to Tasper Britt?

How did it happen that Cashier Vaniman was holding on to his job?

His townsfolk knew Britt's character pretty well, and they had much food for speculation in his case.

There were some who ventured the suggestion that Hittie's remonstrating spirit had come to him in the night watches. Other guesses ran all the way down the scale of probability to the prosaic belief that Britt had decided that it was not profitable to go on making a fool of himself. It was agreed that Britt had a good eye for profit in every line of action; and it was conceded, even by those who did not believe all that was said about spiritist influences in these modern days, that if Hittie really had managed to get at him it was likely that her caustic communications would knock some of the folly out of him.

Egypt did not know Vaniman, the outlander, very well. Gossip about his reasons for remaining were mostly all guess-so; the folks got absolutely nothing from him on the subject. He did not discuss the matter even with Squire Hexter and Xoa. Frank and Vona had definitely adopted the policy of waiting, and he resolved to take no chances on having that policy prejudiced by anybody carrying random stories to Britt, reports that the cashier had said this or the other.

Vaniman took occasion to reassure Mr. Britt on that point, and the latter had displayed much gratitude. "If you don't hurt *me*, Frank, I won't hurt *you*!" Then the usurer's eyes hardened. "Of course I can't expect you to forget that I threatened to blacken your name in banking circles. But in our new understanding I guess we can afford to call it a stand-off."

"If I were staying here simply to wheedle you into passing me on with a high testimonial, I'd be playing a selfish game, and that isn't my attitude, sir. I was anxious to get this job. I felt that I had a right to stand for myself, on my own honesty. But I shall tell the whole story the next time I apply for a position. I'm getting to understand big financiers better," he added, with bitterness.

"Yes, finance is very touchy on certain points," admitted the president. "But I'm glad you're not going to do any more talking here in town. You're somewhat of a new man here, and you don't know the folks as I do. I suppose some talk will have to be made as to why you and I are sticking along together, after you slapped my face in public. You'd better let me manage the story."

"You may say what you think is best, Mr. Britt."

"They're a suspicious lot, the men in this town." The banker surveyed Vaniman, making slits of his eyes. "However, I've grown used to all this recent talk about me being a fool. If it's also said that I'm a fool for keeping you here, I won't mind it. And you mustn't mind if it's hinted around that you're hanging on in the bank because you've got private reasons that you're not talking about."

The cashier greeted that sentiment with an inquiring frown.

"Oh, don't be nervous, Frank!" Mr. Britt flapped his hand, making light of the matter. He grinned. "I won't set you out as being the leader of a robber gang. I'm not like the peaked-billed old buzzards of this place—bound to say the worst of every stranger. You'd better turn to and hate the critters here, just as I do."

Britt's tones rasped when he said that; his feelings were getting away from him. The young man's expression hinted that he was trying to reconcile this rancorous mood with Britt's recent declarations of a new view of life.

"What I really meant to say, Frank, was that such has been my feeling in the past. I'm trying to change my nature. If I forget and slip once in a while, don't lay it up against me."

After that the president and the cashier in their daily conferences confined their discourse to the business of the bank. Britt got into the way of asking Vaniman's advice and of deferring to it when it had been given. "You're running the bank. You know the trick better than I do."

Therefore, it was perfectly natural for the president to bring up a topic of the past, a matter where Frank had given advice that had been scornfully rejected. "I've been thinking over what you said about that stock of hard money in the vault needing a guard. That fool of a Stickney has started a lot of gossip, in spite of my warning to him. There's no telling how far the gossip has spread."

"That kind of news travels fast, sir."

Britt showed worry. "Perhaps I undertook too much of a chore for a little bank like ours. But because we are little and because this town isn't able to support the bank the way I had hoped, I thought I'd turn a trick that would net us more of a handy surplus in a modest sort of a way."

Britt did not trouble himself to explain to the cashier that, by a private arrangement with the city broker, the deal would also turn a neat sum into the pocket of the president of the Egypt Trust Company, hidden in the charge of "commission and expenses," split with due regard to the feelings of broker and president.

"The big fellows are grabbing off twenty-five or thirty per cent in their foreign money deals," went on the banker. "Tightening home credits so as to do it! What's fair for big is fair for little!"

"The profit is attractive, surely," the cashier stated.

"Our stockholders have honored me right along, and I'd like to show 'em that I deserve my reputation as a financier. I'm just finicky enough to want to clean up the last cent there is in it—and that's why I'm waiting for the right market. We've got to hold on for a few days, at any rate. But I reckon you feel as I do, that we're taking chances, now that gossip is flying high!"

"I think the vault should be guarded, Mr. Britt."

"Any suggestions as to a man?"

"I don't know the men here well enough to choose."

"And I know 'em so blasted well that I'm in the same box as you are. They're numbheads."

The two men sat and looked at each other in silence; the matter seemed to be hung up right there, like a log stranded on a bank—"jillpoked," as rivermen say.

"There's one way out of it, Frank," blurted the president. "Nobody cares when I come or go, nights. I may as well sleep here as in my house, all alone. I'll have a cot put in the back room." He pointed to a door in the rear of the bank office.

Vaniman came forward with instant and eager proffer. "That's a job for me, Mr. Britt."

In spite of an effort to seem casual, Britt could not keep significance out of his tone. "It's too bad to pen a young man up of an evening, when he can be enjoying himself somewhere."

"It's because I'm young that I'm insisting, sir."

"And I suppose I'm so old that no husky robber would be afraid of me," returned Britt, dryly. "So you insist, do you?"

"I do."

"I must ask you to remember that you're doing it only

because you have volunteered."

"I'll be glad to have you tell the directors that I volunteered and insisted."

"Very well! We'll have the thing understood, Frank. I wouldn't want to have 'em think I was obliging you to do more than your work as cashier."

Therefore, Vaniman had a cot brought down from Squire Hexter's house, and borrowed a double-barreled shotgun from the same source. He did not consider that his new duty entailed any hardship. He had his evenings for the pachisi games. Xoa insisted on making a visit to the bank and putting the back room in shape for the lodger. But she vowed that she was more than ever convinced that money was the root of all evil.

Frank's slumbers were undisturbed; he found the temporary arrangement rather convenient than otherwise. He kindled his furnace fire before going to the Squire's for breakfast and Britt Block was thoroughly warm when he returned.

There was only one break in this routine, one occasion for alarm, and the alarm was but temporary. Frank heard footsteps in the corridor one evening after he had come back to the bank from the Squire's house. Almost immediately Mr. Britt used his key and appeared to the young man. "I waited till I was sure you were here," the president explained. "What Hexter doesn't know won't hurt him—and I thought I'd better not come to the house for you. I'm sorry it's so late." Britt was anxiously apologetic.

"It isn't very late, sir."

"But it's late, considering what's on my mind, Frank. And

now that I'm here I hate to tell you what my errand is." He fumbled in his pocket and brought out a letter, tapped it with his forefinger, and replaced it. "I got it in the mail after you had gone to supper."

"If it's any matter where I can be of help, sir, you needn't be a bit afraid to speak out."

"You can help, but—" After his hesitation Britt plunged on. "I wrote to that broker that I was feeling a little under the weather and was postponing my trip to the city, and now that fool of a Barnes writes back that he's starting right behind his letter to come up here to arrange about taking over the specie and closing the deal, because the market is just right to act. And the through train, the one he'll be sure to take, hits Levant about two o'clock to-morrow morning. He asks me to send somebody down to meet him. That's all one of those taxicab patronizers knows about traveling conditions in the country. Frank, unless you'll volunteer to go I'll have to go myself. I don't want that man talking all the way up here with old Files's gabby hostler, or with anybody else I send from the village."

Vaniman, even though he tried to make Britt's reasons for the request seem convincing, could not help feeling that the financier's natural secretiveness in matters of personal business was stretched somewhat in this instance. But he gulped back any hesitation and offered to go on the errand.

"Frank, when I was having my run of foolishness I was sorry that you are young. Now I'm mighty glad of it," declared Britt. "I can take your place in yonder on the cot for the night—and I'm going to do it. But I'll be frank enough to say that I'd rather you'd ride to Levant and back in a sleigh to-night than do it myself. Go rout up Files's hostler, borrow his fur coat, and bundle up warm. It's good slipping along the road, and the trip may have a little pep for you, after all."

And, putting away his momentary doubts, Frank reflected on the matter and was honestly glad to vary the monotony of his close confinement to the bank.

So he went and roused Files's hostler, bundled himself in the coat and the sleigh robes, and made a really joyous experience out of the trip to Levant, under the stars and over the snow that was crisped by the night's chill.

He waited beside the station platform, standing up in the sleigh and peering eagerly after the train stopped. He called the name, "Mr. Barnes," until the few sleepy, slouching, countrified passengers who alighted had passed on their way.

It was perfectly apparent that Broker Barnes was not present to answer roll call.

And after waiting, in whimsical delay, to make sure that Mr. Barnes had not come footing it behind the train, Frank whipped up and drove back to Egypt. He felt no pique; he had enjoyed the outing in the sparkling night.

In the gray dawn he again routed out Files's yawning hostler and turned the equipage over to him.

"Hope you found it a starry night for a ramble," suggested the hostler, willing to be informed as to why a bank cashier had been gallivanting around over the country between days, turning in a sweating horse at break of dawn.

Vaniman allowed that it was a starry night, all right, and left the topic there, with a period set to it by the snap of his tone.

He went directly to the bank and admitted himself with his keys.

President Britt came from the back room, with yawns that matched those of the hostler.

"What time did Barnes say he'd be down here from the tavern in the morning?"

"Mr. Barnes did not come on that train, sir."

"Well, I'll be—" rapped Britt, snapping shut his jaws.

"But I haven't minded the trip—I really enjoyed the ride," insisted the messenger.

"Don't tell that to Barnes when he shows up to-night on Ike Jones's stage," commanded Britt. "I propose to have a few words to say about what it means in the country when a city fathead changes his mind about the train he'll take." He was looking past the cashier while he talked. He turned away and picked up his hat and coat from a chair. "I'll be going along to my house, I reckon. You'd better catch a cat-nap on the cot. I found it comfortable. I've slept every minute since you've been gone."

Then Britt hurried out, locking the door behind him.

CHAPTER XII

SOMETHING TO BE EXPLAINED

By noon that day, in the lulls between customers at the wicket, Vaniman had had a succession of run-ins with the demon of drowsiness—a particularly mischievous elf, sometimes, in business hours. Whenever he caught himself snapping back into wakefulness he found Vona's twinkle of amusement waiting for him.

Once she pointed to the big figures on the day-by-day calendar on the wall. The date was February 21st. "Console yourself, Frank, dear," she advised, teasing him. "The bank will be closed to-morrow and you can make Washington's Birthday your sleep day! But I do hope you can stay awake at our play this evening."

"The man who invented sleep as a blessing didn't take into account city brokers who change their minds about trains," he returned. "I hope old Ike Jones will sing that 'Ring, ting! Foo loo larry, lo day' song of his all the way coming up from Levant. It'll be about the sort of punishment that Behind-time Barnes deserves."

A few minutes later the cashier was jumped out of another incipient nap by the clamor of bells. The two horses that whisked past, pulling a double-seated sleigh, were belted with bells. A big man with a lambrequin mustache was filling the rear seat measurably well. Folks recognized the team as a "let-hitch" from Levant.

"Mr. Barnes comes late, but he comes in style and with all his bells," Vona suggested.

The equipage swung up beside the tavern porch and the big man threw off the robes and stamped in, leaving the driver to take the horses to the stable.

Landlord Files had furnished an accompaniment for the clangor of the bells; he was pounding his dinner gong.

The new arrival had a foghorn voice and used it in hearty volume in telling Mr. Files that his music was all right and mighty timely! "And that alligator seems to be calling for his grub, too," he remarked, on his way to hang up his coat. "But he doesn't look any hungrier than I feel."

"Room?" inquired the landlord, hopefully, swinging the register book and pulling a pen out of a withered potato.

"No room! Just dinner. I expect to be out of here by night."

Mr. Files stabbed the potato with a vicious pen thrust. He knew food capacity when he viewed it; there would be some profit from a lodging, but none from a two-shilling meal served to a man who had compared himself with that open-mouthed saurian.

But the guest grabbed the penstock while it was still vibrating. He wrote across the book, with great flourishes: "Fremont Starr. State Bank Examiner. February 21st."

Holman Day

"A matter of record, landlord! Show's I'm here. Tells the world I was here on date noted. Never can tell when the law will call for records. Hotel registers are fine evidence. Always keep your registers."

"I've had that one eleven years, and it 'ain't been filled up yet," averred Mr. Files, inspecting the potentate's signature as sourly as if he were estimating by how much the lavish use of ink had reduced the possible dinner profit. "You're the new appointment, hey? I heard you speak, one time, over at the political rally in the shire town."

"Both my enemies and my friends would have advised you to stay right here on your porch—saying that you could hear me just as well, if you didn't care to make the trip to the shire," said Mr. Starr, lifting the mat of his mustache in a wide smile. "But when they call me 'Foghorn Fremont' I'm never one mite offended. 'Let your light shine and your voice be heard,' is my motto in politics."

"Shouldn't wonder if it's a good one, when they get to passing around the offices," admitted Files. He started on his way to the kitchen.

At that moment President Britt entered, having answered the gong with the promptitude of a fireman chasing a box alarm.

"What have you on the fire, landlord?" called Mr. Starr, absorbed in the dinner topic.

"Boiled dinner!"

Britt did not show the enthusiasm that was exhibited by the other guest.

"Nothing like a boiled dinner after a long ride," Mr. Starr

affirmed. "Plenty of cabbage with mine, if you'll be so kind!"

Files gave Mr. Britt some information that he thought might be of interest. "Here's the new bank examiner. Seeing that you probably have business together, I'll set both of you at the same table." He retired.

After the commonplaces of getting acquainted, the two tacked the boiled dinner.

"Let's see—who's your cashier?" inquired Starr, chewing vigorously behind the mask of his mustache.

"Young fellow named Vaniman. I have let him take full charge of the bank business. He seems to know all the ropes."

"Poor policy, Britt! Poor policy!" stated the examiner, vehemently. "Not a word to say against Vaniman—" He halted on the word and opened his eyes on Britt. "Vaniman! A name that sticks. There was a Vaniman of Verona. Easy to remember! There was some sort of a money snarl, as I recollect."

"It was the young chap's father."

"And you're letting the son run your bank?"

"I'm not the kind that visits the sins of the fathers on the children," loftily stated the president. "Furthermore, a burnt child dreads the fire. I heard a railroad manager say that a trainman who had let an accident happen by his negligence was worth twice as much to the road as he was before. You don't say that I made a bad pick, do you?"

"Not a word to say against Vaniman!" repeated Starr,

slashing his cabbage. "I never *guess* about any proposition—I go at it! But what I'm saying to you, Britt, is what I'm saying to all the easy-going country-town bankers. 'You may have second editions of the Apostle Paul for your cashiers,' I say, 'but every time you sign a statement of condition without close and careful audit you're bearing false witness.' And being a new broom that proposes to sweep clean, I'm tempted to poke it just as hard to slack presidents and directors as I am to an embezzling cashier who has been given plenty of rope to run as he wants! *I'm* on the job *examining* banks!" He was a vigorous man, Examiner Starr! He showed it by the way he went at his corned beef.

President Britt was perturbed; his eyes shifted; he was even pale. "If that's the way you feel about it, I hope you'll give our little bank a good going-over. I was glad to read of your appointment, Mr. Starr!"

"Uncle Whittum isn't on this job any longer," stated the examiner, not needing, in Britt's case, as a banker, to dwell upon the lax methods of the easy-going predecessor.

A half hour later, Starr, with his unbuttoned fur-lined overcoat outspread as he strode, giving him the aspect of a scaling aeroplane, marched from the tavern to the bank with Britt.

Vaniman had his mouth opened to welcome a man named Barnes, but he was presented to Bank-Examiner Starr and surprise placed him at a disadvantage in the meeting. The torpor of drowsiness made him appear stupid and ill at ease in the presence of this forceful man who stamped in and proceeded to exploit and enjoy his newly acquired authority. Mr. Starr hung up his coat and hat and swooped like a hawk on the daybook, at the same time calling for the book of "petty cash."

"First of all, the finger on the pulse of the patient, Cashier," he declared, grimly jovial. "Then we'll have a look at the tongue, and study the other symptoms."

President Britt went away to his own office.

Examiner Starr, confining himself to his announced policy of grabbing in on the running operations of the bank at the moment of his entry, studied the petty-cash accounts and checked up the daybook with thoroughness. He found everything all right and grunted his acknowledgment of that discovery.

Then he began on the ledgers, assuring Vona with ponderous gallantry that he wouldn't get in her way; he averred that he had a comparison system of his own, and showed the pride of "the new broom."

After a time it was apparent that Mr. Starr was having trouble. He added columns of figures over again and scowled; his system was plainly trigged.

"Young lady, where's your comptometer?" he demanded, after he had made a quick survey of the office.

"We have never used one, sir."

"One is indispensable these days in a bank—especially when a bookkeeper can't add a column of figures correctly by the old method."

She flushed and her lips quivered. "I'm sure I do add correctly, sir. My books always balance."

"Add that column, young lady!" He indicated the column with the plunging pressure of a stubby digit, and stood so close to her, while she toiled up the line of figures, that his breath fanned her hair.

Vaniman looked on, sympathizing, feeling sure that the bluff inquisitor had made a mistake of his own.

Her confusion under Starr's baleful espionage sent her wits scattering. She jotted down the total, as she made it.

"Wrong!" announced the examiner. "And your figures are different, even, from the wrong total you have on the books. Try again."

She set her lips and controlled her emotions and went over the work once more.

Starr exhibited figures which he had jotted on a bit of paper that he had palmed. "You're right, as the figures stand! But your book total doesn't agree with those figures. Now what say?"

Vona was distinctly in no condition to say anything sensible; she stared from the figures to Starr, showing utter amazement, and then she mutely appealed to the cashier.

"I'm sure that Miss Harnden is remarkably accurate in her work, Mr. Starr," asserted the young man. "I have been in the habit of going over it, myself, and I have found no errors."

"Oh, you go over it, do you? That's good!" But Starr's tone was not one of satisfied indorsement. He picked up the big book and carried it to the center table. He fished from his waistcoat pocket a small reading glass, unfolded the lenses, and studied the page. He turned other pages and performed the same minute inspection. Then he took the ledger to the window and held page after page against the glass, propping the book in his big hands.

When he turned, Vona was sitting in a chair, trembling, tears in her eyes, apprehension ridging her face.

"Cashier Vaniman, I don't want to hurt this young lady's feelings any more than I have. There's no sense in blaming her until I understand the which and the why of this thing. I have found column after column added wrongly. Perhaps she has done her work, originally, all right. But the pages of this ledger are pretty well speckled with erasures. The two of you will have to thresh it out between yourselves. I'm looking to you as the responsible party in this bank, Vaniman. I'll do the rest of my talking to you. After you have found out what the trouble is you must explain to me."

"There can be no trouble with our books!" But the cashier stammered; his incredulity would not permit him to discuss the matter then or to offer any sort of explanation; in his amazement he could not think of any possible explanation. He could not convince himself that Vona needed other protection than her own thoroughness and rectitude gave her; however, he wanted to extend his protection.

"If anything is wrong with the accounts, you may most certainly look to me, Mr. Starr. I assume full responsibility. I have found Miss Harnden to be most accurate."

"I ought to have been through with this small bank and away by night," grumbled the examiner. "But I'm going to give you a fair show, Vaniman, by waiting over. You've got this evening—and to-morrow is a holiday, and you can take that day, if you need it, to get this tangle straightened out. I'm stopping my work right here." He slammed the ledger shut and tossed it on the girl's desk. "There's no sense in going through your cash in the vault till I can check by the book accounts. But, bless my soul! I can't understand by what rhyme or reason those figures have been put into the muddle they're in. It's coarse work. I'll be frank and say that it doesn't look like a sane man's attempt to put something over. That's why I'm lenient with you and am not sticking one of my closure notices on to your front door. Now get busy, so that you can be sure it won't go up on the door day after to-morrow."

He took down his coat and hat and when he left the room they heard him go into Tasper Britt's office across the corridor.

The stricken lovers faced each other, appalled, mystified, questioning with the looks they exchanged.

"Frank," the girl wailed, "you know I haven't—"

"I know you have been faithful and careful, in every stroke of your pen, dear. Whatever it is, it's not your fault."

"But what has happened to the books?" she queried, winking back her tears, trying hard to meet him on the plane of his calmness; he was getting his feelings in hand.

"I propose to find out before I close my eyes this night," he told her, gravely.

CHAPTER XIII

MISFORTUNE MEDDLES

Shortly before the supper hour, Britt and Starr came into the bank; they wore their overcoats and hats, and were on their way to the tavern, evidently.

"How are you making it, Frank?" the president inquired, with solicitude.

A sympathetic observer would have found a suggestion of captives, caged and hopeless, in the demeanor of the cashier and the bookkeeper behind the grille.

Vaniman peered through the lattice into the gloom where the callers stood and shook his head. "I'm not making it well at all, sir."

"But you must have some idea of what the trouble is."

"There's trouble, all right, Mr. Britt—plenty of it. There's no use in my denying that. But I'm not far enough along to give any sensible explanation."

The president showed real anxiety. "What do you say for a guess?"

Holman Day

"If you are asking me only for a guess, I should say that the ghost of Jim the Penman has been amusing himself with these books," replied the cashier; he was bitter; he was showing the effects of worry that was aggravated by lack of sleep.

"Aha! Plainly not far enough along for a sensible explanation," rumbled Examiner Starr.

"A knave is usually ready with a good story when he has been taken by surprise. Honesty isn't as handy with the tongue. I can only say that something—I don't say somebody —has put these books into a devil of a mess, and I'm doing my best to straighten them."

"I wish you luck," affirmed Starr. "I've been talking with your president and he says everything good about your faithfulness, and about how you have been doing guard duty in the bank of late. Perhaps you're a sleepwalker, Vaniman," he added, with heavy humor.

"I feel like one now," retorted the cashier. "I was awake all last night."

"Ah! Doing what?" asked the examiner, politely, but without interest.

The question hinted that in the talk in Britt's office the president had refrained from mention of Barnes, the broker. Vaniman decided instantly to respect Britt's reticence; the president had shown much caution the night before, even in regard to Squire Hexter. "Oh, merely running around on a little business of my own, Mr. Starr."

Britt did not assist by any reference to his own share in the business. "We may as well start along toward the tavern,

Starr." The president took two steps toward the grille and addressed Vona. "I'm going to take Mr. Starr to the show this evening. I want him to see what smart girls we have in Egypt."

Vona did not reply. She turned to Vaniman with the air of one who has suddenly been reminded of something forgotten in the stress of affairs. But before she had an opportunity to speak there was a tramping of hasty feet in the corridor and her father came in through the door that had been left ajar by Britt. "Good evening, all!" hailed Mr. Harnden, cheerily. "But, see here, Vona, my dear girl, we have been waiting supper a whole half hour. You've got scant time to eat and get on your stage togs."

"This has been a pretty busy day in the bank, Harnden," explained Britt. "Meet Mr. Starr, the bank examiner!"

"Oh, hullo, Starr!" cried Mr. Harnden, shoving out a friendly hand. "Heard you were in town. I know Starr," he told Britt. "I know everybody in the state worth knowing. I told you so."

Mr. Starr was not effusive; there was a hint of sarcasm in his inquiry as to how the invention business was coming along.

"Fine and flourishing!" announced Harnden, radiantly. Then he blurted some news which seemed to embarrass Britt very much; the news also provoked intense interest in Vaniman and the daughter. "All I've ever needed is backing, Starr. Now I've got it!" He clapped his hand on the banker's shoulder. "Here's my backer—good as a certified check. Hey, Tasper?"

"I'm—I'm always ready to help develop local talent," Britt admitted, stammering, turning his back on the faces at the grille. "Starr, we'd better get along toward the tavern. I've had some poor luck with Files when he's off his schedule time!"

"The new combination of Harnden and Britt will make 'em sit up and take notice," persisted the inventor. Forgetting Vona, desiring to impress a skeptic from the outside world, he followed Starr and the banker.

Vaniman and the girl listened to the optimist's fervid declarations till the slam of the outside door shut them off.

"That sounds like an interesting investment, Vona," was the cashier's dry comment. "Mr. Britt seems to be swinging that watering pot of his new generosity around in pretty reckless fashion. I wonder what he'll do next!"

"Frank, I'm afraid!" She spoke in a whisper, staring hard at him. "No, no! Not what you think! I am not afraid because he is buying my father. If Mr. Britt thinks I can be included in that bargain he is wiser in making his money than he is in spending it. But there's something dreadful at work against us!" She had her hand on the page of an open ledger.

"The books can be straightened," he insisted. "I can do it. I'll do it, if I have to call in every depositor's pass book." He pointed to the vault. He was keeping the doors open till his work was done. "As long as the money is there, every cent of it, the final checking will show for itself. And the money will be there! I'm answering for that much! I propose to stay with it till that Barnes shows up."

"I remember now that you told me he would come by the stage to-day."

"So Britt gave me to understand, when I reported that he

didn't come on the night train."

"But I looked out of the window a little while ago—there was no passenger with Jones."

"Has the stage come?" He glanced at the clock and blinked at the girl. "Well, I guess those books had me hypnotized!"

"Small wonder," she said, bitterly. "I tell you I'm afraid, Frank! There's something we don't see through!"

"I don't dare to waste any more time wondering what the trouble is, Vona. I must get on to the job."

"Both of us must."

"It's time for you to be going home."

"I'm going to stay here."

"But, dear girl, there's the play! You have the leading part!"

"The words will stick in my throat and tears will blind me when I think of you working here alone. Frank, I insist! I will not leave you. They must postpone the play."

He went to her and laid her hands, one upon the other, between his caressing palms. "The folks will be there—they are expecting the play—you must not disappoint them. It's as much your duty to go to the hall as it is mine to stay here with the books. And another thing! Think of the stories that will be set going, with the bank examiner here, if it's given out that the play had to be postponed because you couldn't leave the books. Such a report might start a run on the bank. Folks would be sure to think there's trouble here. You must go, Vona. It's for the sake of both of us."

He went and brought her coat and hat.

"I can't go through with the play," she wailed.

"We've got to use all the grit that's in us—whatever it is we're up against. Come! Hold out your arms!" He assisted her with the coat.

He drew her toward the door with his arm about her. "We'll make a good long day of it to-morrow—a holiday. George Washington never told a lie. Perhaps those books will come to themselves in the morning and realize what day it is and will stop lying! Now be brave!"

The kiss he gave her was long and tender; she clung to him. He released her, but she turned in the corridor and hurried back to him. "I shouldn't feel as I do—worried sick about you, Frank! The books must come out right, because both of us have been careful and honest."

"Exactly! The thing will prove itself in the end. The money in that vault will talk for us! I'll do a little talking, myself, when—But no matter now!"

"You have suspicions! I know you have!"

"Naturally, not believing as much in ghosts or demons as I may have intimated to Starr."

She looked apprehensively over her shoulder into the dark corners of the corridor. Then she drew his face down close to hers. "And it's hard to believe in the reformation of demons," she whispered.

"I'm doing a whole lot of thinking, little girl. But I don't want to talk now. Do your best at the play. Hide your troubles behind smiles—that's real fighting! And we'll see what to-morrow will do for us."

"Yes, to-morrow!" She ran away, but again she returned. "And nothing can happen to you here, in a quiet town like this, can it, Frank?" she asked.

"Nothing but what can be taken care of with that shotgun in the back room! But don't look frightened, precious girl! There's nothing—"

But even Vaniman was startled, the next moment. The girl leaped into his embrace and cowered. Something was clattering against a window of the bank. But only the mild face of Squire Hexter was framed in the lamplight cast on the window. He called, when he got a peep at the cashier, who came hastening back inside the grille: "Supper, boy! Supper! Come along!"

Frank threw up the window. "I'll make what's left over from my lunch do me, Squire. I'm tied up here with my work."

"I'll allow the new Starr in our local sky to keep you away from euchre," the Squire grumbled, "but I swanny if I'll let your interest in astronomy, all of a sudden, keep you away from the hot vittles you need. You come along with me to the house."

"Squire, I can't lock the vault yet awhile. I don't want to leave things as they are. I must not."

Vona had come to his side, she understood the nature of his anxiety. "I am just starting for my house, Squire Hexter. I'm going to hurry back with Frank's supper, so that he won't be bothered."

"Bless your soul, sis, even Xoa will be perfectly satisfied with that arrangement when I explain," said the Squire, gallantly. "I'm tempted to stay, myself, if Hebe is going to serve." He backed away and did a grand salaam, flourishing the cane whose taps on the window had startled the lovers.

"You must not take the time, Vona," protested the young man.

"I'll bring the supper when I'm on my way to the hall. Not another word! If I'm to lose the best part of my audience from the hall to-night, I can, at least, have that best part give me a compliment on my new gown—and give me," she went on, reassuring him by a brave little smile, "a whole lot of courage by a dear kiss."

She hurried away.

He was hard at work when she returned, carrying a wicker basket.

Again he protested because she was taking so much trouble, but she laid aside her coat and insisted on arranging the food on a corner of the table, a happy flush on her cheeks, giving him thanks with her eyes when he praised her gown.

"I'm going to look in on you after the show," she declared. "Father will come with me."

Vona remained with him until the wall clock warned her.

She asked him to wait a moment when he brought her wraps. She stood before him in her gay garb, wistfully appealing. "Frank, I was intending to have a little play of my own with you at the hall to-night. I was going to look right past that Durgin boy, straight down into your eyes, when I came to a certain place in the play. I was intending to let the folks of Egypt know something, providing they all don't know it by now. This is what I have to say, and now I'm saying it to the only audience I care for:

"'Twere vain to tell thee all I feel,
Or say for thee I'd die.
Ah, well-a-day, the sweetest melody
Could never, never say one half my love for thee."

Then, after a moment, she escaped from his ardent embrace.

"Remember that, dearest," she called from the doorway.

"I'll remember it every time I start with a line of figures, you blessed girl. And then how my pencil will go dancing up the column!"

After she had gone he pulled the curtain cords, raising the curtains so that they covered the lower sashes; he did not care to be seen at his work by the folks who were on their way to the hall.

Squire Hexter, escorting Xoa, took the trouble to step to the window and tap lightly with his cane. He was hoping that the cashier would change his mind and go to the hall. He waited after tapping but Vaniman did not appear at the window. The Squire did not venture to tap again. "He must be pretty well taken up with his work," he suggested to Xoa when they were on their way. "That's where we get the saying, 'Deaf as an adder.'"

Oblivious to all sounds, bent over his task, Vaniman gave to the exasperating puzzle all the concentration he could muster.

The play that evening at Town Hall dragged after the fashion of amateur shows. The management of the sets and the properties consumed much time. There were mishaps. One of these accidents had to do with the most ambitious scene of the piece, a real brook—the main feature of the final, grand tableau when folks were trying to keep awake at eleven o'clock. The brook came babbling down over rocks and was conveyed off-stage by means of a V-shaped spout. There was much merriment when the audience discovered that the brook could be heard running uphill behind the scenes; two hobble-de-hoy boys were dipping the water with pails from the washboiler at the end of the sluice and lugging it upstairs, where they dumped it into the brook's fount. The brook's peripatetic qualities were emphasized when both boys fell off the top of the makeshift stairs and came down over the rocks, pails and all. Then there was hilarity which fairly rocked the hall.

For some moments another sound—a sound which did not harmonize with the laughter—was disregarded by the audience.

All at once the folks realized that a man was squalling discordantly—his shrieks almost as shrill as a frightened porker's squeals. Heads were snapped around. Eyes saw Dorsey, the municipal watchman, almost the only man of the village of Egypt who was not of the evening's audience in Town Hall. He was standing on a settee at the extreme rear of the auditorium. He was swinging his arms wildly; as wildly was he shouting. He noted that he had secured their attention.

"How in damnation can you laugh" he screamed. "The bank has been robbed and the cashier murdered!"

CHAPTER XIV

A BANK TURNED INSIDE OUT

When the skeow-wowed "brook" twisted the drama into an anticlimax of comicality, the players who were on the stage escaped the deluge by fleeing into the wings.

Vona had been waiting for her cue to join the hero and pledge their vows beside the babbling stream. After one horrified gasp of amazement, she led off the hilarity backstage. Frank was in her mind at that moment, as he had been all the evening; her zestful enjoyment of the affair was heightened by the thought that she could help him forget his troubles for a little while by the story she would carry to him. Then she and the others in the group heard the piercing squeals of a man's voice.

"Somebody has got hystierucks out of it, and I don't blame him," stated the manager of the show. He grabbed the handle of the winch and began to let down the curtain. "I reckon the only sensible thing to do is to let Brook Number One and Brook Number Two take the curtain call."

Then Dorsey's shrill insistence prevailed over the roars of laughter in front; the young folks on the stage heard his bloodcurdling bulletin.

Holman Day

The manager let slip the whirling handle and the pole of the hurrying curtain thumped the platform. Vona had leaped, risking her life, and was able to dodge under the descending pole. For a moment, sick with horror and unutterable woe, she stood there alone against the tawdry curtain, as wide-eyed and white-faced as Tragedy's muse.

Men, women, and children, all the folks of Egypt, were struggling to their feet; the sliding settees squawked and clattered.

She saw Tasper Britt, fighting a path for himself, Starr following. Britt's face, above his blackened beard, was yellow-pale.

Panic was piling the people at the narrow rear doors; the weight of those who were rushing forward wedged all the mass at the exits.

"Vona!" called the manager, pulling at the edge of the curtain to give her passage. "This way! The side door."

The summons helped to put away her faintness; her strength came back to her. Her goal was the bank! In the frenzy of her solicitude for her lover she took no thought of herself.

The others stopped to find their wraps. Vona ran down the street as she was, bareheaded, the ribbons of her stage finery fluttering. She was close behind the first arrivals at the open door of Britt Block. All the other portals were wide open, bank door and grille door. But the door of the vault was closed.

She thrust herself resolutely through the group of men and made a frenzied survey of the bank's interior. Her single quest was for Vaniman; he was nowhere in sight. The books of account were open on the desk, mute evidence for her that he had been interrupted suddenly.

She voiced demands in shrill tones, but the men had no information for her. She called his name wildly and there was no reply.

"I found the outside door open," said Dorsey, raucously hoarse. "I came in, and all was just as you see it."

"But you said that he—that Frank—" Vona pressed her hands against her throat; she could not voice the terrible announcement that Dorsey had made.

"Well, if it ain't that, what else is it?" insisted the watchman.

Then Tasper Britt arrived in the room, followed by the bank examiner; they entered, breathing heavily and running with the tread of Percherons.

"If it ain't murder and robbery, what is it, Mr. Britt?" Dorsey bawled, evidently feeling the authority was then on the scene and was demanding report and action.

"I don't know—I don't know!" the president quavered, staggering to the grille and clutching the wires with both hands in order to steady himself. He was palpably, unmistakably stricken with a fear that was overpowering him.

The outer office was filling; the corridor was being packed by the arriving throngs.

Examiner Starr took command of the situation. He noted the nickel badge on Dorsey's breast. "Officer, put every person except Mr. Britt out of this building!"

But Watchman Dorsey, though he commanded and pushed, was not able to make any impression.

"By my authority as bank examiner, I order this place cleared!" bellowed Mr. Starr. The folks of Egypt showed that they were greatly interested in the volume of voice possessed by "Foghorn Fremont," but they did not retreat. For that matter, the crowd in the room was thoroughly blocked at the door by the press in the corridor.

Starr's attention was wholly taken up by one individual for the next few minutes. Prophet Elias boldly advanced, after worming his way out of the throng; he pushed the examiner aside from the door of the grille and went into the inner inclosure. An intruder who was prosaically garbed would not have prevailed as easily as this bizarre individual with the deep-set eyes, assertive mien, and wearing a robe that put him out of the ordinary run of humanity. But Mr. Starr got back his voice and ordered the Prophet to walk out.

Elias turned slowly and faced Starr. The Prophet's feet were hidden by the robe and he came around with the effect of a window dummy revolving on a support. Starr bawled more furious demands.

But the Prophet did not lower his crest. "'Many bulls have compassed me: strong bulls of Bashan have beset me round. They gaped upon me with their mouths, as a ravening and a roaring lion.'"

Then the Prophet spatted his palm upon the legend on his breast and clacked a disdainful digit off the pivot of his thumb. Tasper Britt, even in his hottest ire, had been restrained in the past by some influence from laying violent hands on this peculiar personage. It was evident that Starr was controlled by a similar reluctance and that his forbearance was puzzling him. When the Prophet got down on his knees, Starr was silent; it looked as if this zealot intended to offer prayer—and the bank examiner did not care to earn the reputation of being a disturber of a religious gathering. But Elias doubled over and began to crawl around the room on his hands and knees, peering intently and cocking his ear and seeming to take much interest in his undertaking.

Until then, in the rush of events, in the haste of gathering at the scene of the tragedy, in the wild uncertainty as to what had happened, nobody had taken the time to study the details of the conditions in the bank inclosure.

Starr ordered Dorsey to stand in front of the grille door and keep out all persons. The examiner was obliged to urge Britt to unclasp his hands and follow him before the door was closed and locked against the crowd.

Vona had stumbled to a chair; she was staring about her, trying to control her horror and steady her mind so that she might comprehend what had happened. Under a stool she saw a crumpled coat; she leaped from her chair, secured it, and sat down again. It was Frank's office coat; both sleeves were ripped and the back breadths were torn. She held it forward in her shaking hands for the inspection of the bank examiner. But Mr. Starr was too intent on other matters to take heed of the pathetic proof of violence. He was particularly concerned with what he had found in one corner.

Literally, thousands of small metal disks were heaped and scattered there. Some of the disks had rolled to all parts of the room. The Prophet had been scraping up handfuls of them, inspecting them, and throwing them toward the corner where the main mass lay.

Holman Day

Starr picked up some of them. They were iron; each disk was perforated.

There were many canvas sacks near the heap of disks; the sacks were ripped and empty. Mr. Starr secured one of them. Its mouth was closed with the seal with which specie sacks are usually secured.

But Mr. Starr saw something else in the corner, an object at which he peered; the gloom made the results of his scrutiny uncertain. He stooped and picked up that object, making it the third of the trinity of exhibits. It was a large square of pasteboard, the backing of an advertising calendar. Starr carried it to the lamp on the table. There was writing on the placard. The characters were large and sprawling. The bank examiner tapped his finger on the writing, calling for the attention of the anguished president. The legend read:

This is a *hell* of a bank!

"Britt, if this is a sample of your whole stock of specie," Starr rumbled, holding a disk between thumb and forefinger, "the profanity is sort of excused by the emphasis needed. I really think I would have been obliged to say the same, after counting up."

"I can't understand it," the president muttered.

"Did you suppose you carried actual coin in those bags?"

"Yes—gold and some silver."

"Had you counted it?"

"I left the checking up to the cashier."

"Where do you think your cashier is, right now?"

Britt flapped his hands, helplessly confessing that he did not know.

In all the room there was a profound hush. The crowd had been straining aural nerves, trying to hear what was being said by the men in authority.

Nobody had been paying any attention to Prophet Elias, who had been crawling like a torpid caterpillar. For some moments he had been rigidly motionless in one spot. He was leaning against the front of the vault, his ear closely pressed to the crevice at the base of the door.

He straightened up on his knees and shouted in such stentorian tones that all in the room jerked their muscles in sudden fright. "Swine! Fools!"

They gaped at him.

"Whilst you're shouting amongst your trash a man is dying on the other side of the door!"

Vona leaped from her chair. She shrieked. She ran to the door and beat her fists against the steel, futilely and furiously.

"In there lies your money-changer, I tell you, Pharaoh, lord of Egypt," the Prophet shouted. "I hear his groans!"

Britt and Starr rushed to the vault and both of them strove clumsily and ineffectually with the mechanism, giving up their attempts after a few moments.

"It's no use!" Britt gulped. "The time lock must be on."

"Oh, for the rod of Moses and the ancient faith that smote the rock in twain!" pleaded the Prophet.

"We'd better use rendrock, seeing that we can't depend on a miracle," called a practical citizen from behind the grille.

"Get sledge hammers and chisels," shouted somebody else, and there followed a surging of the throng, indicating that concerted action was following the suggestion.

The face of the president was twisted by grimaces which resembled spasms. "Wait! Wait a moment! There may be a way!" he called, chokingly. "Let me out through there!"

Then Vona gave over her insane efforts to pry open the vault door with her finger nails. She ran out past Starr, who stopped to lock the grille door. The examiner was too much taken up by other matters to bother with the Prophet, who held to his place at the vault door and was intently scrutinizing something which he found of interest.

Vona forced herself through the press, in company with Starr, and was at Britt's elbow when he unlocked his office door. He tried to keep her out and called to Dorsey. But she slipped past while the door was open to admit Starr's bulky form. Inside, she turned on Britt, who was in the doorway.

"You don't dare to keep me out, Mr. Britt!" She stamped her foot. Her eyes blazed. "You don't dare!"

He blinked and entered and locked the door.

CHAPTER XV

VIA THE PRESIDENT'S PRIVATE WAY

There was a hanging lamp in Britt's office, and the president hastened to light it.

"Do you mean to say that there's another way of entering that bank vault?" Starr demanded when Britt began to twirl the knob of a steel door that guarded his private vault. "I'm beginning to think that the fellow who wrote on that placard had this joint sized up mighty well."

Britt went on with the working of the combination. He was deeply stirred; his excitement had made his temper touchy. "I know of no reason why the president of a bank isn't allowed access to the vault."

"Perhaps not, under proper conditions, but we'll discuss that matter later, Britt. Right now I'm all-fired glad you can get in." He sneered when he added, "Perhaps a regular, time-locked vault does need a safety outlet. I may recommend it for all state banks."

Vona took her stand close to the door, trembling with passionate eagerness. Constantly she appealed to Britt to hurry. When he finally swung open the door she leaped into the vault. He dragged her back, handling her roughly, harshly telling her that it was no place for a girl.

"I don't think it is, either," agreed Starr. "We seem to have considerable love mixed in with this situation, young woman, but this is not the time for it."

He crowded past her, at the back of Britt.

The man ahead stopped and fumbled at what seemed to be a wall of concrete; he pushed open a narrow door which fitted so closely that it had seemed to be a part of the wall.

Mr. Starr grunted.

There was a passage at the right of the inner safe. The light from the lamp outside shed dim radiance. Britt descended a short flight of cement steps, and Starr, following groping with his feet, realized that the way led under the floor of the corridor. He was obliged to crouch almost double in order to avoid the ceiling.

There was another flight of stairs leading up to the floor level.

The two men, mounting the stairs, heard groans.

Vona, undeterred by her treatment, had followed closely on Starr's heels. She urged them to hurry, calling hysterically.

Again the man ahead fumbled at what seemed to be solid wall. Again he was able to open a door of concrete.

But Britt, when he was through the narrow door in the lead, was blocked and stopped. He lighted a match. One leaf of the double doors of the inner safe of the bank vault was flung back across the narrow passage. He dropped the stub of the match and pushed. The door moved only a few inches; it was opposed by something on the other side. The president lighted another match and held it while he peered over the door; there was a space between the top of the door and the ceiling. "It's Vaniman," he reported, huskily. "He's lying against this door. I can't push it any further. He's wedged against the front of the vault."

Then Starr lighted a match. He noted that the space above the door was too narrow for his bulk or Britt's.

"Go tell the guard to send in a chap that's slim and spry," the examiner commanded the girl. "We've got to boost somebody in over that door."

"I'll go. I must go. I'm bound and determined to go!" she insisted, pulling at him, trying to crowd past him.

But it was necessary for Starr and Britt to follow her to the wider space below the corridor in order to allow her to pass them. They demurred, still, but she hurried back up the stairs. Britt knelt and gave her his shoulders to serve as a mounting block. She swung herself over the door, and by the light of the match that Starr held she was able to avoid stepping on the prostrate figure when she lowered herself to the floor.

The men outside in the passage detected the odor of chloroform.

"I have lifted him," the girl cried. "Push back the door."

Britt obeyed. Then he and Starr took the unconscious cashier by shoulders and heels and carried him to the private office.

Britt's office conveniences did not include a couch; the men propped Vaniman in the desk chair and Vona crouched beside him and took his head on her shoulder.

There were no visible marks of injury. He gave off the scent of chloroform. His wrists were crossed in front of him and were secured with a noose of tape. Starr picked up shears from Britt's desk and cut the tape. "Where's your doctor? Get him in here."

"He lives in another part of the town. I didn't see him at the hall to-night," said Britt. "I'll send for him."

But Vaniman began to show such promising symptoms that the president delayed the message.

There seemed to be magic in the touch of Vona's caressing palm on the stricken man's forehead; the words she was murmuring in his ear were stirring his faculties. He opened his eyes and stared at her and at the two men, vague wonderment in his expression.

"What is it—what has happened?" he muttered.

"That's what we want to know," said Starr. "What did happen? Who got afoul of you?"

"I don't know. Who brought me in here?"

"We got you out of the bank vault and brought you here by the way of Britt's private passage."

Vaniman seemed to find that statement unconvincing.

"He didn't know about that passage," stammered the president. "I—I never bothered to speak about it. I suppose I ought to have told you, Frank. That cement panel is a door—with the handle on this side."

The cashier shook his head slowly, as if giving up the attempt to understand.

"I guess the panel fits so closely that you never noticed it was a door," Britt went on, with the manner of one trying to set himself right. "I meant to tell you about it."

"But what happened?" the examiner insisted.

"I don't know, sir."

"Look here! You must know something!"

"Mr. Starr, this is no time to shout and bellow at this poor boy who has barely got his senses back," Vona protested, indignantly.

"You mustn't blame Mr. Starr, dear," said the cashier, patting her hand. "Of course, he and Mr. Britt are much stirred up over the thing. I'm not trying to hide anything, gentlemen. You say you found me in the vault! What is the condition of things in the bank?" He struggled and sat up straighter in the chair. He was showing intense anxiety as his senses cleared.

Examiner Starr, though present officially, was in no mood to make any report on bank conditions just then. "Vaniman, you'd better do your talking first."

"I'll tell all I know about it. I was working on the books, my attention very much taken up, of course. I felt a sudden shock, as I remember it. Everything went black. As to what has been going on from that moment, whenever it was, till I woke up here, I'll have to depend on you for information."

"That's straight, is it?" demanded the examiner, grimly.

"On my honor, sir."

"There's a lot to be opened out and what you have said doesn't help."

"I wish I could help more. I understand fully what a fix I'm in unless this whole muddle is cleared up," confessed the cashier, plaintively. He had been putting his hand to his head. "I think I must have been stunned by a blow."

Starr, without asking permission, ran his hand over Vaniman's head. "No especially big lump anywhere!"

Vaniman spanned a space on his head between thumb and forefinger. "I feel a particular ache right about there, sir."

"Britt, get down that lamp!"

The president brought the lamp from the hanging bracket and held it close to Vaniman's head while Starr carefully parted the hair and inspected. "There's a red strip, but it's not much swollen," he reported. "Of course, we know all about those rubber wallopers that—But this is not a time for guesswork. Now, Vaniman, how about this chloroform odor? Remember anything about an attempt to snuff you that way?"

"No, sir!"

"Why don't you wait until to-morrow and let Frank's mind clear up?" Vona pleaded. She had been standing with her arm about the young man's shoulders, insisting on holding her position even when Starr crowded close in making his survey of the cashier's cranium.

"Young woman, the first statements in any affair are the best statements when there's a general, all-round desire to get to bottom facts," said the examiner, sternly.

"That's my desire, sir," declared Vaniman, earnestly. "But I have told you all I know."

President Britt had replaced the lamp in the bracket. He waited for a moment while Starr regarded the cashier with uncompromising stare, as if meditating a more determined onslaught in the way of the third degree. Britt, restraining himself during the interview, had managed to steady himself somewhat, but he was much perturbed. He ventured to put in a word. "Mr. Starr, don't you think that Vona's idea is a good one—give Frank a good night's rest? He may be able to tell us a whole lot more in the morning."

Then the bank examiner delivered the crusher that he had been holding in reserve. "Vaniman, you may be able to tell me in the morning, if not now, how it happens that all your specie bags were filled with—not with the gold coin that ought to have been there, but with"—Starr advanced close to the cashier and shook a big finger—"mere metal disks!" He shouted the last words.

Whether Starr perceived any proof of innocence in Vaniman's expression—mouth opening, eyes wide, face white with the pallor of threatened collapse—the bank examiner did not reveal by any expression of his own.

"This is wicked—wicked!" gasped Vona.

"Young woman, step away!" Starr yanked her arm from Vaniman's shoulder and pushed her to one side. "Did you know *that*, Mr. Cashier—suspect that—have any least idea of that?"

"I did not know it, sir."

"Why didn't you know it?"

Vaniman tried to say something sensible about this astounding condition of affairs and failed to utter a word, he shook his head.

"How had you verified the specie?"

"By checking the sacks as received—by weighing them."

"Expect somebody else to take 'em in the course of business on the same basis?"

"I was intending—"

Starr waited for the explanation and then urged the cashier out of his silence.

"I intended to have President Britt and a committee of the directors count up the coin with me, sir. But it can't be possible—not with the Sub-treasury seal—not after—"

"If you're able to walk, you'd better go over into the bank and take a look at what was in those sacks, Mr. Cashier." The examiner put a sardonic twist upon the appellation. "The sight may help your thoughts while you are running over the matter in your mind between now and to-morrow morning."

Vaniman rose from the chair. He was flushed. "Mr. Starr, I protest against this attitude you're taking! From the very start you have acted as if I am a guilty man—guilty of falsifying accounts, and now of stealing the bank's money."

There was so much fire in Vaniman's resentment that Starr

was taken down a few pegs. He replied in a milder tone: "I don't intend to put any name on to the thing as it stands. But I'm here to examine a bank, and I find a combination of crazy bookkeeping and a junk shop. My feelings are to be excused."

"I'll admit that, sir. But you found something else! You found me in the vault, you say. It is plain that I was shut in that vault with the time lock on; otherwise it wouldn't have been necessary to lug me out by that other way, whatever it is!" He snapped accusatory gesture at the open door of Britt's vault and flashed equally accusatory gaze at the president. "Do you think I was trying to commit suicide by that kind of lingering agony?"

"Seeing how you admit that you excuse my feelings, Vaniman, I'll admit, for my part, that you've certainly got me on that point. It doesn't look like a sensible plan of doing away with yourself, provided there is any sense in suicide, anyway! You say you were not aware of Mr. Britt's private passage?" he quizzed.

"Most certainly I knew nothing about it."

"I suppose, however, the vault door is time-locked. To be sure, we were pretty much excited when we tried to open it—"

"Verily, ye were!"

The voice was deep and solemn. The sound jumped the four persons in Britt's office. Framed in the door of Britt's vault was Prophet Elias.

"How did you get in here?" thundered "Foghorn Fremont," first to get his voice.

"Not by smiting with the rod of Moses," returned the Prophet, considerable ire in his tone. "I pulled open the door of the bank vault and walked in."

"Britt, you'd better put up a sign of 'Lunatic Avenue' over that passage and invite a general parade through," barked Starr. "I've had plenty of nightmares in my life, but never anything to equal this one, take it by and large!"

It was evident from President Britt's countenance that a great many emotions were struggling in him; but the prevailing expression—the one which seemed to embrace all the modifications of his emotions—indicated that he felt thoroughly sick. He gazed at the open door of his vault and looked as a man might appear after realizing that the presentation of a wooden popgun had made him turn over his pocketbook to a robber. "Walked in? *Walked* in?" he reiterated.

The stress of the occasion seemed to have made the Prophet less incoherent than was his wont; or perhaps he found no texts to fit this situation. "I did not dive through your solid steel, Pharaoh! I used my eyes, after I had used my ears. Here!" His fists had been doubled. He unclasped his hands and held them forward. In each palm was one of the metal disks. "Your bank-vault door was trigged with these—wedged in the crack of the outer flange. I saw, I pulled hard on the big handle—and here I am!"

"But the bolts—" Starr stopped, trying to remember about the bolts.

"The bolts were not shot. You were trying to push back what had already been pushed."

Starr began to scratch the back of his head, in the process tipping his hat low over his eyes. He turned those eyes on

Vaniman. "Speaking of pushing—of being able to push—" But the examiner did not allow himself to go any farther at that time. "Vaniman," he blurted, after a few moments of meditation, "I want you to volunteer to do something—of your own free will, understand!"

Vaniman, pallid again, was fully aware of the effect of this new revelation on his position, already more than questionable. "I'll follow any suggestion, of my own free will, sir."

"We'd better arrange to have a private talk to-night before we go to sleep, and another talk when we wake up. I suggest that you come to the tavern and lodge with me."

"It's a good plan, Mr. Starr," the cashier returned, bravely.

But in the distressed glance which Frank and Vona exchanged they both confessed that they knew he was politely and unofficially under arrest.

"I'll keep Dorsey on the premises and will stay here, myself," proffered the president. "You can be sure that things will take no harm during the night, Mr. Starr."

"So far as your bank goes, there doesn't seem to be much left to harm, Britt," snapped back the examiner. He fished one of the disks from his vest pocket and surveyed it grimly. "As to these assets, whatever they may be, I don't think you need to fear—except that small boys may want to steal 'em to use for sinkers or to scale on the water next summer. What are they, anyway? Does anybody know?"

Britt had plucked one of the disks from his pocket and was inspecting it. He hastened to say that he had never seen anything of the sort till that evening.

Prophet Elias seemed to be taking no further interest in affairs. He went to the door leading into the corridor. It was locked. "I'd like to get out," he suggested.

"Now that the other way through the vaults had become the main-traveled avenue of the village, why don't you go out as you came in?" was Starr's sardonic query.

The Prophet was not ruffled. "I would gladly do so, but the door of the grille is locked."

"Ah, that accounts for the fact that everybody else in Egypt isn't in this office on your heels! Britt, let him out!"

The president obeyed, unlocking the door, and the Prophet joined the crowd in the corridor. Starr went to the door and addressed the folks. "Allow me to call your attention, such of you as are handy to this door, to Cashier Vaniman." He jerked a gesture over his shoulder. "You can see that he is all right. We are giving out no information to-night. I order you, one and all, to leave this building at once. I mean business!"

He waited till the movement of the populace began, gave Dorsey some sharp commands, and banged the door. But when he turned to face those in the office he reached behind himself and opened the door again; the sight of the girl had prompted him. "I suggest that this is a good time for you to be going along, Miss Harnden. You'll have plenty of company."

But she showed no inclination to go. She was exhibiting something like a desperate resolve. "Will you please shut the door, Mr. Starr?"

He obeyed.

"It's in regard to those disks! They are coat weights!"

Starr fished out his souvenir once more and inspected it; his face showed that he had not been illuminated especially.

"Women understand such things better than men, of course," she went on. "Dressmakers stitch those weights into the lower edges of women's suit coats to make the fabric drape properly and hang without wrinkling."

"You're a woman and you probably know what you're talking about on that line," admitted the examiner. "But because you're a woman I don't suppose you can tell me how coat weights happen to be the main cash assets of this bank!" Mr. Starr's manner expressed fully his contemptuous convictions on that point.

"I certainly cannot say how those weights happen to be in the bank, sir. But I feel that this is the time for everybody in our town to give in every bit of information that will help to clear up this terrible thing. I'm taking that attitude for myself, Mr. Starr, and I hope that all others are going to be as frank." She gave President Britt a fearless stare of challenge. "My father has recently had a great deal of new courage about some of the inventions he hopes to put through. He has told me that Mr. Britt is backing him financially."

"Your father is everlastingly shinning up a moonbeam, and you know it," declared Britt.

Starr shook his hand, pinching the disk between thumb and forefinger. "Young woman, I'm interested only in this, if you have any information to give me in regard to it."

Vaniman was displaying an interest of his own that was but little short of amazement.

"The information I have is this, sir! My father said that Mr. Britt's help had enabled him to start in manufacturing a patent door which requires the use of many washers with small holes, and he was saying at home that he'd be obliged to have them turned out by a blacksmith. I happened to be making over something for mother and I had some coat weights on my table. I showed them to my father and he said they were just the thing. He found out where they were made and he ordered a quantity—they came in little kegs and he stored them in the stable. That's all, Mr. Starr!"

"All? Go ahead and tell me—"

"I have told you all I know, sir! That's the stand I'm taking, whatever may come up. If you expect me to tell you that these are the disks my father stored in the stable, I shall do no such thing. The kegs and the disks may be there right now, for all I know." She faced the examiner with an intrepidity which made that gentleman blink. It was plain enough that he wanted to say something—but he did not venture to say it.

"And now I'll go! I think my father must be out there waiting for me. If you care to stay here long enough, I'll have him hurry back from our home and report whether the kegs are still in the stable."

"We'll wait, Miss Harnden!" Starr opened the door.

After she had gone, Britt closed the door of his vault and shot the bolts.

The three men kept off the dangerous topic except as they conferred on the pressing business in hand. They helped Dorsey hurry the lingerers from the building. Then they went into the bank, stored the books in the vault, and locked it.

Starr, especially intent on collecting all items of evidence, found in the vault, when he entered, a cloth that gave off the odor of chloroform. On one corner of the cloth was a loop by which it could be suspended from a hook.

"Is this cloth anything that has been about the premises?" asked the official.

"It's Vona's dustcloth," stated Britt. He had watched the girl too closely o' mornings not to know that cloth!

That information seemed to prick Starr's memory on another point. From his trousers pocket he dug the tape which he had cut from Vaniman's wrists. He glanced about the littered floor. There was the remnant of a roll of tape on the floor. Mr. Starr wrapped the fragment of tape in a sheet of paper along with the roll.

Then Mr. Harnden arrived. The outer door had been left open for him. He had run so fast that his breath came in whistles with the effect of a penny squawker. As the movie scenarios put it, he "got over," with gestures and breathless mouthings rather than stated in so many words, that the kegs of disks were gone—all of them.

Replying with asthmatic difficulty to questions put to him by Starr, Mr. Harnden stated that he could not say with any certainty when the kegs had been taken, nor could he guess who had taken them. He kept no horse or cow and had not been into the stable since he put the kegs there. The stable was not locked. He had always had full faith in the honesty of his fellow-man, said the optimist.

Mr. Starr allowed that he had always tried to feel that way, too, but stated that he had been having his feelings pretty severely wrenched since he had arrived in the town of Egypt.

Then he and Vaniman left the bank to go to the tavern.

Outside the door, a statue of patience, Squire Hexter was waiting.

"I didn't use my pull as a director to get underfoot in there, Brother Starr. No, just as soon as I heard that the boy, here, was all right I stepped out and coaxed out all the others I could prevail on. What has been done about starting the general hue and cry about those robbers?"

Starr stammered when he said that he supposed that the local constable had notified the sheriff.

"I attended to that, myself! Dorsey could think of only one thing at a time. But I reckoned you had taken some steps to make the call more official. The state police ought to be on the job."

"I'll attend to it." But Mr. Starr did not display particularly urgent zeal.

"Well, son, we'll toddle home! What say?"

Vaniman did not say. He was choking. Reaction and grief and anxiety were unnerving him. Starr did the saying. "The cashier and I have a lot of things to go over, Squire, and he plans to spend the night with me at the tavern."

"I see!" returned the notary, amiably, showing no surprise. He called a cheery "Good night!" when he left them at the tavern door.

Landlord Files gave them a room with two beds. Without making any bones of the thing, Examiner Starr pushed his bed across the door and then turned in and snored with the abandon of one who had relieved himself of the responsibility of keeping vigil.

Holman Day

CHAPTER XVI

LOOKED AT SQUARELY

The bank examiner and the cashier were down early to breakfast.

Starr had slept well and was vigorously alert. Vaniman was haggard and visibly worried. Both of them were reticent.

Vaniman felt that he had nothing to say, as matters stood.

Starr was thinking, rather than talking. He snapped up Files when the landlord meekly inquired whether there were any clews. Files retreated in a panic.

"Vaniman," said the examiner, when they pulled on their coats under the alligator's gaping espionage, "this is going to be my busy day and I hope you feel like pitching into this thing with me, helping to your utmost."

"You can depend on me, Mr. Starr."

"I don't intend to bother you with any questions at present except to ask about the routine business of the bank. So you can have your mind free on that point."

They went to the bank and relieved Britt.

"Go get your breakfast and come back here as soon as you can," Starr commanded, plunging into matters with the air of the sole captain of the craft. "And call a meeting of the directors."

The examiner had brought a brief-case along with him from the tavern. He pulled out a card. Britt winced when he saw what was printed on the card.

THIS BANK CLOSED

pending examination of resources and liabilities and

auditing of accounts. Per order STATE BANK EXAMINERS.

Mr. Starr ordered Britt to tack that card on the outer door.

"Isn't there any other way but this?" asked the president.

"There's nothing else to be done—certainly not! I'm afraid the institution is in a bad way, Britt. You say you have been calling regular loans in order to build up a cash reserve—and your cash isn't in sight. I reckon it means that the stockholders will be assessed the full hundred per cent of liability."

He bolted the bank door behind the president.

"Now, Vaniman, did you find out anything sensible about those books, as far as you got last evening?"

"Only that the accounts seem to have been willfully tangled up."

"Then we'll let that part of the thing hang. Get out letters to depositors, calling in all pass books."

After Vaniman had set himself down to that task, Starr went about his business briskly. He prepared telegrams and sent his charioteer to put them on the wire at Levant. Those messages were intended to set in operation the state police, a firm of licensed auditors, the security company which had bonded the bank's officials, the insurance corporation which guaranteed the Egypt Trust Company against loss by burglars. Then Starr proceeded with the usual routine of examination as conducted when banks are going concerns.

For the next few days Egypt was on the map.

Ike Jones was obliged to put extra pungs on to his stage line for the accommodation of visitors who included accountants, newspaper reporters, insurance men, and security representatives.

Finally, so far as Starr's concern was involved, the affairs of the Egypt Trust Company were shaken down into something like coherence. The apparent errors in the books, when they had been checked by pass books and notes and securities, were resolved into a mere wanton effort to mix things up.

Mr. Starr took occasion to reassure Miss Harnden in regard to those books; during the investigation the girl had been working with Vaniman in the usual double-hitch arrangement which had prevailed before the day of the disaster. The two plodded steadily, faithfully, silently, under the orders of the examiner.

"Now that I've seen you at work, Miss Harnden, I eliminate carelessness and stupidity as the reasons for the books being as they are. That's the way I'm going at this thing—by the process of elimination. I'm going to say more! I'm eliminating you as being consciously responsible for any of the wrongdoing in this bank. That's about as far as I've got in the matter of elimination." He thumped his fist on a ledger. "It looks to me as if somebody had started to put something over by mixing these figures and had been tripped before finishing the job."

Then Mr. Starr, as if to show his appreciation of a worthy young woman whom he had treated in rather cavalier fashion at their first meeting, made her clerk to the receiver; the receiver was Almon Waite, an amiable old professor of mathematics, retired, who had come back to Egypt to pass his last days with his son. Examiner Starr, having taken it upon himself to put the Egypt Trust case through, had found in Professor Waite a handy sort of a soft rubber stamp.

Every afternoon, day by day, Starr had remarked casually to Vaniman, "Seeing that we have so many things to talk over, you'd better lodge with me at the hotel to-night!" And daily Vaniman agreed without a flicker of an eyelid. In view of the fact that both of them kept sedulously off the bank business after hours, there was a perfect understanding between the examiner and the cashier as to what this espionage meant. And Vaniman knew perfectly well just why a chap named Bixby was in town!

Having a pretty good knowledge of Starr's general opinions and prejudices, the cashier had squared himself to meet things as they came along. Once or twice Starr gave the young man an opportunity to come across with explanations or defense. Vaniman kept silent.

The cashier explained his sentiments to Vona. "It's mighty little ammunition I've got, dear! All I can do now is to keep it dry, and wait till I can see the whites of the enemy's eyes."

He refrained from any comment on the identity of the enemy. He did not need to name names to Vona. The attitude of Tasper Britt, who kept by himself in his own office; who offered not one word of suggestion or explanation or consolation; who surveyed Vaniman, when the two met at the tavern, with the reproachful stare of the benefactor who had been betrayed—Britt's attitude was sufficiently significant. Vaniman was waiting to see what Britt would do in the crisis that was approaching. "At any rate, I must keep silent until I'm directly accused, Vona. Starr is regularly talking with Britt. If I begin now to defend myself by telling about Britt's operations, I'll merely be handing weapons to the enemy. They can't surprise me by any charge they may bring! I have got myself stiffened up to that point. You must make up your mind that it's coming. Pile up courage beforehand!"

It was a valiant little speech. But he was obliged to strive heroically to make his countenance fit his words of courage. In facing the situation squarely he had been trying to make an estimate of the state of mind in Egypt. He bitterly decided that the folks were lining up against the outlander. As hateful as Britt had made himself, he was Egyptian, born and bred. Vaniman knew what the wreck of the little bank signified in that town, which was already staggering under its debt burden. How that bank had been wrecked was not clear to Vaniman, even when he gave the thing profound consi-deration. He did not dare to declare to himself all that he suspected of the president. Nor did he dare to believe that Britt would dump the whole burden on the cashier. However, if Britt undertook such a play of perfidy, the outlander knew that the native would have the advantage in the exchange of accusation.

Vaniman perceived the existing state of affairs in the demeanor of the men whom he met on the street, going to and from the tavern. He heard some of their remarks. He strove to keep a calm face while his soul burned!

Then, at last, Examiner Starr acted. He employed peculiar methods to fit a peculiar case.

One afternoon Starr sat and stared for some time at Vaniman. They were alone in the bank. Receiver Waite and Vona had gone away.

"Would you relish a little show?" inquired the examiner.

Vaniman had nerved himself against all kinds of surprise, he thought, but he was not prepared for this proffer of entertainment. He frankly declared that he did not understand.

"Seeing that you are doubtful, we'll have the show, anyway, and you can tell me later whether or not you relish it." He opened the door and called. Bixby came in. It was evident that Bixby had been waiting.

"All ready!" said Starr.

"All right!" said Bixby.

"I'll say that Bixby, here, is an operator from a detective agency, in case you don't know it," explained the examiner.

"I do know it, sir!"

Bixby pulled off his overcoat. Under it he wore a mohair office coat. He yanked off that garment, ripped the sleeves, tore the back breadth, and threw the coat under a stool. Then he secured a dustcloth from a hook, produced a small vial of chloroform, and poured some of the liquid on the cloth. He poured more of the chloroform on his hair and his vest. Then he laid down the cloth and got a roll of tape out of a drawer.

He cut off a length and made a noose, slipped it over his wrists, bent down and laid the end of the tape on the floor, stood on it, and pulled taut the noose until the flesh was ridged. He stooped again and picked up two metal disks which Starr tossed on the floor; the detective did this easily, although his writs were noosed.

"Not the exact program, perhaps, but near enough," Starr commented.

With equal ease Bixby laid the disks carefully on the flange of the sill of the vault. Then he took the cloth from the desk, went to the vault, stooped and thumped his head up against the projecting lever. He went into the vault and carefully pulled the door shut after him, both hands on the main bolt.

Starr was silent for some moments, exchanging looks with the cashier.

"Any comments?" inquired the manager of the show.

"None, sir."

"I'll simply say that the chloroform cloth can be put to the nose as occasion calls for. Bixby isn't doing that. I told Bixby that for the purposes of demonstration he might count one hundred slow and then figure that he had used up the oxygen in the vault, and then, if nobody came to open the door, he could—well, he isn't in there to commit suicide, but only to create an impression. I ask again—any comments?"

Vaniman shook his head.

Then the door swung open. Bixby was on his back, his heels in the air. He had pushed the door with his feet, his shoulders against the inner door. He rose and came out. Starr cut the tape with the office shears.

"That's all!" said the manager.

Bixby, not troubling about the torn office jacket, put on his overcoat and departed.

Starr took a lot of time in lighting a cigar and getting a good clinch on the weed with his teeth. He spoke between those teeth. "It's your move, Vaniman."

"I haven't agreed to sit in at that kind of a game," stated the young man, firmly.

"But you'll have to admit that I'm playing mighty fair," insisted the examiner. "When we talked in Britt's office, you and I agreed that it wasn't likely that a chap would run risks or commit suicide by shutting himself up in a bank vault with a time lock on. That's about the only point we did agree on. I'm showing you that I don't agree with you now, even on that point. That being the case, you've got to—show *me*." Starr emphasized the last two words by stabbing at his breast with the cigar.

"The idea is, Mr. Starr, you believe that I framed a fake robbery, or something that looked like a robbery, in order to cover myself." Frank stood up and spoke hotly.

Mr. Starr jumped up and was just as heated in his retort. "Yes!"

"But the whole thing—the muddling of the bank's books—the disks—a man shoving himself into the vault—I'd have to be a lunatic to perform in that fashion!"

"They say there's nothing new under the sun! There is, just

the same! Some crook is thinking up a new scheme every day!"

"By the gods, you shall not call me a crook!"

"You, yourself, are drawing that inference. But I don't propose to deal in inferences—"

"Starting in the first day you struck this town, hounding me on account of matters I had no knowledge of, Mr. Starr, was drawing a damnable inference."

"It has been backed up by some mighty good evidence!"

"What is your evidence?"

The examiner blew a cloud of smoke, then he fanned the screen away and squinted at Vaniman. "If you ever hear of me giving away the state's case in any matter where I'm concerned you'll next hear of me committing suicide by locking myself into a bank vault. Calm down, Mr. Cashier!"

Starr walked close to Vaniman and tapped a stubby forefinger against the young man's heaving breast. "I'm going to give you a chance, young fellow! I staged that little play a few moments ago so that you'd see what a fool house of cards you're living in! I hope you noted carefully that we did not need to go off the premises for any of our props. I, myself, had noted in your case that everything that was used came from the premises. Real robbers usually bring their own stuff. Even that chloroform—"

"I know nothing about the chloroform, sir."

"Well, the vial was here that night, anyway! It's a small thing to waste time on! I don't profess to be at the bottom of the affair, Vaniman. I'll admit that it looks as if there's a lot behind this thing—plenty that is interesting. I've got my full share of human curiosity. I'd like to be let in on this thing, first hand. Now come across clean! The whole story! Tell me where the coin is! It's certainly a queer case, and there must be some twist in it where I can do you a good turn. I've giving you your chance, I say!"

"I have no more idea where that coin is than you have, Mr. Starr. I never touched it. I have already told the whole truth, so far as I know facts."

"Now listen, Vaniman! This town is already *down*! If that gold isn't recovered this bank failure will put the town *out*! The folks are ugly. They're talking. Britt says they believe you have hidden the money!"

"He does say it!" Vaniman fairly barked the words. "No doubt he has been telling 'em so!"

Starr proceeded remorselessly. "I have heard all the gossip about the trouble between you and Britt. But that gossip doesn't belong in this thing right now. Vaniman, you know what a country town is when it turns against an outsider! If you go before a jury on this case—and that money isn't in sight—you don't stand the show of a wooden latch on the back door of hell's kitchen! They'll all come to court with what they can grub up in the way of brickbats—facts, if they can get 'em, lies, anyway! Come, come, now! Dig up the coin!"

Starr's bland persistency in taking for granted the fact that Vaniman was hiding the money snapped the overstrained leash of the cashier's self-restraint. In default of a general audience of the hateful Egyptian vilifiers, he used Starr as the object of his frenzied vituperation.

Mr. Starr listened without reply.

As soon as it was apparent to the bank examiner that the cashier did not intend to take advantage of the chance that had been offered, Starr marched to the door, opened it, and called. The corridor, it seemed, was serving as repository for various properties required in the drama which Mr. Starr had staged that day. The man who entered wore a gold badge— and a gold badge marks the high sheriff of a county. Starr handed a paper to the officer. "Serve it," he commanded, curtly.

The sheriff walked to Vaniman and tapped him on the shoulder. "You're under arrest."

"Charged with what?"

"I'm making it fairly easy for you," explained, Starr, dryly, appearing to be better acquainted with the nature of the warrant than the sheriff was. "Burglary, with or without accomplices, might have been charged—seeing that the coin has been removed—in the nighttime, of course! But we're simply making the charge embezzlement!"

CHAPTER XVII

ON THE FACE OF IT

Squire Hexter arranged for Vaniman's bail, volunteering for that service, frankly admitting that he "had seen it coming all along"! But the Squire was not as ready to serve as Frank's counsel and withstood that young man's urging for some time. The Squire's solicitude in behalf of the accused was the reason for this reluctance. "You ought to have the smartest city lawyer you can hire. I'm only an old country codger, son!"

"Squire Hexter, I propose to let the other side have a monopoly of the tricks. I'm depending on my innocence, and I want your honesty back of it."

In the hope that the folks of Egypt would recognize innocence when they saw it, Vaniman daily walked the streets of the village. The pride of innocence was soon wounded; he learned that his action in "showing himself under the folks's noses" was considered as bravado. The light of day showed him so many sour looks that he stayed in the house with Xoa or in the Squire's office until night. Then he discovered that when he walked abroad under cover of the darkness he was persistently trailed; it was evident that the belief that he had hidden the coin of the Egypt Trust

Company was sticking firmly in the noodles of the public.

The bank, of course, was now forbidden ground for him. The affairs of that unhappy institution were being wound up. Considering the fact that the stockholders had been assessed dollar for dollar of their holdings, and that, even with this assessment added to the assets, the depositors would get back only a fraction of their money, Vaniman could scarcely marvel at the hard looks and the muttered words he met up with on the street.

Furthermore, the insurance company took the stand that the bank had not been burglarized. On the other hand, the security company behind Vaniman's bond refused to settle, claiming that some kind of a theft had been committed by outsiders. Only after expensive litigation could Receiver Waite hope to add insurance and bond money to the assets. The prospects of getting anything were clouded by the revelations concerning President Britt's private entrance to the bank vault. But Britt was not accused of anything except of presuming on too many liberties in running a one-man bank. Under some circumstances Britt would have been called to an accounting, without question. But all the venom of suspicion was wholly engaged with Frank Vaniman, the son of an embezzler.

Squire Hexter, armed with authority and information given him by the young man, had repeatedly waited on Tasper Britt and had asked what attitude the president proposed to take at the trial. Britt had said that he should tell the truth, and that was all any witness could be expected to do or to promise, furthermore, so he told the Squire, he had been enjoined by his counsel to make no talk to anybody.

Vaniman was not sure of his self-restraint during that period of waiting. There were days when he felt like slapping the faces that glowered when he looked at them. He avoided any meeting with Britt. That was easy, because Britt swung with pendulum regularity between house and tavern, tavern and office.

There were days when Vaniman was so thoroughly disheartened that he pleaded with Vona to make a show of breaking off their friendship. She had insisted on displaying herself as his champion; obeying her, he walked in her company to and from the bank with more or less regularity. His spirit of chivalry made the snubs harder to endure when she was obliged to share them in his company.

But Vona staunchly refused to be a party to such deception. She borrowed some figures of speech suggested by the work she was doing in the bank and declared that her loyalty was not insolvent and that she would not make any composition with her conscience.

In her zeal to be of service, one day she even volunteered to interview Tasper Britt on the subject of what had happened to the Egypt Trust Company. On that fresh April morning they had walked up the slope of Burkett Hill, where the sward was showing its first green. He had come to her house earlier than usual so that she might have time for the little excursion. They hunted for mayflowers and found enough to make a bit of a bouquet for her desk in the office.

"One just has to feel hopeful in the spring, Frank," she insisted, brushing the blossoms gently against his cheek. From the slope they could look down into the length of Egypt's main street. "Why, there goes Tasper Britt toward his office and he actually waved his hand to a man—honest! The spring does soften folks. If he does know something about the inside of the dreadful puzzle, as you and I have talked so many times, I do believe I can coax him to tell me."

"I don't want you to coax him, dear. Squire Hexter has put the thing up to Britt, man to man, and I think it better to let it stand that way."

"But if we could get only a little hint to work from!"

"I'm afraid you'll find him as stingy with hints as he is with everything else. He does know—something! I would not put him above arranging that frame-up that put me where I was found that night," he declared, with bitterness.

"No, Frank, I tell you again that I don't believe he knew it was going to happen. When I stood there outside the curtain that night I was looking straight at him, and at nobody else. I don't remember another face. Tasper Britt is not actor enough to make up the expression that I saw. It was simple, absolute, flabbergasted fright!"

They started down the slope and walked in silence.

"He's considerable of a coward," Vaniman admitted, after his pondering. "I'm depending on that fact, more or less. I don't believe he'll dare to stand up as a witness in court and perjure himself. Squire Hexter has a line of questions that he and I have prepared very carefully. Britt will have to testify that I did not have sole opportunity. In considering crimes, it's proving sole opportunity that sends folks to prison!"

She turned away her face and set her teeth upon her lower lip, controlling her agitation.

"I'm trying to face the thing just as bravely as I can, Vona. On the face of it I'm in bad! When I remember how Britt maneuvered with me, I feel like running to him and twisting his head off his neck."

When they arrived in front of Britt Block, Vaniman scowled at the stone effigy in its niche. Then, when his eyes came down from that complacent countenance, they beheld the face of Tasper Britt framed in his office window. The Britt in the bank was distinctly in an ugly mood. And there was a challenge in his demeanor, a sneer in the twist of his features.

"Vona, I'm going in there," Vaniman declared. "There's got to be a showdown, but it's no job for you!"

She offered neither protest nor advice. At that moment the young man was manifestly in a state of mind which sudden resolution had inflamed with something like desperation. When he strode in through the front door Britt disappeared from the window.

Vona, following her lover, put her hand on his arm when he arrived in front of the office door. "Don't you need me with you in there?" She could not hide her apprehensiveness.

"I'm going to hold myself in, dear! Don't be worried. But it's best for me to see him alone."

He waited until she had gone into the bank office.

He did not bother to knock on Britt's door. When he twisted the handle he found that the door was locked. He called, but Britt did not reply. He put his mouth close to the door. "Mr. Britt, I have some business to talk over with you. Please let me in!"

He waited. The man inside did not move or speak. "I'm coming in there, Britt, even if I have to kick this door down."

But the threat did not produce any results. Vaniman stepped

Holman Day

back and drove his foot against the panel, but not with enough force to break the lock. His kick was in the way of admonition. After a few moments Britt opened the door; he had an iron poker in his hand. Vaniman marched in. "You don't need any weapon, sir."

"I think I do, judging from the way you came rushing into this building. Vaniman, I protest. I have said my say to your attorney. I have nothing more to add."

"I'm not here to try the case, Mr. Britt. I'll confess that I did not intend to waste my breath in talking with you. But I could not resist the feeling that came over me a few moments ago." He was standing just inside the door. He closed it. "You informed Squire Hexter that you intend to tell the truth at the trial. That's all right! I hope so. I have no criticism to offer on that point. But there's a matter of man's business between us two, and it belongs here rather than in a courtroom. Do you intend to tell the truth about how you framed me?"

"I don't understand what you mean," returned Britt, stiffly.

"I'll put it so that you can't help understanding, sir. You rigged a plan to have me sleep in the bank nights."

"That was your own suggestion. You asked to be allowed to sleep here."

"You intend to say that in your testimony, do you?"

Britt took a firm hold on the poker. "I most certainly do."

"You cooked up an excuse to send me off on a wild-goose chase in the night."

"I know nothing about your going anywhere in the night—except that Files's hostler is saying that you hired a hitch for some purpose."

Vaniman knew that appeal and protest would be futile—realizing the full extent of Britt's effrontery. However, in his amazement he began to rail at the president.

Britt broke in on the anathema. "I was not nigh the bank that night. I was asleep in my own house. You'd better not try any such ridiculous story in court—it will spoil any defense Hexter may manage to put up for you. Vaniman, it's plain enough why you hired that hitch! Why don't you tell where you hauled that money?"

"I'm not going to do to you what I ought to do, Britt. I'm into the hole deep enough as it is! But let me ask you if any jury is going to believe that I was lunatic enough to hire a livery hitch, if I was hauling away loot?"

"It's my idea, Vaniman, that you were trying to work a hold-up game on the bank, knowing that you were done here," stated Britt, coolly. "But something went wrong before you had a chance to offer a compromise. Naturally, you thought we'd do 'most anything to keep our little bank from failing."

The young man beat his fist upon his breast. "Have you the damnation cheek, Britt, to use me, the victim, to rehearse your lies on?"

"I'm giving you a little glimpse of the evidence. If the hint is of any use to you, you're welcome."

"Britt, have you turned into a demon?" Vaniman demanded. He stared at the usurer with honest incredulity.

Holman Day

"I've had enough setbacks, in recent days, to craze 'most any man, I'll admit. But I'm keeping along in my usual course, doing the right thing as I see it."

"Britt, I have never done you an injury. Are you going to ruin me because a good girl loves me?"

"I have too much respect for that young lady to allow her name to be dragged into a mess of this sort," stated the amazing Britt. "And I think that she'll wake up after she has come to a realizing sense of what a narrow escape she has had."

Vaniman stood there, his hands closing and unclosing, his palms itching to feel the contact of Britt's cheeks. There was venom in Britt's eyes. This outrageous baiting was satisfying the older man's rancor—the ugly grudge that clawed and tore his soul when he sat alone in his chamber and gazed on the girl's pictured beauty. Every night, after he puffed out his light, he muttered the same speech—it had become the talisman of his ponderings. "Whilst I'm staying alone here he'll be alone in a cell in state prison."

Vaniman understood.

He turned on his heel and walked out of Britt's office.

In the street the young man met Prophet Elias, who was adventuring abroad under his big umbrella. Vaniman was in a mood to poke ruthless facts against his aches. "Prophet, you ought to know whether any of the folks in this town believe that I'm innocent. Are there any?"

Elias, ever since he had flung to the cashier the sage advice about keeping his eye peeled, had used texts rarely in his infrequent talks with Vaniman.

"Oh yes, there are a few," he said, with matter-of-fact indifference. "But they didn't lose money by the bank failure."

"What do you think about me?"

The Prophet cocked his eyebrow. "'Can a man take fire into his bosom, and his clothing not be burned?' Britt, the bank, the girl! Three hot torches, young sir! Very hot torches!" He walked on. Then he turned and came back and patted Vaniman's arm. "You didn't keep your eye peeled! The young are thoughtless. But four good old eyes will be serving you while you're—*away*! Mine and Brother Usial's."

"Thank you!" said the young man, and he went on his way. He was reflecting on that text the Prophet had enunciated.

Might it not apply as well to Tasper Britt?

CHAPTER XVIII

A PERSISTENT BELIEF

Vaniman was indicted; he was tried; he was convicted; he was sentenced to serve seven years in the state prison. He refused to allow Squire Hexter to appeal the case. He had no taste for further struggle against the circumstantial evidence that was reinforced by perjury. His consciousness of protesting innocence was subjugated by the morose determination to accept the unjust punishment.

The general opinion was that he was a very refractory young man because he would not disclose the hiding place of the gold.

Even the warden of the prison had some remarks to make on that subject. The chaplain urged Vaniman to clear his conscience and do what he could to aid the distressed inhabitants of a bankrupt town. This conspiracy of persistent belief in his guilt put a raw edge on his mental suffering.

His only source of solace was the weekly letter from Vona. Her fortitude seemed to be unaffected; her loyalty heartened him. And after a time hope intervened and comforted him; although Vaniman had only a few friends on the job for him in Egypt, he reflected that Tasper Britt had plenty of enemies who would operate constantly and for the indirect benefit of Britt's especial victim. The young man felt that accident might disclose the truth at any time. But every little while he went through a period of acute torture; he had a wild desire to break out of his prison, to be on the ground in Egypt, to go at the job of unmasking Britt as only a man vitally interested in the task could go at it!

Sometimes his frenzy reached such a height that it resembled the affliction that pathologists call claustrophobia. He stamped to and fro in his cell, after the bolts had been driven for the night; he lamented and he cursed, muffling his tones. And a man named Bartley Wagg, having taken it upon himself to keep close tabs on Vaniman's state of mind, noted the prisoner's rebellious restlessness with deepening interest and coupled a lot of steady pondering with his furtive espionage.

Wagg was a prison guard.

After Vaniman was committed, Wagg complained of rheumatism and asked the warden to transfer him from the wall where he had been doing sentry-go with a rifle and give him an inside job as night warder. And the warden humored Wagg, who was a trusted veteran.

Wagg made regular trips along the cell tiers during the night. He padded as noiselessly as a cat, for he had soles of felt on his shoes. Many times, keeping vigil when his emotions would not allow him to sleep, Vaniman saw Wagg halt and peer through the bars of the cell. The corridor light showed his face. But Wagg did not accost the prisoner. The guard acted like a man who, whatever might be his particular interest in Vaniman, proposed to take plenty of time in getting acquainted.

Holman Day

Once, after midnight, Wagg found the prisoner pacing; Vaniman dared to relieve his feelings by groans, for the chorus of snores served as a sound-screen.

"Sick?" inquired the guard, whispering.

"No."

"If you ever are, don't be afraid to call on me when I pass. I've got a good heart."

"Thank you!"

"I've really got too good a heart to be tied up to a prison job," volunteered Wagg. "I hate to see sorrow."

"Sorrow is about all you have a chance to see in this place."

"Yes," admitted the guard, sliding away.

The warden had given Vaniman a bookkeeper's job. But the prison office was a gloomy place and the windows were hatefully barred Through the bars he could see convict toilers wheeling barrows of dirt. They were filling up a lime-quarry pit within the walls. In the old days convicts had quarried lime rocks. But in the newer days of shops the quarry was abandoned and had been gradually filled with stagnant water. When the prison commissioners decided that the pool was a menace to health, a crew was set at work filling the pit. Vaniman envied the men who could work in the sunshine. He was everlastingly behind bars; the office was not much better than his cell. The bars shut him away from opportunity to make a man's fight for himself. Every time he looked at a window he was reminded of his helplessness. It seemed to him that if he could get out into the sunshine and toil till his muscles ached he would be able to endure better the night of confinement in the cell.

He blurted out that much of confession to Wagg when the guard discovered him pacing in the narrow space a few nights later.

"I sympathize!" whispered Wagg. "I know all about your case!" Then Wagg passed on.

The next night he halted long enough to say that, knowing all about the case from what the newspapers printed, he realized just why Vaniman found it so tough to be locked up.

Then Wagg refrained from saying anything for several nights. The prisoner was quite sure that the guard had something on his mind outside of a mere notion of being polite; in the case of Wagg, so hardened a veteran, politeness to a prisoner would have been heresy. Wondering just what Wagg was driving at, Vaniman found the guard's leisurely methods tantalizing in the extreme. One night the prisoner ventured to take the initiative; he stuck out his hand to signal the guard.

Wagg, it was manifest, was not so much a master of facial control that he could suppress all signs of satisfaction. He looked pleased—like a man who had employed tactics that were working according to plans and hopes.

"Sick?"

"Yes—heart and soul! Body, too! Isn't there any way of my getting a job wheeling that dirt?"

Wagg made his noiseless getaway. He departed suddenly, without a word. Until the next night Vaniman was left to wonder to what extent he had offended the official.

But Wagg showed no signs of unfriendliness when he halted, after midnight, at the cell door. "Feel any better?"

"No!"

"I reckon I understand. Of course I understand! Most of 'em that's in here haven't anything special to look forward to when they get out. Your case is different. Everything to look forward to! No wonder you walk the cell."

On he slid, silently.

Vaniman had read the *Arabian Nights* tales, as they were divided in the literal translation. He reflected whimsically on the methods of the story-teller who, "having said her permitted say," was wont to stop right in the middle of a sentence for the sake of piquing interest in what was to follow.

The next night the prisoner's interest was heightened into real amazement. Wagg stuck his hand through the bars and waggled it invitingly.

"Take it!" he urged, sibilantly.

For a dizzy instant Vaniman was moved by the expansive hope that his plight had appealed to this man; he hastened to take what Wagg offered. It was a small cube of something.

"Eat it!" said the guard.

Holding it close to his face, to make an inspection in the dim light, the young man caught the scent of the cube. It was a piece of soap. He made sure by putting it to his nose.

"Just a little at a time—what you can stomach," Wagg urged.

He passed on.

But Vaniman did not obey; he was unable to comprehend what this sort of fodder signified; he broke the cube into bits, thinking that a saw might be hidden. It was only soap—common soap. He put the bits away in the portfolio he was allow to have in his cell.

Wagg was a bit testy the next night when Vaniman confessed that he had not eaten any of the soap.

"You've got to show absolute confidence in me—do what I tell you to do," insisted the guard.

"I can't eat that soap. It will make me sick!"

"You've said it! But eat that soap—a little at a time—and see what the prison doctor says. It isn't easy to fool prison doctors—but I've been on this job long enough to know how."

That was Wagg's longest speech to date. His earnestness impressed the young man. He managed to eat a bit of the soap after the guard had departed. He ate more in the morning before his release from the cell. He put some crumbs of the soap in his pockets and choked down the hateful substance when he found an opportunity during the day.

That night Wagg had a few more words to say on the subject. "One of the biggest birds they ever caged at Atlanta fooled the doctors and got his pardon so that he could die outside the pen. Did he die? Bah-bah! Soap! Just soap!"

"So you think the pardon plan can be worked in my case, do you?"

"Pardon your eyes!" scoffed Wagg. "That isn't the idea at all!"

He fed the soap to the prisoner for many nights, but he did not give any information. However, Wagg had the air of a man who knew well what he was about, and Vaniman was desperate enough to continue the horrible diet, having found that Mr. Wagg was a very touchy person when his policies were doubted or his good faith questioned.

Then, one day the prison doctor, who had been observing Vaniman for some time, took the bookkeeper into his office and examined him thoroughly; he gravely informed the warden that the young man had symptoms of incipient kidney trouble and ought to be less closely confined.

When Vaniman found himself out in the sunshine, intrusted with the sinecure of checking up barrow-loads of dirt which convicts wheeled past him where he sat in an armchair provided by the warden from his office, the prisoner perceived that the Wagg policies were effective in getting results.

Having added respect for Mr. Wagg's ability in general, Vaniman was not surprised to find the guard following the favored prisoner into the new field of operations. The young man was quite sure that the guard had not opened up on his principal plan.

One morning Wagg came with a stool and a rifle and located himself close beside the armchair; he sat on the stool and rested the rifle across his knees and smoked a corncob pipe placidly. And there was plenty of opportunity for talk, though Wagg obtrusively kept his face turned from Vaniman's and talked through the corner of his mouth.

"Now you see, I hope! In a prison you've got to step light and go the other way around to get to a thing. I'm favored here, and I'm supposed to be nursing rheumatism." He leaned forward to knock out his pipe dottle and found an opportunity to give Vaniman a wink. "I arranged to come off the wall—knowing all about your case. I could ask to come out here, having found that night work didn't help me! Sunshine is good. But you couldn't ask for sunshine. When a prisoner asks for a thing, they go on the plan of doing exactly opposite to what he seems to want. From now on, having seen how I can operate, I expect you to do just what I tell you to do."

Vaniman looked at the rifle. Wagg waved it, commanding a convict to hurry past.

"Yes, sir! You've got to do just as I say!" insisted the guard when the convict had gone out of earshot.

"How can I help myself?"

"Oh, I don't mean that I'm going to team you around with this rifle! I want you to co-operate."

"Don't you think I can co-operate better if you give me a line on what all this means?" pleaded the prisoner.

"Sure and slow is my policy. I'm not just certain that I have you sized up right, as yet. I'm of a suspicious nature. But I'm finding this sunshine softening." Mr. Wagg rambled on, squinting up at the sky. "Seven years is a long while to wait for a good time to come. Figuring that your time will be paid for at the rate of about ten thousand dollars a year, while you're in here, helps to smooth the feelings somewhat, of course. But now that you're in here you're counting days instead of years—and every day seems a year when you're looking forward. The newspapers said it was about seventy-five thousand dollars in good, solid gold."

Wagg bored Vaniman with a side glance that was prolonged until a toiling convict had passed to a safe distance. The young man was eyeing the guard with a demeanor which indicated that the tractable spirit commended by Mr. Wagg was no longer under good control. However, Vaniman did manage to control his tongue.

After the silence had continued for some time, the guard slipped down from the stool and marched to and fro with his rifle in the hook of his arm, affording a fine display of attention to duty.

After he had returned to his stool, Wagg gave the ex-cashier plenty of time to take up the topic. "Considering my position in this place, I reckon I've said about enough," suggested the guard.

"I think you have said enough!" returned Vaniman, grimly.

"What have you to say?"

"I didn't take that money from the Egypt Trust Company. I don't know where it is. I never knew where it went. And I'm getting infernally sick of having it everlastingly thrown up at me."

"I thought I had you sized up better—but I see I was wrong," admitted Wagg.

"Of course you're wrong! You and the chaplain and the warden and the jury! I didn't take that money!"

"I didn't mean I was wrong on that point," proceeded Wagg,

remorselessly. "But I had watched you bang around your cell and I concluded that you was ready to make about a fifty-fifty split of the swag with the chap who could get you out of here. If you're still stuffy, you'll have to stay that way—and stay in here, too!"

He took another promenade, pursuing his regular policy of starting the fire and letting the kettle come aboil on its own hook.

"What good would it do me to escape from this prison—to be hounded and hunted from one end of the world to the other?" Vaniman demanded, when Wagg had returned to the stool. "I do want to get out. But I want to get out right! I have a job to do for myself when I'm out of here!" Mr. Wagg nodded understandingly. "And that job is right in the same town where I have been living."

"Exactly!" agreed the guard. "And speaking of a job, you don't think for one moment, do you, that I'd be earning a fifty-fifty split by boosting you over that wall or smuggling you out of the gate to shift for yourself? Small wonder that you got hot, thinking I meant it that way. My plan will put you out right! My plan is a prime plan that can be worked only once. Therefore, it's worth money."

"Damn it, I haven't the money!" Vaniman, exasperated by this pertinacity, was not able to control his feelings or his language.

"It's too bad you are still at the point where you *think* you haven't got it," returned Mr. Wagg. "I'm a terrible good waiter. Reckon I have showed that kind of a disposition already. When you get to the other and sensible point where you want to be out of here, and out right, with nobody chasing and hectoring you, you and I will do business on the fifty-fifty basis. It may seem high," he pursued. "But all prices are high in these times. They're so blamed high that I'm in debt, simply trying to give my family a decent living. The state won't raise my wages. The state practically says, 'You'll have to do the best you can!' The state owes me a living. So I'll grab on to the assets that the state has hove into my reach, and will speculate as best I know now."

"You think I'm your asset, eh?"

"You're not worth a cent to me or yourself until I operate. And when you're ready to have me operate—fifty-fifty— give me the high sign. And something will be done what was never done before!"

Then Wagg carried his stool to the lee of a shop wall, seeking shade—too far away for further talk.

CHAPTER XIX

AND PHARAOH'S HEART WAS HARDENED

By the wiles of Wagg and a soap diet Frank Vaniman had been able to secure his modest slice of God's sunlight.

There was aplenty of that sunshine in Egypt. It flooded the bare hills and the barren valleys; there were not trees enough to trig the sunlight's flood with effective barriers of shade.

Tasper Britt walked out into it from the door of Files's tavern.

He had just been talking to the landlord about the tavern diet. His language was vitriolic. Even Vaniman could not have used more bitter words to express his detestation for soap as a comestible.

Britt's heat in the matter, the manner in which he had plunged into the diatribe all of a sudden, astonished Mr. Files tremendously. Britt seemed to be acting out a part, he was so violent. Usually, Britt did not waste any of the heat in his cold nature unless he had a good reason for the expenditure. There seemed to be something else than mere dyspepsia concerned, so Files thought. He followed Mr. Britt and called to him from the door. Britt had stopped to light his cigar.

190   Holman Day

"I've had my say. I'm all done here. Let that end it," declared the departing guest.

There were listeners, the usual after-dinner loafers of the tavern's purlieus. Mr. Britt did not seem to mind them. He even looked about, as if to make sure of their numbers.

"All you needed to do was to complain in a genteel way, and I would have been just as genteel in rectifying," pleaded Files.

"The people of this town are still saying that I'm a hard man. If that's so, I'm waking up to the reason for it—your grub has petrified me. My real friends have noticed it." Here was more of Britt's unwonted garrulity about his private concerns. "Some of those friends have taken pity on me. I have been invited to board with the Harnden family."

Mr. Britt did not look around to note the effect of that piece of news. He gazed complacently up into the sunshine.

He made quite a figure—for Egypt—as he stood there. Mr. Britt had "togged out." His toupee, when he first flashed it, had signified much. But the manner in which he had garbed himself for summer was little less than hardihood, considering the sort of a community in which he lived. He was "a native." The style of his attire declared that he was completely indifferent to any comments by his townsmen— and such a trait exposed in a New England village revealed more fully than his usurious habits the real callousness of the Britt nature. There was not a man in sight who did not have patches either fore or aft, or both! Mr. Britt wore a light, checked suit with a fitted waist, garishly yellow shoes, a puff tie of light blue, and a sailor straw with a sash band. He was a peacock in a yard full of brown Leghorns. But nobody laughed at Mr. Britt. Nobody in Egypt felt like laughing at anything, any more. They were accepting Britt, in his gorgeous plumage, as merely another strange item in the list of the signs and wonders that marked the latter days in Egypt.

More tawdry than ever appeared Prophet Elias's robe in that sunshine, though his umbrella did seem to comport better with the season. He stood in front of Usial's home. For a long time he had been keeping his tongue off the magnate of the town. For some weeks he had been away somewhere. To those who indulgently asked where he had been he replied tartly that he had volunteered as a scapegoat for the woes and sins of Egypt, had gone in search of a wilderness, and had come back because all other wildernesses were only second-rate affairs compared with the town from which he had started.

The Prophet seemed to feel that the appearance of Mr. Britt required comment. He raised his voice and made that comment:

"'And why take ye thought for raiment? Consider the lilies of the field, how they grow; they toil not, neither do they spin; and yet I say unto you that even Solomon in all his glory was not arrayed like one of these.'"

The Prophet bestowed a momentary benefit on gloomy Egypt—the listeners did manage to crease their countenances with grins; Britt surveyed those grins before he turned his attention to Elias. But all he did turn was his attention— silent, bodeful, malicious scrutiny. The onlookers were considerably surprised by Britt's silence; they wondered what controlled his tongue; but they were not in doubt on one point—every man of them knew that when Tasper Britt wore that expression it meant that he had settled upon the method of his revenge in the case of one who had offended him.

After a few moments Britt turned from his stare at the Prophet and dropped what was nigh to being a bombshell; it was more effective because it had nothing to do with the matter in hand.

"Listen, fellow townsmen! We all know that we ought to put our shoulders to the wheel and do something for poor Egypt. I propose to start off." He pointed to the old Britt mansion. "I'm going to tear down my house."

The men of Egypt goggled at him.

"Aye! And start off with it?" queried the Prophet. "Good riddance!"

But Mr. Britt was not troubling himself about the mouthings of Elias.

"I shall put a crew on it to-morrow. A city contractor will arrive here this afternoon with equipment and men. But he can also use all the local men who want to work. All who will pitch in can hire with him at the regular scale of wages. As soon as the site is cleared I shall start work on a new house. The plans are drawn. I have them here."

He snapped the rubber bands off a roll which he carried under his arm. He exhibited a watercolor facade elevation, stretching his arms wide and holding the paper in front of his face. The men came crowding around. They saw the drawing of a pretentious structure with towers and porticoes. Britt, holding the architect's broad sheet so that his features were hidden, explained the details of his project in regard to rooms and grounds. There was a hateful expression on the hidden face; it was the face of a man who hoped he was stirring jealous envy in those whom he wished to punish.

"It will be a mansion to the queen's taste, when you get it done," observed one man; he took advantage of the fact that Britt could not see him and winked at a neighbor. But if the man hoped to get a rise out of the builder in regard to a possible queen, he was disappointed.

Another citizen was more venturesome: "I'm taking it for granted that you don't intend to keep old-bach hall in a house like that, Tasper!"

Britt took down the shield. He displayed a countenance of bland satisfaction. "I don't think I'll be allowed to do it," he retorted, answering jest with jest. "You know what women are when they see a good-looking house needing a mistress." He rolled the paper up carefully. "And now, talking of something sensible, I hope you're going to turn out in good numbers when that contractor begins to hire. And pass the word!"

Nobody showed much enthusiasm. One man with a querulous mouth suggested: "It will seem like helping waste money, tearing down a stand of buildings that ain't in any ways due to be scrapped; I ain't sure but what it will seem like a worse waste of money, building a palace in a town like this. Don't you expect to be taxed like Sancho?"

"Until we get some kind of legislation or court action to make our town acts legal, the taxation question isn't worrying me much," said Britt, grimly. "I'll take my chances along with the rest of you on getting an act allowing us to compound with creditors."

"Probably can be arranged," said a man with the malice against the usurer that prevailed in the oppressed town. "We're sending a good man to the next legislature."

But Britt, in that new mood of his, was refusing to be baited. He began to look about. "Where is that person who calls himself a Prophet?"

The others joined with Britt in making a survey of the landscape. Nobody had been paying any attention to Elias, whose voice had been stilled since the one-sided affair with Britt.

"There he is," announced a man.

The Prophet was patrolling. He was marching to and fro in front of Britt's house. Then he walked in through a gap in Britt's fence and went to the house and peered in at one of the windows. He had lowered and folded his big umbrella and carried it under his arm.

"I call on all of you to note what he did then," called Britt. "He has been doing that lately."

The Prophet returned to the road. Then he seemed to be attacked by another idea. He went back through the gap in the fence and peered in at another window.

"I repeat, he has been doing that. I was getting ready to take proper measures to handle him. Something better than talking back to a lunatic! But I didn't reckon I'd have such good luck as this! Twelve men right here for my witnesses! Look hard at him, men!"

They did look, though they did not comprehend what Britt's excited insistence signified. He pulled out a notebook and pencil and handed it to the nearest man. "Mark down two! Mark it down—and all of you take due notice."

The Prophet returned to the highway and came slowly pacing

along toward the group.

"All of you saw, did you? All of you ready to bear witness?" demanded the magnate.

He stepped out in front of Elias when the latter came near. Britt shook the roll of drawings under the Prophet's nose. "Listen here, my man! I didn't bother to talk to you a few minutes ago. Now I'm talking. You've been a vagabond in this town for a long time. The only thing that has protected you from the law in such cases made and provided has been the roof of a man who ought to be a tramp along with you. Right now, before the eyes of a dozen citizens, you have committed two separate and distinct breaches of the law. You have trespassed on my property. In the past I have sent men to jail for sixty days for one offense of that sort. On my complaint, backed by these witnesses, you'll see sixty days on one case—and I'll have you re-arrested on the other count the moment you step foot out of the jail." He paused.

"Yes?" said the Prophet, mildly inquiring.

"I'm a fair man, and I call the attention of these witnesses to what I say now. I'll give you a chance. Walk out of this town and stay out, and I'll not prosecute."

The Prophet shook his head.

"Do you refuse to go?"

For a man who dealt so exclusively in texts, the Prophet was rather vulgarly blunt when he replied, "You bet!"

Britt received that manner of retort with the air of a man who had been tunked between the eyes. It was some moments before he could go on. "Don't you realize what the judge will say when I show up your willfulness?"

The Prophet was even more amazing in his new manners. He stuck out his tongue, put his thumb to his nose, and wriggled his fingers.

"Well, I'll be condemned!" Britt gasped.

"Sure! When all the evidence is in about you!"

The magnate of Egypt lowered the roll that he had brandished so constantly. After a few moments of silent challenge with the eyes, he turned and walked away.

But he heard the mumble of men's laughter behind him, and his anger and the determination not to be put down in this style in his own town helped him to get back some of his self-possession. He whirled on his heels and strode to the enigma of Egypt.

"Who are you, anyway?" he demanded.

But Prophet Elias was his usual self once more. He had assumed that air which a practical man like Britt found an aggravating, teasing pose or a kind of lunacy with which common sense could not cope. Elias slowly spread his umbrella. He stood beneath it and declaimed:

"'And Moses and Aaron did all these wonders before Pharaoh; and the Lord hardened Pharaoh's heart, so that he would not let the children of Israel go out of his land.'"

"You let me tell you something! There's one man going out of this land mighty sudden—and he's going to the county jail in charge of a constable."

When Britt started away that time he kept on going. He went to the office of Trial-Justice Bowman and swore out a warrant. A constable served it and the Prophet was haled before the justice. On the evidence presented, Bowman sentenced a person known as "the Prophet Elias" to serve sixty days in the county jail. Within an hour after the Prophet's defiance he was on his way with the constable in a side-bar buggy.

The Prophet had not opened his mouth to give out even one text. He had not opened his mouth, either, to give his name; the writ designated him merely by his sobriquet. But there was a queer little wrinkle at each corner of that closed mouth.

CHAPTER XX

NO STRAW FOR THE BRICKS

Mr. Harnden banged his pulpy fist on the board at which so he had declared, Tasper Britt was to sit.

"I have ruled a happy home by love in the past. Don't force me to rule it otherwise now."

He was obliged to lower his eyes to a level at last because his neck ached. He was forced to turn those eyes in his daughter's direction, for her gaze was of that compelling quality which causes the object of regard to return the scrutiny.

"I tell you, I'm not lowering myself by taking in boarders," the father insisted. "I have become tied up in a business way with my friend Britt. We need to be in conference right along. They're going to tear down his house. Shall I let it be said that I left a friend ahungered and without a roof? Shall—"

"Father, I'm no longer patient enough to listen to any more of that nonsense," said Vona.

"But it isn't nonsense," put in the mother. "Poor Tasper is left without a home. Files's vittles have nigh killed him. He was always used to home cooking. He—"

"Please! Please!" protested the girl, impatiently. "We're three grown-ups. Let's be honest with one another. I, at least, have been honest—ever since I declared myself under this roof last winter."

"If you're bound to put your father's and your mother's close friendship for a man strictly on the business basis, we'll have it that way," agreed Mr. Harnden, trying to straightedge his little bunghole of a mouth and failing.

"Very well, father! We shall get along better. I'm not in any position to dictate in our home—"

"Well, I should say not!" exploded the master.

"But I have worked and turned in my money to help support it, and I have my personal rights here."

Mr. Harnden had more success in arranging the expression he assumed then; he looked hurt; he had been very successful with that expression in the past. "Any farseeing man has his ups and downs, Vona. Is it kind to twit your father—"

She protested more impatiently still. "I am simply presenting the business side of the matter. I say, I have earned some rights to be comfortable in my own home. On the plea of friendship for a man whom I detest, you are proposing to destroy that comfort. Is your friendship for that man greater than your love for your daughter?"

Mr. Harnden rose and stuck out his frontal convexity and wagged a forefinger. "Now you're getting off the question of business—just as you accused me of getting off it!" He

Holman Day

slapped his breast. "I'm a business man these days. I'm no longer a man with visions, needing a daughter's sacrifices, like you have twitted me of being. Keep still! I'm talking!" he squealed. He was displaying more of the new and cocky demeanor that had been his for some time. He had been especially set up for a few days prior to his announcement that Tasper Britt was coming into the Harnden home as lodger and guest at table. "Business it is! Britt will pay board enough, seeing that he has come to my—*my* terms, so that your mother can keep a hired girl for the first time in her life. Are you so selfish as to want to have your mother—my wife—go on potwalloping in the kitchen for the rest of her days? If that's so, you'll find that my pride will override your selfishness."

"Father, I will stay at home and do all the work, if you'll keep our home from being desecrated by that man!"

Mr. Harnden reared his crest and advanced one foot. "I have raised my daughter to be a lady and will keep her so! I'm now in a position to do it without any of her help."

Vona stood up then. But not to fling angry retort at her father! She knew that she was able to conquer the raging self that was urging her to tell both of them what she thought of their idiotic persistency in backing the attentions of Britt. Being victor over herself in that conflict with self where so many fail, she felt courage to battle in another quarter. Since Frank had been penned up where he could not fight, she had felt that she was the champion for their mutual interests, and she was resolved to keep on valiantly. "Father, you know how I stand in the matter of Frank Vaniman."

"I have broken your engagement with that jailbird."

"Vona, I have told you repeatedly that I will never consent to your marrying that man," shrilled Mrs. Harnden. "What does the Bible say about obeying your parents?"

The girl was tensely suppressing her emotions. "The outsiders merely know that I am engaged to marry him. But both of you know that I am married to him."

Mr. Harnden sat down in order to express his emotions; Mrs. Harnden stood up. Their duet of disavowal of any such knowledge was keyed high.

"You heard me when I married him—in your presence—under this roof. The legal formality can wait. But I am married. In my heart I am married. It is enough for me until he comes back to me. And what God hath joined together let not man put asunder!" She said it reverently, with all her soul in her tones, all her woman's resolution of loyalty in her eyes.

They tried to say something, but in the face of her demeanor of firmness their opposition was futile, and they probably realized it, for they became silent and allowed her to speak on.

"If you do not choose to consider my feelings in the matter, I'll not complain. You are master and mistress of the home. I tell you now, as I have told you before, that if Tasper Britt had come out with the whole truth Frank would not be in prison. You must not expect that I will sit at table with a man who has so persecuted my—husband!" She hesitated a moment before she spoke the last word. She caressed it with loving inflection. A moment later her cheeks were burning hotly. She went out into the hall, got her sunshade, and left the house.

She still had her work at the bank; the progress of liquidation was slow. Tasper Britt, from his office window, saw her coming. She wore no hat. The parasol framed the face that was still glowing after her battle for the sanctity of her love.

"It's worth it!" he muttered; but not even to himself did Britt mention what the price was.

Mr. Harnden's comment, delayed for some minutes, was that the girl was putting it almighty strong.

"It's her loyalty. She can't help it. She takes it from me," declared the mother, pouring another cup of tea for her shaken nerves.

"She does, hey?" Mr. Harnden's voice indicated that he was not commending the quality mentioned.

His wife was decidedly tart in her retort that he ought to be thankful for the loyalty that enabled her to put up with all the privations of the past.

"Well, let the past be the past. I've got my feet placed now— and that hired girl is coming to-morrow." The idea of his new prosperity revived Mr. Harnden's natural optimism. "That jailbird hasn't been away from her long enough for her to be weaned from her foolishness about him. He's safe away for seven years, and a whole lot can happen in that time— even to that loyalty that women seem to set such store by. My friend Britt comes here—into our family! That's understood. If Vona wants to eat off'n the mantelshelf in her room, well and good till she's tamed. And now—to work—to work!"

Mr. Harnden was truly very much up-and-coming those days. He rose and shook out first one leg and then the other, with the manner of a scratching rooster. The movements settled the legs of his trousers. He had a new suit of his own. It resembled Tasper Britt's. That new suit and the yellow gloves and the billycock hat excited some interest in Egypt; the new hitch that Harnden possessed excited much more interest. He was driving a "trappy" bay nag, and his new road wagon had rubber tires. Nor was Mr. Harnden doing any more inventing, so he declared to the public. The public, however, did declare behind his back that he must have invented something in the way of a system to be able to wear those clothes and drive that hitch. To be sure, there were some who insisted that the matter of Vona was still potent with Britt and that Britt's money was behind Harnden. But there were more who were certain that it was not the style of Britt to invest in any such remote possibility as a girl who openly declared that she proposed to wait seven years for the man of her choice.

Harnden had a new business; he was selling nursery stock. But that business did not account for his prosperity. He was taking town orders for his goods—taking orders on the town treasury, orders that had long been creased in wallets or had grown yellow in bureau drawers or had been dickered about at a few cents on the dollar and accepted when a debtor had nothing else with which to pay. Mr. Harnden said he was ready to take town orders at any time. He optimistically declared that his faith in the old town was firmly fixed. That optimism was entirely in accord with Mr. Harnden's past professions; and nobody wondered much, because he was so foolish. But he was not wholly a fool in that matter. He had only about a fifty-per-cent faith in Egypt—he insisted on that much discount when he took in a town order. Even at that rate, Ossian Orne did insist that Harnden was a complete fool. Orne would not take town orders for his nursery stock. But Orne's nose was out of joint, it was generally agreed. Harnden's lithographs showed apples twice as big as Orne's book did; the pears fairly oozed sweetness from their plump, pictured mellowness; there were peaches that provoked folks to make funny noises at the corners of their mouths when the optimistic Harnden flipped a page and brought the fruit to view. Nobody had ever heard of a peach tree growing among the rocks of Egypt. On the other hand, nobody supposed that a town order on the Egypt treasury was worth anything, as things stood. There were folks who bought peach trees!

And in the meantime there was much clatter in and about the old Britt house, tumble of timbers and rip of wainscotings and snarl of drawing nails. Out from the gaping windows floated the powdery drift of the plastering which the broad shovels had tackled. The satirists said that it was noticeable that the statue of Tasper Britt in the cemetery had settled down heavier on its heels, as if making grimly sure that Hittie was staying where she could not interfere.

In the meantime, also, Tasper Britt and a hired girl had become fixtures in the Harnden home—and the hired girl was quite in love with Vona and in entire sympathy with her stand; the girl brought to Vona's room the tidbits of all the meals and offered to put tacks in Britt's doughnuts if that would help matters any.

Vona was entirely serene in her companionship with her father and her mother. As for Tasper Britt, in sitting room or hall, on the street or on the lawn of the Harndens, he was ignored as completely, yet sweetly, as if he were an innocuous dweller in the so-called Fourth Dimension—to be seen through—even walked through—a mere shade, uninterred, unhonored, and unwarranted.

Tasper Britt, relentlessly on the job of punishing those who had poisoned his pride and his peace of mind, acknowledged to himself that the attitude of this girl was reacting on him in the way of more acute punishment than he was dealing out to anybody just then, except to Vaniman. Through the latter the girl was punished. But that punishment had steeled her to the stand she was making in the case of Britt. The god of the machine pondered on the case and constantly found himself in a more parlous state of mind because he did ponder.

Mr. Harnden tried his best to cheer the morose Britt. Some days the usurer-suitor wanted to cuff the optimist; some days he felt that he would go crazy unless Harnden could extend some hope, suggest some way of changing the girl's attitude.

All the time Mr. Harnden was very cheerful and extremely busy; his nag kicked up the dust along all the roads. His book of lithographs was dog's-eared with much thumbing, but he had served as a human vacuum cleaner in sucking up most of the town orders. Mr. Harnden was very free with information, customarily. But when folks asked him whatever in the world he expected to do with those town orders he was reticent as to any details of his plans. He considered that his optimism of faith in the future of the town covered the matter. He said so. He let it go at that.

One day Harnden roamed far afield and went to the shire.

The next day he came back from the shire.

After supper he sat in a wicker chair on the lawn with Tasper Britt, who was wearing a new suit of white flannel and who scowled when Vona passed along the walk without even a glance in that direction, though Britt had twitched up his trousers leg to show a particularly handsomely clocked sock.

Mr. Harnden did a lot of talking that evening. Every now and then, as if to fortify his optimistic courage, he declared, "After all, business is business—and the trend of the times is to make the most of opportunity."

Holman Day

Britt was showing interest in what Harnden was saying—interest and satisfaction, too. But all at once that interest was diverted and the smooth satisfaction was wrinkled by a scowl. Britt swore roundly and struggled up from his chair.

Prophet Elias was passing along the street. He flapped his hand in a greeting contemptuously indifferent and went on his way toward Usial's cot.

"Oh! I was intending to tell you about him," avowed Mr. Harnden, "but I've had more important things to talk over!"

Britt gave to this blunderheaded news purveyor the tail end of the malevolent stare that he had been bestowing on the Prophet's back.

"I heard about it when I was over to the shire town. A city lawyer showed up the other day and deposited cash bonds and got out a writ, and got Elias out, too, and the case has been appealed. Looks like the Prophet has footed it back here again. But I suppose you can arrest him on that other case of trespass."

Britt did not show especial alacrity in starting anything else in the case of the new arrival in town. He sat down. "Who was the lawyer? Who sent him?"

"Guess he didn't say. Let the money do the talking for him. And money can talk! Now, as I was saying, to get back to our regular business, it's up to you to name the ones that Dowd will tackle. Say, where are you going?"

Britt was on his feet and moving rapidly. "Somewhere to do some thinking away from that carpet-loom, shuttle-tongued, infernal mouth of yours!"

Mr. Harnden, astonished and much hurt, watched the usurer till he tramped into Britt Block.

But Mr. Harnden had too much important business of his own on his mind to use time in wondering how a Prophet had managed to get out of jail.

CHAPTER XXI

BLOOD OUT OF TURNIPS

In the past Mr. Harnden had regularly referred to Egypt as a good jumping-off place; he emphasized the jest by pointing to the ledge outcroppings which indicated that the landscape would not sag under the weight of the most energetic jumper. Then away he would go!

His detractors said that he was in the habit of coming home when affairs were in such a bad way with him that he could not stay anywhere else.

His wife and daughter had never admitted anything of the sort, even to each other. They affectionately welcomed Mr. Harnden when he came; after he had stoked the fires of his faith, and they had darned his socks and mended his shirts, they gave him the accustomed encouraging and loving Godspeed when he went away again under a full head of optimism. They always agreed with him, on each going-away, that this was surely the time when Opportunity was waiting outside.

But for many weeks Opportunity had seemed to be camping with Mr. Harnden right in his own home town. He was brisk, radiant, and apparently prosperous.

Therefore, when he announced in the bosom of his family that he proposed to go away for a time, his wife and daughter were frankly astonished.

It was directly after breakfast on the morning following Mr. Harnden's return from the shire town.

He did not display his usual jocose manner when he referred to Egypt as a jumping-off place. Vona found a sort of furtive uneasiness in the way he glanced out of the window and fingered his vest-pocket equipment. And he trod to and fro with the air of a man stepping on hot bricks.

"But you have said you are doing so well in your new business, father!" Vona's straightforward gaze was disconcerting.

Mr. Harnden kept on with his patrol. "Confound it. I've got to get into towns where there's more dirt if I'm going to sell any more nursery stock!"

"Oh, is that it? But I happened to go up in the attic and I found your sample books thrown behind a trunk, and I was afraid—"

"Afraid of what?" he demanded, with childish temper.

"Afraid you were giving up what seems to be a sure thing. The other ventures have been such uncertainties!" she returned, her business woman's composure unaffected by his reproachful stare.

"The books were all smutched up—too many dirty fingers afoul of them. I shall get new ones—providing I stay in that line." He was not convincing. "We'll see—we'll see! I've got to be moving. These are busy times for me."

"But you don't say when you're coming back, Joe!" quavered his wife.

"Why should I begin to set dates now, when I never have in past times?"

"Oh, I suppose it's because we've got so used to having you at home," she confessed.

"I'm leaving matters in better shape than I ever did before," said Mr. Harnden, pompously. "I have been worried about my home in the past when I have had to be absent on my business. We have Tasper in the house now. And he will not only guard and protect, but he will pay as he goes. I may not go far or stay long. Just let it stand that way. Tell inquiring friends that. I'll keep you posted. You know what my business is; it takes me here—it takes me there." He gave his wife a peck of a kiss and patted Vona's shoulder when he passed her. He picked up a valise in the hallway.

The girl followed him. "Father, always when you have been away, mother and I have felt perfectly comfortable and safe here in our home. If Mr. Britt hasn't the sense or the good taste to go somewhere else to board, won't you suggest to him that he'd better do so?"

"Nothing of the sort, Vona!" declared Harnden. "That contractor has brought a lot of strangers here to work on Britt's house, seeing that the men of this town are biting off their noses to spite their faces! I wouldn't take a minute's peace, knowing that my home is unprotected, unless I felt that a friend of mine was here as guardian. Oh, I know what you mean! But I have the safety of my family to consider instead of a girl's whims."

She did not argue the matter. His peppery impatience was

increasing. This time he was not departing with his customary bland hopefulness. She knew the sort of selfishness her father possessed and how he avoided scenes that troubled his smug serenity. But on this occasion he seemed to be impelled by some urgent reason outside of mere anxiety to be away from complaining tongues.

He hurried out of the house and went to the stable, and she said no further word.

Ten minutes later he drove away, flinging a kiss to his womenfolks from the finger tips of the yellow gloves.

He headed directly out of the village and drove at a good clip.

However, one might have concluded that Mr. Harnden's destination was not as clearly settled in his mind as the haste of his departure suggested. When he came to four corners he pulled up and looked to right and to left and to the straight ahead. Mr. Harnden was too well acquainted with all the roads of Egypt and its environs to be confused by anything except strictly personal and peculiar doubts which had nothing to do with the matter of destination. He looked up into the heavens, as if he really wished that he might be able to escape from Egypt by flight. Then he did literally what the Yankee phrase suggests by way of synonym for taking counsel—"he looked between the horse's ears." He narrowed his eyes in meditation and spoke aloud. "I reckon it's only general nervousness on account of overwork and women's foolishness. There ain't one chance in ten that they'll get around to it to-day."

Arriving at that comfortable conclusion, Mr. Harnden lighted a cigar and chirruped to his horse and drove straight on.

The road zigzagged through an alder swamp for some distance, and the horse footed along slowly because a portion of the way was patched with sapling "corduroy." And with the impulse of a man who had been obliged to waste time, and saw an opportunity to get on, Harnden whipped up when he was again facing a smooth road. Therefore he came suddenly around the bend of the alders into cleared country and abreast a farm. It was a farm made up of the alluvial soil of the lowlands and was a rather pretentious tract of tillage, compared with the other hillside apologies of Egypt. And the buildings were in fairly good repair. It was the home of Jared Sparks Grant, the first selectman of the town.

Mr. Harnden did not look to right or left as his horse trotted past. He did not appear to be interested in the affairs of Egyptians that day—even in the case of the town's chief executive. When Harnden was hailed raucously he did not pull up, though he heard his name. After a few moments a gun banged behind him.

"I'm saving the other barrel," the voice announced, after Harnden had steered his horse from the gutter into the road; the animal had been frightened by the pattering of shot in the foliage of a tree overhead. "You'll get it straight, Harnden, unless you drive back here!"

When Harnden wheeled the horse and returned he perceived a dooryard group which he had affected not to see a few moments before.

There were Jared Sparks Grant, his son, his womenfolks, his hired man; Mr. Harnden recognized all of them, of course. He also recognized Deputy-sheriff Wagner Dowd from the shire town. Dowd had a couple of helpers with him. It was plain that the shotgun which had halted Mr. Harnden had been very nigh at hand and ready for use; there was a look about the folks in the dooryard which suggested an armed truce, now prolonged, for the handling of the new arrival.

"Don't you realize what's going on here?" demanded Selectman Grant, his weapon in the hook of his arm.

"No!" asserted Mr. Harnden.

"I know a blamed sight better! You can't look at this deputy sheriff without turning redder than one of the apples in that fake picture book of yours. You know what you have been doing in this town."

The selectman's tone was offensively harsh and loud. Mr. Harnden was moved to show a little spirit, having been cornered—and feeling protected by the presence of an officer of the law. "I have been doing business!"

"Scooping in town orders, you mean!"

"Taking them in the due course of my business, Mr. Selectman. I had a right to do it!"

"And what did you do with those orders?"

"I passed them on—still in the course of my business."

"And you don't know into whose hands they have come?"

"Oh no!"

The selectman stepped close to the carriage and brandished his gun. "While this town was staggering along, trying to find a way out, only a hellion would take and make a club out of those orders and hit us the last and final clip with 'em. You've done it, Harnden! For the sake of the dirty money you've done it. They were letting those orders rest easy till we could get the legislature and have things put into some condition where we'd know what's what. Through your work some land pirate has got hold of those town orders. There isn't a cent in the town treasury. You know it."

He whirled away from Harnden and shook the gun at the deputy sheriff.

"I sha'n't believe your law, Dowd, till I've been and talked with Squire Hexter."

"Go and talk! But in the meantime a good lawyer has told me what to do and has given me the documents, and I'm not trying the case in your dooryard. I have levied on those oxen and I shall take 'em along."

"Do you hear that, Harnden? That's what you have done to your town," bellowed the infuriated selectman. "He says there's a law allowing a creditor to levy on the property of any citizen of a town to satisfy a judgment. Judgment has been secured on those town orders. They are jumping on me first."

"It's what the lawyer told me to do," insisted the officer. "'Start with the selectman,' says he. 'That shows the others where they get off.' Grant, I'm here with the papers and the right to act." He advanced close to the selectman, waggling admonitory forefinger. "I've been excusing your feelings. I don't blame you! This is tough. It's the penalty you pay for living in such a town. But I don't propose to stand for any more of that gunplay. Hand it over!"

Grant hesitated. The officer snatched away the gun, broke it down, and pulled out the undischarged shell. He put that into his pocket and shoved the gun under the seat of a wagon.

"You can have this gun back after the war is over. Now to business! You claim that the oxen are exempt because you have no horses. All right! I see you have a dozen cows. I'll take three of those. I'm fair, you see! You're only entitled to one cow. But keep nine. I'm going to spread the thing around town till I have enough to satisfy this judgment. It's for one hundred and ninety dollars. What say, now? Do you want to pay a fine for obstructing an officer?"

Selectman Grant shook his head. The flame of his rage had died down into sullen rancor. He went along to Harnden's carriage and suddenly nipped that gentleman's nose between toil-calloused index and middle fingers. "They tell me there's no law against doing this," he said between his yellow, hard-set teeth, as he twisted at the nose, while Harnden's eyes ran water. "If there is a law, I hope you'll stay handy by in this town and prosecute while we're heating the tar and getting the feathers ready."

Sheriff Dowd took advantage of Selectman Grant's preoccupation with Harnden. He gave off orders to his helpers and they lowered the bars of the barnyard and started away with the cows.

There was a general disintegration of the group. Mrs. Grant led the lamenting womenfolk into the house. Mr. Harnden did not really extricate his nose; Grant twisted so violently that he broke his own grip, and his victim laced the whip under the horse's belly and escaped.

Within ten minutes Selectman Grant was whipping his own horse in a direction opposite to that which Harnden had taken. Mr. Grant was hot after law.

Squire Hexter gave him the law, and cold comfort.

"They can do it, Jared. Outsiders can get hold of unpaid town orders and put on the screws if they're that heartless. It isn't done once in a dog's age. But, as I say, it can be done when a creditor is ugly enough. Harnden didn't say, did he, just who brought the orders?"

"I wouldn't have believed him if he did say! But he didn't say."

"And you don't know the man who secured judgment?"

"Never heard of him."

"I will try to trace the matter, Jared. No, keep your wallet in your pocket. There's no charge. It's a case where the interests of the citizens in general are concerned. I'm the regularly elected town agent, as you know!" The Squire smiled. "I'll take a town order for my pay." He looked out of the window. "It's about time for somebody else to come larruping up here after law! Don't hurry, Jared! Wait and hear what's happened to the neighbors!"

The selectman sat gloomily, elbows squared on his knees, and waited. Almost opposite the Squire's office the rattle-te-bang business on Britt's premises was going on.

"I wonder whether Tasper will dare to go ahead and build his palace after he hears the latest news," suggested the Squire. "You must be told, Jared, that after the live stock of the town has been thinned down to the essentials permitted by law, then the farms and general real estate can be levied on."

Grant lifted his haggard face and stared at the Squire. "Then, outside of the cook stove and my clothes, I don't know whether I'm worth a blasted cent, hey? They can dreen me slow with a gimlet, or let it out all at once with a pod auger, can they? That's what the law can do *to* me, you say! What can it do *for* me, Squire Hexter?"

"Well, Jared, they'll take your cows over to the shire and auction them off for what they'll bring. You can sue this town and recover the real value of the cows, along with interest at twelve per cent. That is to say, you can get judgment against the town for that amount."

"And then I can go over to my neighbor's and grab away any loose property I can find of his?"

"You can do it!"

"Look here, Squire, that makes it nothing except a game of 'tag, you're it,' and a case of 'I've got my fingers crossed'! The whole of us running around in circles, and the lawyers picking up all the loose change we drop from our pockets. Where do we wind up?"

The Squire shook his head slowly and reached down and stroked one of Eli's ears. "Eli was telling me that Jones thought he had invented perpetual motion when he tied a piece of liver to a pup's tail and set the pup to revolving; but the pup wore out."

Grant sat for some minutes and harkened to the bang of the hammers across the way. "I don't understand how a farseeing man like Tasp Britt dares to build a good house here," he growled.

"Oh, the pup may be worn out by the time it is finished—or those towers may mean that he intends to list it as a meetinghouse and have it exempted from taxation, Jared. We shall see!"

But whatever it was that the selectman saw, as he sat there and stared at the wall of Squire Hexter's office, it evidently was not serving in the way of comfort.

The Squire's prediction about other seekers for law was fulfilled before long. The deputy sheriff had proceeded on his travels. The afflicted parties came up the Squire's stairs. Arden Young reported that three of his best cows were driven away. George Jordan and his cousin J. O. Jordan each surrendered two faithful moolies. It was plain that Sheriff Dowd proposed to make sure that there was auction material enough to yield one hundred and ninety dollars, along with the costs.

"Jared," suggested the notary, "you'd better have an accounting and find out how many of those town orders were issued when the reckless spirit was on. Somebody has decided to milk the old town. It is being done scientifically, seeing that this first mess is so modest. But we need to know about how many messes we're expected to give down."

Inside of a fortnight there were two more milkings.

At about that time Tasper Britt started proceedings to foreclose a couple of mortgages. The debtors despondently declared that they would not attempt to redeem the property; they told Britt that he could have it for what he could get out of it. The usurer tried to show disinclination to take over real estate in Egypt, but he did not make a very good job of the pretense. He had the air of a man who expected to be obliged to tussle for something, but had had the something dropped into his grasp when he merely touched the holder's knuckles.

Britt had a map of the town in his office desk. He began to color sections with a red crayon. According to Mr. Britt's best judgment in the matter, he was in a fine way to own a whole town—a barony six miles square—at an extremely reasonable figure. From the selectman down, nobody seemed to feel that Egypt property was worth anything. As to beginning suits against the town, nobody felt like paying lawyers' fees and piling up costs. It was like tilting against a fog bank. And in a veritable fog bank of doubt and despair the unhappy Egyptians wandered around and around.

Holman Day

CHAPTER XXII

THE TAUT STRING SNAPS

Frank Vaniman's mother was allowed to visit him once a month at the prison. She was not present at his trial. She had respected his earnest wishes in that matter.

When she came to him she smiled—she did not weep. When she smiled he wanted to weep. He realized how much that display of calm courage was costing Martha Vaniman. He remembered how bravely and steadfastly she had brought that same heroine's quality to the support of his father when she had taken Frank with her to the prison; they used to walk in through the gloomy portal hand in hand, and, though her face was serene, her throbbing fingers told him what her heart was saying to her.

Her husband had thankfully accepted that little fiction of her fortitude; her son, under like circumstances, did the same. Between mother and son, as between husband and wife, was the bond of an implicit faith in the innocence of the accused. Love was not shamed, no matter how the outside world might view the matter.

The prison warden was a fat man, full of sympathy. He gave the mother and son the privileges of his office, and to those reassuring surroundings the mother brought Frank's sister on one of the regular visits.

After Mr. Wagg's guile gave Vaniman his outdoor job, the mother brought Anna each month, for the school vacation season was on. The sun was bright out there in the yard. One could look up into the fleecy clouds, over the walls, and forget the bars and the armed guards.

In fact, one day, Anna's ingenuous forgetfulness of the true situation provoked real merriment for the little party—Guard Wagg included. Anna surveyed apprehensively several particularly villainous-looking barrowmen who passed and expressed the devout hope that Frank always saw to it carefully that he locked his bedroom door nights.

Before all the zest of that joke had evaporated, Mrs. Vaniman departed; it was a part of her helpful tact in alleviating the grievous situation in which Frank was placed. She always came with the best little piece of news she could provide for the meeting; for the parting she reserved a bit of a joke.

Mr. Wagg chuckled for a long time after the visitors went away. Gradually his face became serious. "Of course, I have to sit here and listen to what's said, because that's my duty. But, as I have told you before, all family matters simply pass into one ear and out of the other."

"I'm mighty grateful for the way you have treated us," said Vaniman.

"The fact that we haven't done business as yet hasn't changed me—never will change me. That mother of yours is so fine a woman that she deserves every favor that I can grant her, for her own sake. And, she being so fine a woman, I was sorry to hear what you wormed out of her this day—that she has gone back to work in the store again."

"It was the one big happiness in my life in Egypt, Mr. Wagg, to feel that at last my mother was having the little rest and comfort that she deserved. I used to look ahead to the time when I could give her what I was able to give her while I was at work. I had a dreadful struggle with her, getting her to leave her work. The only way I ever did get around her was to complain that she was spoiling my prettiest dream by staying in the store. And now it's all to do over again. I haven't even the realization of the dream to help me here."

"It's tough—realizing what you could do if you had the chance, and not being able to do it," averred Mr. Wagg. He lighted his pipe and slid off his stool. "A woman earning her living these days has to do a terrible lot of hard work in seven years."

And having, after his usual custom, lighted a fire under the kettle, Mr. Wagg went to a distance and allowed the contents to boil.

The contents did boil that day, when Vaniman had an opportunity to do some concentrated thinking.

That morning he had received his weekly letter from Vona. She confessed to him that for some weeks she had refrained from telling him that Tasper Britt was a member of the household. She explained under what circumstances Britt was there and what her attitude was and would continue to be. She had not written anything about the matter, she said, on account of her anxiety to keep petty troubles and worries away from one who was suffering from such cruel injustice. But now that her father had gone away for an indefinite stay, leaving Britt as general guardian, she wrote to Vaniman to anticipate any rumors which might reach the young man from another quarter.

She did not state that this intrusion by Britt into her home was perpetual persecution where she was concerned; Vaniman felt that she did not need to say so. His imagination pictured the situation. He had become morbid. He admitted it, but he could not help himself. He had done his best to keep his judgments sane and his hopes untarnished. But he was judging Britt by what Britt had already done, and he was in a mood to believe that Britt would be able to go ahead and accomplish a lot more in the way of hideous deviltry. The thought of Britt in that house—a girl there with no other protection than the presence of a silly mother—made for agony of apprehension that was excruciating.

One of his most precious dreams had just melted into drab reality—his mother was compelled to go back to her toil.

His other dream—the one that was consoling him through the dreary wait of seven years behind bars—was threatened by the malevolence of a man who was showing himself to be a veritable fiend in his machinations.

Vaniman put some questions to himself. Who on God's green earth had a more imperious call to be out—to be free to fight for himself and the innocent? Would not a lie be holy if it should open prison doors and allow a guiltless man to go forth and battle with the guilty? Did not the end justify all the means? The state had declared that his liberty must be forfeited. Had the state the right to take away his reason? Vaniman told himself that he was on the straight road to lunacy.

He leaped up, in the frenzy of his determination forgetting that there were preliminaries yet to be attended to.

Holman Day

"Sit down there, Convict Two-Seven-Nine, or I'll bore ye!" bawled Guard Wagg, with a mighty volume of tone. A deputy warden was crossing the yard. He flourished a commendatory salute to the vigilant warder.

"Good stuff, Bart! Always on your job, eh?"

"Always!" agreed Mr. Wagg.

The warden went on his way and the guard marched to the convict with a manner which expressed a determination to give No. 279 an earful. He stood over Vaniman, who had dropped back to the chair, and the two of them swapped stares.

"I want to get out—I want to get out!" whimpered Vaniman.

Mr. Wagg nodded.

"What must I do?"

"Whack up with me—fifty-fifty. Haven't I told you times enough?"

"But, I mean, what must I do to help?"

"I don't need any of your help. I only want you to say that you'll lead me to that money."

Vaniman drew a deep breath. "I will lead you to that money."

"Some men would make you swear that you know just where the coin is," proceeded Wagg. "But I'm playing my own hunch in this thing on that point. Furthermore, I have talked with a chap named Bixby." He looked hard at the ex-cashier.

"Bixby tied your little game into knots, didn't he?"

Vaniman admitted that fact by a rueful sag of his chin.

"Confidence—mutual confidence in each other!" Mr. Wagg walked away. When he came back past Vaniman, patrolling, he snapped: "No more talk! No more need of talk. Never can tell when talk may trip us. From now on, sit tight!"

After that, though days passed, Wagg had not one word for the amelioration of the convict's impatience. Then, one day, Wagg changed his job again. Vaniman was kept at the same work, if work it could be called. He caught glimpses of Wagg. The guard was busy on the opposite side of the big pit. He had two or three convict helpers. They began to operate drills in the side of a rocky hillock which towered considerably above the level of the yard.

News circulates inside prison walls despite the inhibition on communications between the inmates. Vaniman got information piecemeal from convicts who stopped near him on the pretense of spitting on their hands to get a new grip on their barrow handles. He learned that the plan was to mine the hillock and rig a blast that would tip it into the pit for filling. The barrow work was proving too slow an operation and the prison commissioners wanted the outside men put back into the shops where they could earn money for the state.

It was evident that Guard Wagg was having a great deal of trouble with his helpers. He was continually bawling them out with a violence whose volume reached the ears of Vaniman.

One day Wagg perceived the warden inspecting the work from the edge of the pit near Vaniman; the guard came trotting around.

"Warden, I'm an expert on quarry work, as you know," he panted. "I'm doing my best to show you that I haven't forgotten what I learned over at Stoneport, and to back up what I promised you and the commissioners after I gave you the tip as to what could be done with that hill. Much obliged to you for allowing me all the dynamite I need. But, demmit! I haven't got anybody with brains to help me handle it. It's notional stuff, sir. It hates a blasted fool." He pointed a finger at the men across the pit. Their striped suits suggested the nomenclature he used "Those potato bugs will do something to blow us to blazes sure'n there's air in a doughnut hole!"

The warden showed his concern. "Don't you know of some man who is used to dynamite?"

"That ain't it, sir. A fool gets used to it, till he's too cussed familiar. I want a man with brains enough to be polite to it."

The warden, making a general survey of the scene, beheld Vaniman. "A man who knows enough to be a bank cashier ought to have brains, Wagg. How about Number Two-Seven-Nine?"

Mr. Wagg contemplated Vaniman and took plenty of time for thought. "I'll try him," he said, without enthusiasm. "I hadn't thought of him—but I'll try him."

Directed to do so by the warden, Vaniman went to his new work with Wagg. The latter exhibited no especial symptoms of satisfaction at securing such a helper. He told the young man that his particular care would be the dynamite—to handle the boxes, store them in the little shed, unpack the sticks, and follow the drills, planting the rendrock ready for the blast that was to topple the hillock into the pit. Mr. Wagg explained to the warden, after a time, that the dynamite could be planted more safely and to better advantage when the drillers were off the job. Therefore, Vaniman was detailed to help during the noon hour while the prisoners were at dinner.

But, even when they were alone together, day after day, Mr. Wagg maintained his reticence. Once in a while he did wink at Vaniman. The winks grew more frequent when Mr. Wagg began to connect up the dynamite pockets in the hill with wires. One afternoon, near knocking-off time, he stepped into the shed where Vaniman was covering up his boxes for the night. "When you leave your cell in the morning," said the man who had promised freedom, "hide in your pockets all the letters and little chickle-fixings you intend to carry away with you. You won't be going back into that cell again, Number Two-Seven-Nine."

CHAPTER XXIII

NO VOICE FROM THE PIT

It was a night of wakefulness and of tremors for Vaniman. His was the acute expectancy of one who was about to set out on strange adventures, but whose orders were sealed and whose destination was unknown. Wagg's stolid appearance of knowing just what he was about had been a steadying aid in helping the young man control his doubts; in issuing his final, curt commands Wagg did not abate his confidence; Vaniman felt that he was in no position to demand more candor.

He forced himself to eat his breakfast when it was pushed under his cell door. The messes that were daily dabbed into the compartments of the tin tray were never appetizing; that morning his emotions made everything as tasteless as sawdust. But he ate for strength's sake; he did not know what form of endurance would be demanded of him.

He put only a few of his letters into his pocket. Cells were inspected every day after the convicts went forth to their toil. He did not dare to excite suspicion by taking away any noticeable amount of his possessions.

The forenoon work went on as usual. And Mr. Wagg gave no

signs that this was the day of days according to his plans. He constantly warned the convicts not to meddle with any of the wires. He was even peremptorily short with a deputy warden who came poking around. The warden asked if there was any danger.

"There's always danger when a hill is full of wired-up, canned thunder," stated Mr. Wagg. "I maintain, as I always have maintained, that it's notional stuff. You'll kindly remember that I told you so."

The warden departed with an air that revealed how much he had been impressed.

With the crisis so near, irritability pricked Vaniman's state of nervous tension. He began to resent Wagg's contemptuous silence in regard to details. That the guard's plans were concerned in some way with the mined hillock was evident enough. But an explosion which merely would create a diversion to assist in an escape was not a device that would effectively solve his difficulties, Vaniman reflected. Wagg's general stolidity made him seem rather stupid; the young man felt that his own wits ought to be enlisted in the affair. In the stress of circumstances he hankered to co-operate instead of being a sort of Ludlam's dog, dumb and driven.

However, toward noon, Mr. Wagg was displaying a certain amount of tension of his own and his demeanor did not invite complaints or recrimination. The convict decided that there was nothing for it except to let Mr. Wagg do the wagging.

When the noon bell clanged from the tower, the pit-job prisoners filtered into groups from their occupation in the yard and others filed from the doors of the shops. They shuffled their way in double lines through the gaping door of the main building, received their tins of food, and went to

Holman Day

their cells.

As usual, Vaniman remained with Wagg.

The warders on the walls relaxed their vigilance when the heavy door was closed behind the last men of the lines. The guards went into the sentry boxes and set down the heavy rifles.

Wagg made a general survey of the scene. No person was moving in the open area of the yard. The veteran of the guard was well acquainted with the customary habits and movements of the noon hour. He knew that the men in the main guardroom were reduced to a shift of two while the others went to their dinners; the two men were in the habit of giving the deserted yard only indifferent attention. But Mr. Wagg had provided against even casual glances.

For purposes of his own, which a boss did not need to explain, he had nailed boards together to form something like a door, six feet square. The thing had been leaning against the dynamite shed for some days.

Quite casually, Mr. Wagg went and lifted away this square of boarding, holding to the traverse braces on which the boards were nailed. He trudged along, carrying it, and came to where Vaniman was standing, observing and wondering.

"Scooch!" snapped Wagg. "Walk along. Don't show yourself past this shield!"

It was a true shield. Wagg carried it straight up and down. Vaniman obeyed instantly. He had a mental flash that Wagg did know exactly what he was about in his tactics. Lacking all idea of the scheme, Vaniman had not the heart to begin to ask for any details of the big plan at the crucial moment. He allowed himself to be an automaton. It was easy to do one thing at a time, as Wagg commanded; knowing nothing about what Wagg intended to do. Vaniman was not in a position to delay matters by doubts as to the best way of doing the thing. He walked behind the board screen, conscious that his movements were hidden from the men in the guardroom and, for that matter, from the eyes of anybody in the prison building.

After a walk of a few rods Vaniman found himself close to a big chimney; it served a shop which had been unused since the crew had been at work on the job of filling the pit. Wagg set down the shield on its edge, as if needing to rest for a moment.

"Open that chimney door and dodge in. Pull the door to behind you."

At the base of the chimney Vaniman beheld the iron door provided for the convenience of cleaners and repair men. The padlock of the door was unhooked. He lifted the door from its latch, crawled into the chimney, and pulled the door shut. A moment later, waiting in the stifling darkness, he heard the rattle of metal against metal and the snap of the padlock. There was the tramp of departing feet. Gradually he became able to see about him in some degree. Away up above him was a square of sunlit sky at the top of the shaft. He saw in one corner a large pail with a cover; inside it were several bottles. Also, there was a bundle of clothing.

Judging from the amount of food, it was rather evident that Mr. Wagg expected prison-bird Two-Seven-Nine to play chimney swallow for some little time!

Wagg had made a quick job of locking in Vaniman. The guard tipped the upper edge of the shield inward till it rested against the chimney. He reached around the end of the boarding and snapped the padlock. Then he lifted his burden and went on.

About that time a lazy man in the guardroom rolled slow gaze upon the yard. He saw Wagg moving with the burden and watched until Wagg laid it down flat on the ground. He opined that it was a part of the bomb-proof shelter that Wagg proposed to build in order to watch the hillock-smashing at close range. The other guard confirmed that opinion, having information straight from Wagg, himself.

"When does she bust?"

"Next week, so he cal'lates!"

But Mr. Wagg, returning slowly, keeping to the side of the pit farthest from the hillock, was at that moment down to seconds in his figuring how long it would be before the crawling fire on a fuse would reach and sever a cord and trip a certain trigger.

"I reckon she's about due," muttered Mr. Wagg. He stopped without easy jumping distance of the corner of a shop and slowly lighted his pipe as an excuse for stopping.

His reckoning was correct.

The hillock heaved. The mining had been skillfully done; the mass of rocks and earth was hoisted from behind and slid toward the pit. There was a tremor of the ground under the prison and its yard as if Thor had thunked viciously with his heaviest hammer. When startled men shot glances from the windows that were handiest for observation, the hill was toppling into the pit. In the forefront was the dynamite shed, splintering under the tons of moving rock. Instantly the last sliver of the shed was swallowed up, and then other tons of dirt and rock went piling into the pit, burying the shattered structure in crashing depths from which lime-rock dust came puffing in clouds.

On the edge of the pit a man was dancing wildly in an aura of dust. The man was Wagg. He came staggering away from the pit, his arms folded across his eyes.

"I saw him!" he squalled, when officers met him in their race across the yard from the prison. "He was in the shed. I told him to keep away from them wires. I've been telling everybody to keep off'n them wires. But everybody has been bound and determined to fool with 'em." He pulled down his arms and shot accusatory digit at the deputy warden whom he had previously rebuked. "Only this day I had to warn you not to fool with them wires. He must have done it. I saw him go under. It's Gawd-awful. I'll never forget it—how he looked. Gimme water!"

He sucked from the edge of the tin dipper which a man brought, suffling like a thirsty horse. He rolled up his eyes and surveyed the warden, who had arrived.

"Number Two-Seven-Nine—you say he has gone?" The warden's countenance registered honest horror; but Mr. Wagg's simulated horror was even more convincing in its intensity.

"He's gone! He's under the whole of it!" Wagg dropped the dipper and collapsed on the ground. "My nerve is all busted, Warden. I sha'n't ever have any more grit to be a guard. I ask to be discharged. Here and now I beg to be fired!"

"I'll arrange a furlough for you, Wagg," said the warden, with understanding sympathy. "You're entitled to a lay-off with pay. It was a terrible thing to see!"

"And his mother!" mourned the guard. "Break it to her easy!"

"A dreadful—dreadful affair," insisted the warden.

He started toward the edge of the pit. "And the prison commissioners, the way state finances are, will never go to the expense of having all that rock moved to dig him out."

"Probably not, seeing that he's under the whole of it," agreed Wagg. "He was a likable chap, spite of what he had done to get in here. Poor Two-Seven-Nine!"

One of the inside guards had arrived at the scene of mourning. He was greatly excited. "And I guess it's poor Two-Eight-Two! He's missing from the noon count-up, Mr. Warden!"

Wagg struggled upon his feet. He was not simulating the new phase of his emotions. He looked distinctly frightened. "There's only one under there. I saw him go. Who is Two-Eight-Two?"

"One of the pair sent down from Levant for breaking and entering in the nighttime."

"He wasn't in my crew—he wasn't on outdoor work," shouted Wagg.

"What was his job?" demanded the warden.

"Harness shop," reported an officer. He called to another guard and started into the building indicated.

All those in the yard waited anxiously, their eyes on the door where the guards had entered. Promptly the officers came out. One propelled a convict, clutching the collar of the dingy prison coat; the other carried a length of narrow ladder that was fashioned from strips of leather. "I reckon he hid out to work on this," said the guard.

"Didn't you know that you couldn't get away with anything of that sort?" the warden demanded, angrily.

The convict looked past the warden, straight into the eyes of Wagg. "You never can tell what you can get away with till you try it," Two-Eight-Two declared. There was a touch of insolence in his manner.

"Into the doghole with him!" the warden commanded.

Wagg surveyed the departure of the convict. The man contrived to twist his head around and look behind him; and he disclosed a grin. But he was hampered by the clutch on his collar and Wagg was not sure that the grin was intended for him, though the consciousness that the convict might have beheld what was on the inner side of that shield of boards was a thought which troubled Mr. Wagg's complacent belief that a good job had been well done.

He continued to watch the man until the narrow door which opened from the yard, admitting to the doghole cells, swallowed up the convict and his guard. All that time a sort of quivery feeling was inside Wagg. He actually found himself in frantic mental search of some kind of a lie to be used in case the convict whirled and pointed to the big chimney and got over an accusation. But the man did not look around again.

"I can plainly see that you are in a bad way, Wagg," affirmed the warden. Fervently did Mr. Wagg agree in his heart.

"Your leave of absence dates from this moment, if you say so."

"I may have to go on to stone work again if I don't get back my grit, warden. I'd like to have the run of the yard for a day or so, in order to look over just how that blast worked. Seeing that it cost a human life, I'd like to get full value of experience out of it."

"Come and go as you like, Wagg. I'll lend you a key to the small door beside the wagon entrance in case you don't want to ring in through the guardroom."

Mr. Wagg expressed his gratitude in proper terms and allowed that he would go and lie down for a time in order to calm himself. Again he urged the warden to break the news gently to Vaniman's mother and respectfully requested that Guard Wagg's sympathy be included in the condolence in the official letter.

The newspapers of that afternoon contained an account of the tragic happening at the state prison.

That night, too, Vona Harnden kept vigil, her door locked against her mother, whose fatuous commonplaces of commiseration were like files against the raw surface of the girl's agony.

The front parlor of the Harndens had been converted into a sleeping room for Tasper Britt. Vona's room was over the parlor. She could hear the rasping diapason of his snoring. He appeared to be sleeping with the calm relaxation of a man who had been able to eliminate some especial worries from his mind.

Furthermore, that night, the chairman of the prison

commissioners had a talk with the warden over the telephone. The warden made a guess as to how many thousands of tons of rock were piled above the body of the unfortunate victim.

"The taxpayers will never indorse the project of digging out that pit to recover the body of a convict, no matter who he is," declared the commissioner. "I don't mean to sound brutal, but we must let it stand as it is. Enter the reports of witnesses and declare the man officially dead. Here is one case, at least, Mr. Warden, when there's no doubt about a man being dead."

However, shortly after twelve o'clock that night—and the night being particularly black with an overcast sky—Bartley Wagg opened the iron door of the big chimney and called forth Frank Vaniman and led him out through the little door at the side of the carriage entrance.

There was a conveyance waiting there, a good-sized van, drawn by a solid-looking horse. Mr. Wagg lifted the flap of the van's cover.

"Crawl in!" he commanded. "You'll find plenty of room along with the rest of the camping kit. Roll yourself up in the tent and take it easy. My nerves have been shocked by the terrible affair and I'm going into the mountains to recuperate. Doctor's orders!" He was grimly serious.

He mounted the seat of the van and drove away with his passenger and the outfit.

CHAPTER XXIV

THE SHADE WHO STALLED

Mr. Wagg did not hurry. He used several days for his trip to Egypt. He drove leisurely along roads which led through small towns and out-of-the-way places. That plan afforded him opportunity and excuse for pitching a tent to serve as shelter during the night stops. And after the tent was pitched and the dusk descended, Vaniman was able to come thankfully from the hateful restraint of the van and stroll along the woodland aisles and get the kinks out of his anatomy.

But, although he eased his body, he was unable to ease his mind. He had not expected to enjoy his questionable freedom, anyway. Liberty was of value to him only as he might be able to use it in his fight for his rights as an innocent man. He could not freely use his liberty until he had cleared his name and thereby justified his escape from the prison. Now he was wondering whether he would have allowed Wagg to proceed as he did had the guard apprised him of the full details of the plan. The sweat of anguish stood out on him as he pondered in the jolting van; he found no pleasure in the respite of the peaceful woods.

By the plot of Wagg he had dealt his loved ones the cruel blow that sudden death inflicts on the affections. In spite of what he hoped to gain from his freedom, Vaniman was accusing himself, realizing what his mother, his sister, and Vona were suffering. It was his nature to draw fine distinctions in points of honor; he was ashamed in the presence of Wagg; and in the consideration of the interests of self, he felt that his liberty was exacting too great a price from others. To all intents and purposes, outside the knowledge of one man to the contrary, he was dead, and he had deprived his best beloved of hope and peace of mind. The one man in the secret profanely declared that if Vaniman made an attempt to communicate with any person in the world until their particular business had been settled, the whole project was in danger. "I don't care how much dependence you put in your mother's good sense. She's a woman, and women slop over when they're all wowed up! She'd have to tell your sister, wouldn't she? She couldn't let your sister go on suffering. And your sister's too young to be trusted. Vaniman, the toughest part is over for 'em. That's a cinch! They'll go on sorrowing, of course, but they'll be feeling more reconciled every day. Mourners always do. Mourners can't help seeing the bright side, after a time. Think of that and quit your foolishness. You have made a trade with me. Till your part of that trade is carried out you ain't a free agent to do what you want to do in your own affairs."

The worry over his inability to carry out that trade was mingled with the young man's general bitterness of regret because he had challenged Fate so boldly.

"There's one thing about it," Mr. Wagg pursued, "the quicker you come across with me the sooner you can do what you darnation want to on your own hook. I have worked a thing that could be worked only once. You're out—and you're out right. Nobody is chasing you. Take another name, show up in some other part of the country, and you'll live happy ever after."

Holman Day

He dwelt on that theme whenever the two talked, and he played all the variations. Furthermore, he complained because Vaniman was not showing his gratitude in more hearty fashion. "I catch you looking at me like a youngster would look at a bumblebee crawling across his bare foot. I don't ask to be taken into your bosom as your main and particular chum—understand that! But while there's business on between us I expect pleasant looks, even if you don't feel like handing me conversation."

Mr. Wagg was doing practically all the talking on that trip. He had emerged from his cocoon of taciturnity. He explained that naturally he was a great talker, but that prison rules had pretty nigh paralyzed his tongue and he was trying to get it back into good working order once more.

He made an especial point of vaunting himself upon the success of his scheme of deliverance. He tackled the thing from all angles. He played it up as the greatest achievement that ever had been worked in behalf of a convict. Mr. Wagg, serving as board of appraisal of his own feat, kept boosting the value. It was evident that he was suspecting that Vaniman, out and free, was in the mood that is characteristic of the common run of humanity: urgent desire is reckless about price; possession proceeds to haggle and demur.

"And there's one thing about it," insisted Wagg, "we've got to keep on going ahead. We can't back up. We can't dissolve partnership. And the trade has got to stand as it was made— fifty-fifty."

"I'm not going back on the trade."

They were sitting close to each other on a tussock behind their little tent. Mr. Wagg leaned close and bored Vaniman with earnest gaze. "We'll fetch Egypt on to-morrow's hitch.

Of course, you're going to stick close to me, and you can bet that I'm going to stick close to you till the whack-up has been made. No shenanigan! Now, seeing how far I have gone in doing my part, don't you think it's about time for you to come across?"

Vaniman spread his hands. "How can I? Wait till we get to Egypt." Right then he had no notion of what he was going to do when he arrived in Egypt. He had not dared to look the proposition squarely in the face. He did not even analyze his feelings. He was dimly conscious that he was pitying Wagg. That ambitious person was in for a grievous disappointment. To be sure, Wagg had insisted on following a current belief and persisted in building his hopes on a fallacy and had forced human nature until weak human nature had snapped under the strain. Wagg had refused to believe the truth; he had preferred to indulge his own delusion in regard to the treasure of the Egypt Trust company. Nevertheless, Vaniman was ashamed—and he was afraid.

Britt was the crux of the situation—that was evident enough! Britt knew where the coin was. Vaniman was sure on that point. Britt had so maneuvered that wild-goose errand to Levant that he had made the affair furnish opportunity to himself and fix the odium on Vaniman. In spite of what the young man knew of Britt's lust for money, he believed that the usurer had worked a scheme to ruin a rival instead of merely operating to add to his riches. But Vaniman knew Britt well enough to reach the conclusion that, once having the hard cash in his possession, and the blame fastened on another man, Britt was allowing avarice to stand pat on the play.

But if, now being on the job in person, he could rig a scheme to make Britt disclose, what could be done for coadjutor Wagg? There was a reward posted for information leading to the recovery of the money. Britt had offered that reward. He had made quite a show of the thing in the public prints. He pledged himself to pay the sum of two thousand five hundred dollars from his own pocket, and Vaniman bitterly realized just why Britt had adopted that pose. Would Wagg be content with the sop of the reward?

The man who had been declared dead knew that he must play for time. He ran over various plans in his head. He did not feel like blurting out the truth to Mr. Wagg and asking what that effectually compromised gentleman was going to do about it. He needed Mr. Wagg. He thought of pleading that the summer landscape was so much different from the winter lay of the land, when the snow was heaped in the gullies and on the hills, that he was bothered in remembering just where he had planted the treasure that night; he reflected that he might show Mr. Wagg a hole in the rocks and assert that some of the persistent Egyptian gold hunters had undoubtedly located the money and taken it for themselves; being moved to more desperate projects, he meditated on the plan of coming across to Wagg with the whole story, showing him that Britt must be guilty, and thereby turning a blackmailer loose on the magnate with plenty of material to use in extorting what Wagg might consider fair pay for the work he had put in.

But Vaniman was freshly free from prison walls. Just then he was psychologically incapable of standing up for himself as a real man ought. His sense of innocence had not been able to withstand that feeling of intimidation with which a prisoner becomes obsessed. Right along with him was the man who had been persistently his guard in the prison. Wagg's narrow rut of occupation had had its full effect on his nature. His striated eyeballs had a vitreous look; they were as hard as marbles. Vaniman knew that he could not look at those eyes and tell a convincing lie. In view of Wagg's settled convictions in the matter of the treasure, the real truth might be harder to support than a lie.

Vaniman went into the van like a whipped dog into a kennel and lay awake and wrestled with his difficulties.

During the progress of the pilgrimage the next day Wagg halted frequently. Vaniman could hear the conversations between his charioteer and the natives of the section. Mr. Wagg was seeking information and at the same time he gave out a modest amount of revelation about himself and his need of a retired spot where he might recuperate. He explained that he wanted to find a camp in some place so remote that nobody would be coming around jarring his nerves.

Eventually he got on track of what he wanted. A native told him about an abandoned log house on the top of a mountain called "Devilbrow."

"They used it for a fire-warden station in the days when Egypt had enough timber to make it an object to protect it," said the man. "You'll be plenty lonesome up there. You can get your wagon within half a mile. Pack your truck on your hoss's back and lead him the rest of the way. That's what I used to do. I was warden till I found myself trying to carry on conversations with tumblebugs and whippoorwills."

When Wagg had driven along far enough so that the native could not overhear, he hailed Vaniman through the trap in the top of the van.

"Did you hear that?"

"Yes."

"Is that Devilbrow within grabbing distance of what we're after?"

Vaniman returned a hearty affirmative. He had been able to see those craggy heights from his window in Britt Block. The thought that what he wanted to grab and what Mr. Wagg wanted to grab were not exactly mated as desired objects did not shade his candor when he asserted that Devilbrow was just the place from which to operate.

"All right!" chirruped Wagg. "Us for it!" He displayed the first cheeriness he had shown on the trip. He whistled for a time. Then he sang, over and over, to a tune of his own, "Up above the world so high, like a di'mond in the sky." This display of Wagg's hopeful belief that the fifty-fifty settlement was near at hand served to increase Vaniman's despondency.

Obeying the native's instructions as to the route, Wagg soon turned off the highway and drove along a rutted lane which whiplashed a slope that continually became steeper. Soon he pulled up and told Vaniman to get out and walk and ease the load on the horse. Wagg got down and walked, too.

The trail up Devilbrow was on the side away from the village of Egypt. The way was through hard growth. There were no houses—no sign of a human being. Wagg's cheerfulness increased. And he said something which put a glimmer of cheer into Vaniman's dark ponderings.

"There's no call to hurry the thing overmuch. If I recuperate too sudden and show up back home it might look funny, after the way I bellowed about my condition. There's plenty of flour, bacon, and canned stuff in that van. I reckon we'd better get our feet well settled here and make sure that nobody is watching us; the money is safer in the hole than with us, for the time being. My pay is going on and the future looks rosy."

A cock partridge rose from the side of the lane and whirred away through the beech leaves that the first frost of early autumn had yellowed.

"And I've got a shotgun and plenty of shells! Son, let's forget that we have ever been in state prison. In the course of time that place is about as wearing on a guard as it is on a convict."

The log camp was behind a spur of the rocky summit and was hidden from the village below. Wagg commented with satisfaction on the location when they had reached the place. The van had been concealed in a ravine which led from the lane. The work of loading the horse with the sacked supplies, and the ascent of the mountain, had consumed hours. Twilight was sifting into the valleys by the time they had unloaded the stuff and stabled the horse in a lean-to.

There was a stove in the camp, and the place was furnished after a fashion with chairs and a table fashioned from birch saplings. The blankets of Wagg's camp equipment made the bunks comfortable.

Wagg had been the cook as well as the captain of the expedition. He did better that evening with the wood-burning stove than he had done with the oil stove of his kit.

After supper, before he turned in, Vaniman went out on a spur of Devilbrow and gazed down on the scattered lights of the village of Egypt. As best he could he determined the location of the Harnden house. He felt as helplessly aloof as if he were a shade revisiting the scene of his mortal experiences.

CHAPTER XXV

THE FIRST PEEP BEHIND THE CURTAIN

The next day Wagg went out and shot two partridges and contrived a stew which fully occupied his attention in the making and the eating. He had suggested to Vaniman that he'd better come along on the expedition after the birds. Vaniman found a bit more than mere suggestion in Wagg's manner of invitation. With his shotgun in the hook of his arm he presented his wonted appearance as the guard at the prison. It was perfectly apparent that Mr. Wagg proposed to keep his eye on the promiser of the fifty-fifty split. But Wagg did not refer to the matter of the money while they strolled in the woods.

As a matter of fact, days went by without the question coming up.

Wagg had previously praised himself as a patient waiter; the young man confessed in his thoughts that his guardian merited the commendation. Wagg was plainly having a particularly good time on this outing. He displayed the contentment of a man who had ceased to worry about the future; he was taking it easy, like a vacationer with plenty of money in the bank. On one occasion he did mention the money in the course of a bit of philosophizing on the situation:

"I suppose that, when you look at it straight, it's stealing, what I'm doing. I've seen a lot of big gents pass through that state prison, serving sentences for stealing. Embezzlement, forgery, crooked stock dealing—it's all stealing. They were tempted. I've been tempted. I've fell. I ain't an angel, any more than those big gents were. And you know what I told you about mourners chirking up, after the first blow! I figure it's the same way in the bank case. They have given up the idea of getting the money back. They're still sad when they think about it, but they keep thinking less and less every day. They've crossed it off, as you might say."

The two who were bound in that peculiar comradeship were out on the crag where they could look down upon the distant checker board of the village. Vaniman, in the stress of the circumstances, wondered whether he might be able to come at Wagg on the sentimental side of his nature.

"The little town must have gone completely broke since the bank failure. Innocent people are suffering. If that money could be returned—"

He did not finish the sentence. Mr. Wagg was most distinctly not encouraging that line of talk.

"Look here, Vaniman, when you got away with that money you had hardened yourself up to the point where you were thinking of your own self first, hadn't you?"

The young man did not dare to burst out with the truth—not while Wagg was in the mood his expression hinted at.

Wagg continued: "Well, I've got myself to the point where I'm thinking of my own self. I'm as hard as this rock I'm sitting on." In his emphasis on that assertion Wagg scarred his knuckles against the ledge. "After all the work I've had in getting myself to that point, I'm proposing to stay there. If you try to soften me I shall consider that you're welching on your trade."

Wagg made the declaration in loud tones. After all his years of soft-shoeing and repression in a prison, the veteran guard was taking full advantage of the wide expanses of the big outdoors.

"What did I do for you, Vaniman? I let you cash in on a play that I had planned ever since the first barrow of dirt was dumped into that pit. There's a lifer in that prison with rich relatives. I reckon they would have come across with at least ten thousand dollars. There's a manslaughter chap who owns four big apartment houses. But I picked you because I could sympathize with you on account of your mother and that girl the papers said so much about. It's a job that can't be done over again, not even for the Apostle Peter. Now will you even hint at welching?"

"Certainly not!"

But that affirmation did not come from Vaniman. It was made in his behalf by a duet of voices, bass and nasal tenor, speaking loudly and confidently behind the two men who were sitting on the ledge.

The younger man leaped to his feet and whirled; the older man struggled partly upright and ground his knees on the ledge when he turned to inspect the terrifying source of sound.

So far as Vaniman's recollection went, they were strangers. One was short and dumpy, the other was tall and thin. They wore slouchy, wrinkled, cheap suits. There was no hint of threat in their faces. On the contrary, both of the men displayed expressions of mingled triumph and mischief. Then, as if they had a mutual understanding in the matter of procedure, they went through a sort of drill. They stuck their right arms straight out; they crooked the arms at the elbows; they drove their hands at their hip pockets and produced, each of them, a bulldog revolver; they snapped their arms into position of quick aim.

Wagg threw up his hands and began to beg. Vaniman held himself under better control.

But the men did not shoot. They returned the guns to their pockets and saluted in military fashion, whacking their palms violently against their thighs in finishing salute.

"Present!" they cried. Then the dumpy man grinned. Wagg had been goggling, trying to resolve his wild incredulity into certainty. That grin settled the thing for him. It was the same sort of a suggestive grin that he had viewed on that day of days in the prison yard.

"Number Two-Eight-Two!" he quavered.

"Sure thing!" The dumpy man patted the tall man's arm. "Add one, and you have Number Two-Eight-Three—a pal who drew the next number because we're always in company."

"And we're here because we're here," stated the other,

The short man fixed his gaze on the ex-cashier. "You don't realize it yet, but this is more of a reunion than it looks to be on the surface. You two gents have seen how we're fixed in the gun line, and we hope the understanding is going to make the party sociable."

"You may be thinking that this is only another case of it

being proved how small the world is, after all," remarked the tall man. "Not so! Not so! We have followed you two because we have important business with you. We have had a lot of trouble and effort in getting here. Bear that in mind, please!"

The new arrivals were quite matter-of-fact and Wagg was helped to recover some of his composure. "The two of you are three-year men—robbery in the nighttime," he declared, out of his official knowledge. "What in blue blazes are you doing outside the pen?"

"Attending to the same business as you are—after a slice of the bank coin," replied the short man, carelessly.

Wagg got to his feet and banged his fists together. "Do you dare to walk right up to a guard of the state prison and—and—" He balked in his demand for information; Mr. Wagg was plainly afflicted with a few uncomfortable considerations of his own situation.

"We do!" the convicts declared in concert. Then the dumpy man went on: "And whatever else it is you're wondering whether we dare to do, we'll inform that we dare. Once on a time we had occasion to express our opinion of a bank. I wrote out that opinion and left it where it would be seen. Not exactly Sunday-school language, but it hit the case." He turned away from Vaniman's frenzy of gasping interrogation. He confined his attention to Wagg. "A prison guard, say you? You're a hell of a guard!"

"Opinion indorsed!" said the other convict.

For a few moments there was complete silence on the summit of Devilbrow. Somewhere, on an upland farm in the distance, a cow mooed. Then a rooster challenged all comers.

"That's the word, old top!" agreed the tall man. "It expresses my feelings," He clapped his hands against his legs and cried in his tenor, imitating the singsong of the rooster, "We're here because we're he-e-ere!"

Then he and his fellow sat down on a ledge outcropping that overtopped and commanded the position of the other men. The convicts surveyed Vaniman and Wagg with a complacent air of triumph. "Are you willing to take things as they stand, or do you feel that you can't go ahead till your curiosity has been scratched?" inquired the short man.

"Curiosity!" stormed the ex-cashier. "Do you dare to call the feeling I have in me curiosity?" He thumped his fist against his breast.

"And how about my feelings, with escaped convicts racing and chasing all over this country?" shouted the guard. "What has happened to that prison since I've been off my job?"

"One at a time!" The dumpy man put up his hand to shut off the stream of questions that were pouring from Wagg. "The young fellow has his innings first. He has more good reasons for rearing and tearing. It's easy enough to get out of a state prison when you have a trick that can be worked once." He winked at Wagg. Then he directed his remarks strictly at Vaniman.

"I'm going to talk free and open. We're all in the same boat. We're a couple of pots, and both of you are kettles, all black. Now, listen! I'm Bill." He stuck his finger against his breast and then tagged with it his pal at his side. "He's Tom. Bill and Tom have been humble and hard-working yeggmen, never tackling anything bigger than country stores and farmers' flivvers. Once on a time they were in a barn, tucked away waiting for night, and they heard a man running a double shift of talk—beating down the farmer on the price of cattle and blowing off about gold coin hoarded by the bushel in a rube bank."

Stickney's unruly mouth! Vaniman understood. "So, says Bill to Tom: 'Why not go up like everything else is going up these days?' Says Tom to Bill: 'I'm on.' We took our time about it, getting the lay of the land. We went down to the big burg to buy drills and soup and pick up points on how to crack a real nut. Equipment up to that time had been a glass cutter and a jimmy for back windows and padlocks."

He was humorously drawling his confession. He stopped talking and lighted a cigarette. Impatience that was agony urged Vaniman, but he controlled himself. Wagg did not venture to say anything. His thoughts were keeping him busy; he was mentally galloping, trying to catch up with the new situation.

"And let me tell you that when Bill and Tom got back up here, they had colder feet than the weather accounted for. General headquarters, that camp!" He jerked thumb gesture toward the log cabin. "It had been our hang-out in times past when we operated in this section. Handy place! Finally got up courage enough to go to the job. Fine night for it! Deserted village. Peeked into Town Hall and saw the general round-up. Light in the bank. Bill was boosted up by Tom and got a peek over the curtain. One fellow inside adding figures—much taken up. Bank-vault door wide open. Front door unlocked. Crawled in. Kept crawling. Crawled into bank room. Grille door wide open. Bill up and hit fellow with rubber nob-knocker—it snuffs, but is not dangerous. Tom is handy by with the chloroform—always carried it for our second-story work."

The young man began to stride to and fro, striving by using

his legs to keep from using his tongue.

The narrator snapped the ash off his cigarette. "Bill and Tom looked at each other. Did they expect such easy picking? They did not. The stuff had been fairly handed to 'em. They dragged the stuff out—all the sacks of it. Transportation all planned on. Couple of handsleds such as we had seen leaning up against the houses in the village. Slipped the fellow into the vault with his hands tied and shut the door with a trig so that he couldn't kick it open right away. Idea was that anybody stepping in later would think he had gone home; we intended to put out the light; nothing desperate about us; we wouldn't shoot the bolts. Bill said to Tom that there'd be a hunt for the fellow when he failed to show up at home, wherever he lived, and he'd sure be pulled out of the vault in good season. Thoughtful, you see! Not bloody villains. Simply wanted time for our getaway. Slow pulling up this hill with handsleds! But we slit a bag to make sure of what we would be pulling. And we kept on slitting bags. And—" the short man shook his head and sighed. "You say it, Tom. I'm trying to be sociable in this talk with these gents— showing a full and free spirit in coming across with the facts. But I don't trust myself!"

"Nor I!" declared Tom. "We'd better not spoil a pleasant party."

"Well, Bill wrote his sentiments, as they occurred to him at the time. Then we heard somebody hollering at the front door that we had left open. We ran and jumped behind the door of the bank office. The fellow who galloped in ran a few times in circles and then he galloped out. He might have noticed a rhinoceros if the rhino had risen up and bit him. But he paid no attention to Bill and Tom behind the door. And Bill and Tom walked out. And we managed to get clear of the village just as that Town Hall crowd broke loose.

"Says Bill to Tom, when they were on their way: 'It's plain that banks are bunk, like everything else these days. Let's stick to our humble line where we know what we're doing.' But, having been studying bank robbing, we had got ourselves nerved up to take desperate chances—and we bulled the regular game in Levant. Coarse work, because we were off our stride. All due to the bank. The bank stands liable for damages. We're up here collecting. Cashier, consider what regular and desperate cracksmen would have done to you! Considering our carefulness where you were concerned, and the trouble we have been put to in getting out and chasing you, what say?"

Again Vaniman got a strong grip on his emotions. He was a fugitive; these cheeky rascals had his fate in their hands; he was not in a position to reply to their effrontery as his wild desire urged. He did not dare to open his mouth just then with any sort of reply; he did not trust himself even to look their way.

"Think it over," advised the short man, composedly. "But please take note that there are now four of us in on the split, and that quartering it makes easy figuring."

Mr. Wagg was not composed. This threat to disrupt his fifty-fifty plan brought him out of something that was like stupor. "You belong back in state prison, and I'll see to it that you're put there."

The man who called himself Bill was not ruffled. He waved his arm to indicate the spread of the landscape. "Doesn't being up here above the world lift you out of the rut of petty revenge? Can't you see things in a broader way? I can. I feel like praising you for that job you put up to get our valuable friend out where he can help all four of us. For many a day, after I saw that you had this friend out in the yard and were interested in him, I tended less to making harness pads and more to watching you through the shop window. I was interested in the gent, too. Tom and I had made up our minds to be as patient as possible for seven years—and then be rusticating up in these hills, right on hand to help him in the chore of digging it out of whatever hole it's hidden in. Couldn't let you monopolize him—absolutely not, Mr. Guard! Do you think I was hiding out that noon only by luck and chance? No, no! I saw you monkeying with the chimney door that forenoon. I saw how you were hopping around and I got a good look at your face. Says I to myself, Tom not being handy, 'There's something to be pulled off, and I'll make sure how it is pulled.' That's how I happened to be on the business side of that shield, Mr. Guard. It was good work. It leaves our friend pretty comfortable, so far as the dicks are concerned. Tom and I have got to keep dodging 'em. We didn't have your advantages, you know—Tom and I didn't! We simply did the best we could in getting out—realizing the value of time."

The short man was employing a patronizing tone, as if accomplishing an escape from state prison was merely a matter of election of methods. All of the guard's official pride was in arms. He advanced on the convict and shook a finger under his nose. "How did you get out? You don't dare to tell me. It was an accident. You didn't use any brains. You don't dare to tell, I say!"

"Oh yes, I do!" The convict was placid. "I'll tell you because you'll never dare to open your mouth on the matter. Furthermore, you've got to understand the position Tom and I are in right now in regard to a third party. That party is a trusty—he gets out in three months from now and has been having the run of the corridors as a repair man."

Wagg growled something.

"Oh yes, he will!" asseverated the convict. "He'll come out on time! A fine show of yourself you'll make trying to dutch him. The pen is mightier than the sword, but inside a prison pen the little screw driver has 'em all faded when a trusty is the repair man. Cell door, tier door, attic door—all attended to; ventilator grating likewise. Rope in ventilator, up rope— out goes rope and down rope! Roof, wall, drop! Rear window of second-hand shop. Outfit! Hike! Good start, till morning shows the cot dummies! Truss rods of Wagner freight, blind baggage to Levant on the 'tween-days train. Into the bush—and here!"

"With this added by me," put in the other convict. "That trusty was a pal in the old days. He understands his friends' financial interest is in this thing, and how we needed to get out sudden to tend to that interest. We have given him our word. He took that word like it was a certified check. And he's going to cash in on that word!"

"He sure is!" declared the short man. "We pass words instead of checks in our business, and a man who lets his promise go to protest is crabbed for keeps. We have incurred obligations so as to get in at the split." He spread out his palm and tapped a digit into the center of it. "Cash—here!"

"Strictly on a business basis, of course," said the tall man. "We don't call for a special split for that trusty. It's a personal debt incurred by Bill and me. We ask nobody to pay our personal debts. All we ask is that debts due us be paid. And we're drawing a sight draft on you gents. Bill and I are probably only a few jumps ahead of the dicks. Where's the coin?"

He brutally thrust the question at Vaniman. The young man turned to Wagg, seeking support in that crisis, believing that the affair could be held on the basis of two against two in the interests of further dilatory tactics. Wagg had been showing indignant protest against the demands of the interlopers. But his corrugated face was smoothed suddenly. He had evidently decided to cash in on the new basis. "That's what I want to know—and what I have been trying to find out. Where's the coin?"

The realignment—three against one—was menacing. Vaniman surveyed the faces—the glowering demanding countenances, the eyes in which money lust gleamed. He knew that the men were in a mood where the truth would serve him in sad stead. He had no knack as a liar. He understood how little chance he had of convincing those shrewd knaves by his inept falsehoods in that extremity. He had already meditated on the plan of running away from Wagg. His reasons for escaping from this intolerable baiting were now threefold.

"It's too near sunset for a job that will take us a long way through the woods," he blurted.

"I'll admit I'm so tired I can't count money till I've had a night's sleep," confessed the short man. "But you make your promise now and here, Mr. Cashier. When?" He emphasized the last word.

"To-morrow!"

"A promissory note—dated and delivered. Don't let it go to protest. That's language you can understand, Mr. Bankman."

Vaniman walked off toward the cabin and the three men followed him.

CHAPTER XXVI

THE SHOW-DOWN

His troubles and his trials had not wholly dulled youth's sense of the ludicrous in Vaniman. He sat down that evening to the meal that had been prepared by Guard Wagg, late of the state prison, for three fugitive convicts, also late of that institution. The chimney of the kerosene lamp was smoky and the light was dim, therefore Vaniman's grin was hidden from his companions. Undoubtedly it would have produced no especial wonderment in them if they had noted his cheerful visage. They were decidedly cheerful, themselves. Mr. Wagg was no longer exhibiting the official side of his nature; he was receiving compliments on his biscuits. The three who had aligned themselves against Vaniman seemed to be getting along in a very friendly fashion, being bound by a common interest.

From biscuits in hand the conversation passed to the prison fare in retrospect. Wagg admitted that the fare was a disgrace to the state. From that point it was easy to go on and agree with the short man and the tall man that the prison was mismanaged generally and that a man was lucky in being able to get away from such a place—no matter whether he was a guard or a prisoner. The incongruous friendliness increased Vaniman's amusement.

He looked at the two knaves who had recently enlightened their victim in such a matter-of-fact manner. He admitted that the comedy overbalanced the tragedy, in view of the fact that the job had resolved itself into petty sneak-thievery. Taking into consideration the trick money they had found, there was considerable farce in the affair. However, Vaniman, looking ahead to the threatening to-morrow, perceived tragedy looming again.

Victim, criminals, guard of the criminals, they were breaking bread in a temporary comradeship of a bizarre nature—a money quest. But that money interest which bound them of an evening would be a disastrous problem on the morrow, if one man attempted to stand out against three.

The one man made up his mind that there was a risky resource for him—to flee and take his chances alone in the woods; he had decided to put his own personal interpretation on the promise, "To-morrow!"

Right after supper he turned into his bunk, in order to simulate slumber and avoid the questions that he could not answer.

The two new arrivals had had much to say about their weariness. He expected that they would promptly eliminate themselves as obstacles to flight. Mr. Wagg, at any rate, had shown a confiding disposition all along.

But the tall man and the short man conferred *sotto voce* and let it be known that they had suspended payment of confidence currency for the time being.

"The idea is," explained the short man, "this being a pleasant party, and all interests being common, it would be a shame to have it broken up. Tom will sit there in the door for two

Holman Day

hours—then he wakes me and I sit there. We're not accusing anybody inside of wanting to leave; but who is sure that somebody from the outside may not stroll along and want to come in? Seeing that we went down to the pen from Levant, it may be thought—providing they do any thinking at the state prison—that we have come back here to start in where we left off. On the other hand, providing they don't do any thinking, they may come up into this section because a reasoning man never would believe we'd take chances by coming back into an old stamping ground. Either way it's looked at, we've got to be careful. Therefore, we hope that gents of a pleasant party will consider this double-shift arrangement as being for the general good of all hands."

Mr. Wagg was pleased. He said so unhesitatingly, but not tactfully. He declared that he would mortally hate to be surprised keeping the company he was in.

Vaniman was able to stay awake through most of the two watches. But the short man on sentry go was more vigilant than the tall man had been; two hours of sleep and the keen hope for the morrow conspired to keep the guard alert. In despair the young man loosed his hold on the hateful verities and slipped into slumber.

He was suddenly awakened by a pinching grip on his arm. He opened his eyes upon broad day and upon the face of the tall man. He was aware that the short man was shaking Wagg awake in the next bunk. "Two men coming up the side of the mountain; got a slant at 'em through the trees; they're after us!"

"Sho!" demurred Wagg. "They're only bird hunters."

"We're taking no chances on 'em being jailbird hunters! Are there any holes here in the rocks?"

"Plenty," stated Wagg. "And the three of you better hunt them holes, no matter who is coming."

The short man, the tall man, and Vaniman needed no urging on that point. They ran, crouching low, and scrambled out of sight among the ledges of the craggy peak of Devilbrow.

Wagg lighted his pipe and went out and sat on the bench beside the camp's door, and when the two early visitors came puffing up the hill and confronted him he was to all appearances enjoying the delights of a bland fall morning and the comfort of an unruffled conscience. He jumped to his feet and hailed one of the men with a great show of cordiality; the man was one of the deputy wardens of the state prison.

Mr. Wagg hopefully and guilelessly expressed the conviction that the officer had followed along into the wilderness in order to join in the process of recuperation.

The deputy asserted that Mr. Wagg was wrong to the extent of a damsite, or something of the sort, and reported some recent happenings at the state prison, Mr. Wagg listening with appropriate, shocked, official concern. He opined that it was a long shot, figuring that the convicts had fled back to the region of Levant. The warden agreed. "But the Old Man is bound to have us tip over every flat rock, Bart. He got a call-down for that accident—and this matter on top of it has made him sore. I'm up here this far because I got a line on you at Levant."

"You did, hey?" Mr. Wagg gazed off across the landscape, as if wondering how much of a trail he had left.

"You dropped 'recuperates' like a molting rooster drops feathers, Bart," averred the warden, jocosely. "That was my trail. Reckoned I'd come and tip you off so that you can do a little scouting for the good cause."

Mr. Wagg threw out his chest. "You can leave this hill section to me. Always on the job! That's my motto."

The deputy said he knew that, stated that he would probably spend a week along the highways and in the villages of the section, got a drink of water from a spring near at hand, and departed with his aide.

And after the two were far down the slope, Mr. Wagg called in his campmates with the caution of a hen partridge assembling the brood after the hunter has passed. "It means that we've got to stick close by this camp and mind our business for a week, at any rate," he said, after he had reported the conversation.

Vaniman could not keep the complacency out of his countenance. He caught the short man squinting at him with a peculiar expression. "It would be mighty dangerous for any one of us to go far from this camp," said the young man.

"It sure would!" agreed the convict, sententiously.

Vaniman was promptly conscious that his innocent air had not been convincing.

He became more fully aware of that fact when the tall man and the short man resumed guard duty that night, turn about. It was plain that they proposed to hang grimly to the token in their possession until the token could be cashed in for the coin.

The confinement behind prison bars had tested Vaniman's powers of endurance; this everlasting espionage by the men who had set themselves over him tried him still more bitterly. They lacked the sanction of the law which even an innocent man respects while he chafes. While that situation continued he was prevented from taking any step toward clearing up his tangled affairs. He could look down on the roofs of the village of Egypt and meditate savagely—and that was all. Vona had apprised him of Britt's plans regarding a mansion. He could see that structure was taking shape rapidly. Men swarmed over it like bees over a hive. He did not doubt the loyalty of the girl. But he was left to wonder how long her loyalty to the memory of a dead man would endure.

Day by day, through dragging hours, he suffered from the agonizing monotony of the camp. But the future offered only a somber prospect. After this respite in the insistence of the treasure seekers, he could expect only ugly determination when they dared to make a move in the matter. They had plenty of leisure for talk. They were already spending that money! Wagg was even more impatient than the others.

Through Vaniman had been cruelly tortured by thoughts of the injustice that had been visited on him, by his reflections that the Egyptians had shown him no consideration, he had nursed the hope that he might contrive to give them back their money after he had dragged from Britt the truth.

But at last, in his new spirit of loneliness, in the conscious-ness that no man's hand was offered to him in the way of help, he entered upon a new phase of resolution. He had gone into prison with youth's ingenuous belief that the truth would prevail. He had permitted a lie to aid in prying his way out, and now he was paltering with evasions and making no progress except toward more dangerous involvement. One afternoon sudden fury swept the props out from under caution.

Holman Day

He leaped up from the rock on which he had been sitting, pondering, the rumble of the conspirators' conversation serving as obbligato for the cry his soul was uttering. He was between them and the sunset sky.

"The truth!" he shouted.

The three men peered at him, shading their eyes. He seemed to tower with heroic stature. He came at them, shaking his fists over his head.

"You are thieves and renegades. I don't believe you know the truth when you hear it. But you're going to hear it."

He tackled Wagg first. He set the grip of both of his hands into the slack of the shoulders of the amazed guard's coat and yanked Wagg to his feet and shouted, with his nose barely an inch from Wagg's face, "I told you the truth at first. I said I didn't know where the money was. You gave me a chance to get out by a lie. I'm human. I took the chance."

He threw Wagg from him with a force that sent the man staggering; the guard stumbled over a rock and fell on his back.

He turned on the convicts. By his set-to with Wagg he had gained their full attention. "You low-lived scoundrels, do you know an honest man when you lay eyes on him? I declare that I am one. Dispute me, and I'll knock your teeth down your throats—guns or no guns. I don't know where the money is. I never touched that money. I didn't know what was in those sacks. If you were decent men, with any conception of an oath before God, I'd swear to the truth of what I say. I won't lower myself to make oath! I make the statement. And now let some of you—or all three of you— stand up in front of me and tell me that I'm lying. Come on!

It's an open field!"

They did not stand up. Wagg merely sat up.

"Say something! Some one of you! Say something!" pleaded Vaniman through his set teeth.

The convicts kept their sitting. Vaniman went on adjuring them to stand up and say something. They showed no resentment when he called them names, and they indicated no relish for battle.

"Hold on a minute!" pleaded the short man. "You seem to have your mind well made up as to what we'd better not say. I may have to eat state-prison grub again, and I'll need my teeth. Won't you kindly drop a hint as to what would suit you in the line of talk?"

"You can tell me whether you think I'm handing you the truth or not."

"I think you are," agreed Bill, readily.

"So do I," asserted Tom.

"How about you, Wagg?" Vaniman demanded, resolved on clearing the matter up once for all.

But the lethargic Mr. Wagg was manifestly unable to turn his slow wits on the single track of the mind and start them off in the opposite direction.

"No matter about him now," said the short man. "Give his mind time. A toadstool grows fast after it gets started."

This meek surrender helped Vaniman to regain his poise. "If

you're willing to take the truth from me, men, I'll meet you halfway. You have been frank and open with me. Men who pretend to be better than you, they have lied to me and about me. That's why I was sent to state prison."

"Tom and I couldn't do business like we do if we lied to folks of our kind. Didn't we cash in our word to the trusty? Being in the hole, as you are right now, you'll excuse me for saying that we consider you one of our kind."

"Thank you," returned the young man, accepting that statement at face value.

The short man lighted a cigarette and pondered for a few moments. "You didn't take the money. Tom and I believe what you say. Wagg will catch up with the procession later. All right, Vaniman! But seeing how anxious you were to get out and up here, it's likely that you have a pretty good idea as to who did take the money. If you need any help in squaring yourself, I'll call your attention to the fact that here are a couple of gents who have a little spare time on their hands."

Vaniman was then in no mood to balance the rights and the wrongs of the case. "I have started in on the basis of the whole truth, and I'm coming through, men. I'm following your lead. I was framed in that bank matter. There was a man who had the opportunity to exchange junk for that gold. He made that opportunity for himself by working on my good nature. The man is Tasper Britt, who was the president of that bank. He took the money. He knows where it is."

"Do you think he is the only one who knows?"

"Naturally, he wouldn't be passing the word around."

"You're a bank man—you had the run of the premises—you

had a chance to know the general style of his ways! What do you guess he did with it?"

"I'm sticking to the truth—and what I actually know. I'm not guessing."

"Not even when you say he took the money?"

"I didn't see him take it. But he had a private entrance to the vault. Everybody was so determined to plaster the guilt on to me that no move was made against Britt on account of that back door of his. I was railroaded by perjurers—and Britt was the captain of 'em."

"There's a corner on 'most everything these days, but it's really too bad for a man like Britt to have a corner on so much valuable knowledge," sighed the short man.

And the tall man sighed and agreed.

Mr. Wagg was catching up. With the appearance of a man who had been running and was out of breath he panted, "What's—what's gong to be done about it?"

Vaniman made no suggestions. Having cut the knot of his own entanglement where these men were concerned, he felt no spirit of alacrity about inviting them farther into his personal affairs; he realized that he had merely shifted the course of their dogged pursuit of that money. In spite of his feelings toward Britt, he was dreading what might come from the disclosures he had just made. He had reason to distrust the tactics such men might employ. His relief arising from the show-down was tinged with regret; he was still sorry for the innocent losers in Egypt. To employ two escaped convicts and a recreant prison guard in his efforts to prevail on Britt and secure the rights due an innocent man promised to involve him more wretchedly.

"Vaniman, suppose you take command and give off your orders," said the short man.

"I haven't any sensible plans. I admit that. I have been so pestered and wrought up by the everlasting bullyragging about the devilish money that I haven't had a chance to figure out a way of getting at the man who has ruined me," Vaniman complained. He strode to and fro, snapping his fingers, revealing his sense of helplessness.

"Suppose we sleep on the thing—the whole four of us," suggested the short man. "I said sleep, please note! This general show-down has cleared the air up here a whole lot, I'll say! And Wagg has steered away the dicks! They won't be strolling in, and till we have settled on a plan I'm sure nobody will feel like strolling out. The night watch is disbanded."

He marched off toward the camp. The others trailed on behind him.

CHAPTER XXVII

THE STIR OF THE YEAST

Mr. Delmont Bangs was naturally of an observant nature. While he was in Egypt he was keeping his eyes particularly wide open. He was looking for two men wanted by the state. Mr. Bangs was the deputy warden who had gone up to the summit of Devilbrow in order to view the landscape o'er and pass the word to Mr. Wagg. Mr. Bangs rode along every highway and byway, day after day, not missing a trick. He was not especially sanguine in regard to locating the missing convicts in that section, but he was obeying the warden's orders; after a day or so he was also obeying an impulse to satisfy his curiosity in lines quite apart from his official quest.

He spent his nights at Files's tavern and grabbed his meals wherever he happened to be.

But after a time he found that housewives were unwilling to give him anything to eat. He was sure that they had not soured on him because he was a state catchpole. When he first arrived in town and gave out the news of his mission and issued a general call for tips he was welcomed heartily by everybody; the women, especially, hoped that he would find the villains and put them where they could not threaten unprotected females. Mr. Bangs had not been able to spend his money for food at farmhouses; the women would not accept any pay, and gave him their best.

However all at once they could not be induced to give food or even to sell it. They acted as if they did not care to be bothered; some of them declared that they were too busy to do cooking. They would not allow Mr. Bangs to stick his nose into their houses; they snapped refusal at him from behind doors only partially opened and foot-braced.

Men with whom Bangs conversed wore an air of abstraction. They plainly were not interested in Mr. Bangs or in the convicts whom he was pursuing. He tackled them on all sorts of subjects, hoping to hit on the topic which was absorbing so much of their attention. He went so far as to ask them bluntly what they were carrying on their minds besides hair. Those who were not surly looked scared.

Even the barn doors were no longer frankly open. There was a mysterious sort of subsurface stir everywhere. There was expectancy that was ill disguised. Mr. Bangs, a stranger, perceived that strangers, for some unexplained reason, had ceased to be popular in Egypt. One day a man gruffly told him that detectives would do well to go off and do their detecting in some other place. That was pretty blunt, and Mr. Bangs informed his helper that he, personally, had had about enough of the gummed-up, infernal town. He declared that he was going to leave. Mr. Bangs was more certain about his departure when he arrived back at Files's tavern that evening. Mr. Files informed him that there would be no more accommodations at the tavern after that night. Mr. Files, questioned, refused to say whether he intended to close the tavern or was merely going away; he would reveal nothing about his further plans.

Mr. Bangs went out and sat on the porch bench with his helper, and irefully asked that bewildered person what the ding-dong the matter was with the dad-fired town, anyway?

In default of specific knowledge the aide tried to be humorous. He told Mr. Bangs that it looked as if the hive was getting ready to swarm. His facetiousness fell flat; Mr. Bangs scowled. The helper became serious.

"I've been watching the old hystrampus they call the Prophet. Everywhere we've been the past few days, he seems to be just coming or just going. Noticed him, haven't you?"

"Of course I've noticed him."

"I don't know what his religious persuasion is, because he hasn't done any talking where I could overhear him. But he seems to be getting busier all the time. Do you know what he preaches?"

"I'm working for the state prison, not the state insane asylum."

"Well," drawled the other, "though I don't know what he's preaching, the general fussed-up condition here in this town reminds me of what happened in Carmel when I lived there as a boy. One of them go-upper preachers struck town. He finally got most of our neighbors into a state of whee-ho where the womenfolks made ascension robes for all concerned and the menfolks built a high platform and they all climbed up on it and waited all one night for Gabr'el's trump to sound."

"What's that got to do with this town?" demanded Mr. Bangs, impatiently.

"Why, considering how near busted the town is—and all the timber cut off and the farms run out—I wouldn't wonder a mite if the right kind of a preacher could get 'em into a frame of mind where they'd be willing to start for anywhere—even straight down, provided they couldn't arrange matters so as to go straight up, like the Carmel folks planned on. Not as how I say that these folks are going to get up and hump it out of Egypt! But there's a whole lot of restle-ness in 'em! That's plain enough to be seen!"

"If there's half as much of it in 'em as there is in me, right now, they'll all follow me when I drive out of town in the morning," declared Mr. Bangs. "And what that king pin, name o' Britt, is building that palace over there for is beyond my guess."

"Expects to grab off the girl of the Vaniman case," said the aide, who had put himself in the way of hearing all the local gossip.

Mr. Bangs lighted a fresh cigar. "Say, I'd like to find out whether this stir here is a go-upper proposition. I'd join the party and go up, too, if I thought I could locate that cashier and find out where he hid that mess of gold."

"Try the ouija board," giggled the aide.

However, in his desperate desire for information in general Mr. Bangs proceeded to try something which suited better his practical turn of mind.

He hailed Prophet Elias, who had appeared in the open door of Usial Britt's shop. The gloom of the autumn evening was deepened by vapor which came drifting from the lowlands after the night air had chilled the moisture evoked by the sun from the soil. The open door set a patch of radiance on the dun robe of the dusk. The light spread upon the vapor, was diffused in it, furnished an aura of soft glow in the center of which stood the robed figure.

Deputy Bangs's first hail, when Elias opened the door and stood revealed, was contemptuously brusque; he used the tone he commonly employed toward his charges in prison; he perceived at first only the queer old chap, the dusty plodder of the highways, the man of cracked wits. Bangs spoke as an officer, peremptorily: "Say, you! Come over here. I want to talk with you!"

The Prophet made no move, either with his feet or his tongue. In the haze that lay between him and Bangs, the man of the robe seemed to tower and to take on a mystic dignity which had been lacking in the candid light of day. After the silence had continued for some time Bangs spoke again. His new manner showed that his eyes had been reprimanding his tongue. "Excuse me! I didn't mean to sound short. But would you kindly step across here? Or"—the eyes certainly had shamed the tongue and had humbled it—"or I'll come over there, if you'd rather have it that way."

The Prophet strode along the misty path of light and stood in the middle of the road. "Talk—but I must ask you to talk to the point and in few words. I have no time to waste on gossip."

"All right! Few words it is! What's the matter with this town all of a sudden?"

"Ask Pharaoh. The kingdom is his."

"I don't get you!"

The deputy's helper pulled his chief's sleeve and hissed some

Holman Day

rapid words of explanation, more fruit gathered from local gossip.

"Oh, so that's what you call him? However, I'm asking you. You ought to know. I've seen you all over the lot, talking with everybody."

"Ask Pharaoh!" repeated the Prophet, sonorously.

The helper nudged Bangs with a swift punch. "If you feel like taking that advice, boss, here's your chance. There's Tasper Britt."

The magnate of Egypt was revealed suddenly, coming from the direction of his new mansion. He strode past Elias. "Ask Pharaoh!" advised the Prophet once more, and Britt halted. He came back a few steps and addressed the men on the tavern porch:

"Can't a man who is deputy warden of our state prison find something for amusement better than stirring up a lunatic?"

"I'm not trying to find amusement—not in this town," returned Mr. Bangs. "I'm after information. He refers me to you—or so I take it!"

"What information?"

"There's something the trouble in this town and I'd like to know what it is."

"There it is," barked Britt, pointing to Elias. "That's the principal trouble—a lunatic spreading lunacy like smallpox."

"But what is it all about?" insisted Bangs, "What's this new excitement?"

"I know nothing about any excitement, sir. I attend to business instead of gossip. If you can make it your business to take this pest to state prison, where he probably belongs if his record could be dug up, the town of Egypt will be all right again."

"Pharaoh, I have a message of comfort for you," stated the Prophet. "This night do I depart from the land of Egypt. I go and I shall not return."

For some moments Britt did not find words with which to reply. Then he mumbled something about good riddance and shaking the dust from the feet.

"I shall shake all the dust from my feet this side of the border line," said Elias. "Your land of Egypt cannot spare any soil."

"You are getting away just in time," rasped the usurer. "I have been tolerating you since you got back from jail because I've been too busy to tend to your case."

"Ah!" commented Elias, mildly.

This subtle humility goaded Britt's wrath more effectually than the Prophet could have prevailed with resentful retort.

"The next time it wouldn't have been a bailable trespass case. Do you dare to tell me why you kept looking in at the windows of my house?"

"I was looking for the closet."

"What closet?"

"For the closet where you keep the skeleton. But rest this night in peace, Pharaoh. I am going away."

"I can sleep better for knowing that you are out of this town."

"Then promise me that you will sleep to-night—sleep soundly. That thought will cheer me as I go on my way." Britt started along, making no reply. "I bespeak for you sleep without dreams," the Prophet called after him. "Your dreams, Pharaoh, might be colored with some of the realities—and that would be bad, very bad for your peace of mind."

Once more Britt strode back from the vapors. "Are you trying to provoke me to smash my fist into your face? Are you trying to cook up a blackmail damage suit by the advice of that crook lawyer who bailed you out? I'm beginning to see why a lawyer was enough interested in you to get you back into this town."

"You guess shrewdly, Pharaoh. You have avoided the deep plot against your wealth. Let the thought make you sleep soundly to-night. I'm glad to make my confession and hope it will add to your peace of mind."

Usial Britt had appeared in the door of his cottage; he leaned lazily against the jamb. "It will be a fine night for sleeping," he remarked, amiably. "This fog is sort of relaxing to the nerves!"

"Hold one moment, Pharaoh!" pleaded Elias. The appearance of the hated brother had started the magnate off once more. "I am anxious to make your night a peaceful one. If you see me go away, knowing that I shall not return again before your face, the comfort of your knowledge will lull you to sleep. Wait!"

He stepped to the door of the cottage, reached inside, and secured a long staff. He picked up from the floor a huge horn—a sort of trump. He settled the curve of the instrument over his shoulder. He blew a long and resounding blast. Then he marched away, taking long strides. He loomed in the first stratum of the vapor, the radiance from the open door showing him as an eerie figure; then the fog swallowed him up. Every few moments he sounded a mighty blast on the trump. The blare of the horn rolled echoes afar in the murk. Steadily the volume of the sound decreased; it was plain that the Prophet was traveling at good speed.

"Well, I'll be dimdaddled!" grunted Mr. Bangs. His was the only comment on the departure of Prophet Elias from the land of Egypt—that is to say, the only comment passed by the group in front of Files's tavern. Tasper Britt went his way toward the Harnden home, his lodgings still. Usial Britt closed his cottage door. Bangs found the sticky chill of the fog uncomfortable. He and his helper went in and upstairs to their rooms.

CHAPTER XXVIII

THE SHADE WHO MEDDLED

Sometime in the night Vaniman awoke, not suddenly, or with the sense of having been disturbed, but torpidly, with the feeling that he had been especially deep in slumber. He recovered his senses slowly. Therefore, only gradually did he become aware of a peculiar new condition of affairs in the camp. He wondered idly, trying to make up his mind as to what was different in the place this night. He heard the "yeak-yeak" of the crickets outside. He heard nothing else. Then he understood. His three comrades were not vocalizing their slumber in snores. He had endured the torture philosophically night after night.

His surprise awakened him fully. He listened, but he could not hear the sound of breathing. He rolled out of his bunk and investigated. The light in the camp was merely the reflection of the paler hue of the night outside, filtering through the open door and the single window. But he perceived that he was alone in the place—the bunks were empty.

His primitive life in the camp had inured him to new habits; he had been removing only his shoes and his coat when he went to bed. He pulled on his shoes—he did not bother with coat or hat. He rushed out of doors and called aloud, hoping that his panic was exaggerating his apprehensions. There was no answer.

Then his fears took definite shape and sought for confirmation. He ran to the horse hovel. The animal was gone.

Standing there, bitterly conscious of what had happened and acutely aware of what was likely to happen with those three miscreants on the trail of the treasure that they coveted, Vaniman accepted his full measure of responsibility. He did not excuse the passion which had prompted him to open his heart in regard to Tasper Britt. It was plain that they intended to unlock the secret of the money by the use of Britt, going to any lengths of brutality the occasion might demand. To get at Britt they would be obliged to invade the Harnden home. The thought of what might develop from that sortie wrought havoc in Vaniman's soul! His fears for Vona and her mother spurred him to action even more effectively than his conviction that his own cause was lost if the men were able to force the money from Britt. If they were captured it would be like them to incriminate Vaniman as an accomplice; if they got safely away with the treasure there could be no revelations regarding Britt's complicity in its concealment. Britt certainly would not tell the truth about what had happened to him; the fugitives would hide their secret and their plunder.

If ever a victim of devilish circumstances had a compelling reason to play the game, single-handed and to the full limit of desperation, so Vaniman told himself, he was the man.

He ran from the hovel to the peak of the crag that overlooked the village of Egypt. He beheld below him a vast expanse of grayish white, the fleecy sea of the enshrouding vapor. He heard no sounds, he saw no lights. He had no notion of the hour. Wagg had accommodated him with the time of day, when he asked for it, just as Wagg loaned him a razor and doled his rations, persistently and with cunning malice working to subdue the young man's sense of independence.

But in this crisis all of Vaniman's courage broke from the thralls in which prison intimidation and a fugitive's caution and despair had bound it during the months of his disgrace.

No matter how long the others had been on their way! They would be obliged to go the long route around the hill, and were hampered by the van; their grim forethought in taking the vehicle to transport their booty, as if they were sure of succeeding, was another element that wrought upon Vaniman's temper.

As he was, without coat or hat, he leaped from the crag, as if he were trying to jump squarely into the middle of the village of Egypt. He had taken no thought of the steepness of the slope or the dangers of descent. He slipped and rolled for many rods and a rain of rocks and earth followed him and beat upon him when he caught a tree and clung to it. He went on more cautiously after that; blood trickled from the wounds on his face where the sharp edges of rocks had cut. He thrust himself through the scrub growth, opening a way with the motions of a swimmer, his hands scarred by the tangled branches. There were other steep places that were broken by terraces. When he was down from the rocky heights on which the vapor did not extend and had entered the confusing mists, he was obliged to go more slowly still, for he narrowly missed some nasty falls.

Fierce impatience roweled him. He would not allow himself to weaken his determination by thinking on what he would do after he arrived at the Harnden home. He had set that as his goal. Above other considerations he placed his frenzied resolution to protect Vona. He realized that he must protect her even from himself—from the shock she would suffer by his unprefaced appearance, this lover who would come like one risen from the dead! The scoundrels who came seeking Britt in her home would not be as terrifying as the visitor who would seem to be a specter—the shade of the convict whom a mountain had crushed, so said the official reports of the tragic affair.

The fact that he was rushing to meet in combat three men, armed and desperate, worried him less than his anguished concern in behalf of the girl who was unprepared for his advent by hint or warning.

At last he came to the pasture slopes where he was more sure of his footing. He ran. When he heard the rumble of wheels he stopped in order to listen, trying to distinguish the location of the sound in the fog, which made direction uncertain. He knew it must be late. Few vehicles were moved in Egypt after dark. He suspected that what he heard was the van.

However, he was puzzled by what he was hearing. Either there were many vehicles, or else the echoes were playing pranks in the mists which enwrapped all objects. Under the pall of fog all sounds were exaggerated. To right and left, near at hand and far away he heard the rumble of wheels, the creak of whiffletrees, and the plodding feet of animals.

He heard, too, an occasional, dust-choked bleat or a plaintive lowing.

But a sound that was repeated regularly he could not understand, nor could he determine the direction from which it came. It was sound diffused like the fog itself. It was mellowed by distance. He recognized the notes as the winding of some sort of a horn or trump.

Holman Day

Vaniman's ears were telling him nothing definite. He hurried on down the hill so that he might make his eyes serve him at closer range. In order to see what was going on in the highway he was obliged to go close to the wall which bordered it; though the fog hindered, it helped, for in the obscurity he was well hidden among the bushes.

First he saw a hayrack go past. Two horses drew it. It was piled high with household goods, and women and children were on top of the load. Two cows were hitched on behind. By the time the fog had hidden this conveyance a wagon of the jigger type rumbled past. It was as heavily loaded as the hayrack. He heard other vehicles coming—he heard still others far down the road on their way.

He was urged by a furious desire to shout—to ask what all this meant. But he did not dare to run such risks. There was a wall between him and the rest of humanity until his sorry affairs could be straightened.

The highway gave him a clew as to his whereabouts; he had been lost in that wallow of vapor, unable to distinguish north from south. He retreated from the wall and stooped as he ran along behind the screen of the wayside alders. He had an affair of his own to look after, no matter what the rest of Egypt was doing.

In spite of his haste, he carefully scrutinized each item in this singular parade of the night, keeping near enough to the road for that purpose. It seemed like some sort of a migration. He wondered how comprehensive it was. He wanted to be sure that nobody in whom he was especially interested passed him without his knowledge. There was every kind of an equipage that would convey people or property. Nobody was talking. So far as was possible, the human beings in the procession seemed to be trying to make a secret of the affair.

Mothers hushed their children when the youngsters chattered or whimpered. Men merely whispered commands to the horses.

All at once Vaniman beheld the van. It was holding a place in the parade and was moving with the decorous slowness of the other vehicles. On the driver's seat with Wagg were the two convicts. The comrade whom they had deserted waited until it had passed; then he ran out into the road and ducked along close to the rear of it.

They were coming away from the village of Egypt. To what extent had they succeeded in their rascally errand? What burden were they conveying? Vaniman could not curb his wild desire to find out. He had had plenty of experience in dodging into that van. He lifted the flap and leaped in. There was black darkness in there. He put out his hand cautiously. It touched a man. The move that the man made was a sort of fruitless struggle, indicating that his limbs were secured in some way.

Vaniman, in that crisis in his affairs, was not affected by squeamishness. He used his hands. He immediately discovered that the man was tied up hand and foot with torn cloth, strips of sheets or something of the kind. The man's only apparel was a nightshirt. Around his neck, so Vaniman's touch told him, was a leather cord to which keys were attached. Tasper Britt had told his cashier that he always carried his keys to bed with him in that fashion, and he had advised Vaniman to employ the same caution.

This prisoner in the van was certainly the magnate of Egypt. Vaniman found that a towel was bound tightly across the bearded mouth; the young man even ran his hand over the bald pate, now divested of its toupee.

There was no gold in the van. Vaniman made sure of that after he had satisfied himself as to the identity of Britt.

While the young man was endeavoring to steady his whirling thoughts, striving to plan some course of action by which he could turn the situation to his personal benefit, his attention became taken up in another quarter. Through the trap he heard the voice of the short man. "Quick! Off the road. Nobody's in sight!"

The van lurched and the front of it dipped with a violence that drove Vaniman and Britt against the end. Up came the front and the rear sagged. Then the van went bumping and swaying over uneven ground. The claw-clash of the branches of trees against the sides informed Vaniman that the men had driven into the woods.

When the vehicle halted, the young man crawled forward and huddled down into as compact a ball as he could make of himself.

He heard the three men dismounting. "I'll tell the world that this is a handy night for us, whatever it is that's going on in this burg!" It was the voice of that ever-ready spokesman, the short man. "There would have been a head at every window if we had been obliged to go teaming around all by ourselves, in the night. But they wouldn't have noticed a couple of giraffes and a hippopotamus in that procession."

"I couldn't see that they even paid any attention to those women squalling upstairs when we did the job," was the tall man's opinion. "Handy night, say you? Why, that man we braced up to and asked where was Britt's boarding house, he seemed to have so much of his own business on his mind that he wasn't wondering a mite what our business with Britt might be."

"Get busy!" said the other convict. "That business is only just beginning."

There was a stir of feet.

"Hold on!" It was the voice of Wagg, mumbling cautiously. "Tie your handkerchiefs over your faces like I'm doing."

"Right!" the short man agreed. "Always leave 'em guessing when you say good-by!"

A few moments later Wagg lifted the flap; Vaniman saw him outlined against the fog. The convicts reached in and pulled Britt out, and the flap was dropped.

"Look out!" the short man warned. "Loosen that towel only a little and hold your clutch on his gullet, bo! We're not any too far from that road, and we'll understand the good news if he'll only whisper it."

After a few moments he went on. "Man, we've got you—got you foul! You know where that gold coin is. Shut up! No argument. You tell us where it is. Then you won't get hurt. If you don't tell us, you *will* get hurt. Get busy with your mouth!"

In spite of his abhorrence at this method of extorting the truth, Vaniman was conscious of a feeling of comradeship with the three rapscallions at that moment. They were merely seeking loot. He was seeking the re-establishment of his honor and his love. He waited in the tense silence, straining every nerve to hear. No sound came to him. He wondered whether Britt, cowed, was whispering the information.

"Get busy, I tell you!"

Evidently the prisoner was obstinate.

Minute after minute the short man labored with the captive, the snarl in his insisting voice deepening into the diapason of malevolent threat.

But Britt said no word.

Vaniman, feeling that all the prospects of his life were at stake, decided to play a waiting game. In spite of their culpable motive, the men outside were serving as his aides in the crucial moment. They were demanding information which the usurer owed to the innocent.

"Oh, very well," said the master of ceremonies. "We'll go on with the rest of the program, then. One of you bring that side lamp and light it. And help me get this towel tighter. He's going to try some squalling."

Vaniman saw the flare of the lamp past the edge of the flap. He set his teeth and decided that he would not interfere. When he heard sounds which, muffled in the towel, were like the whines and grunts of a tortured animal, he stiffened his determination to await the issue.

"Now loosen the gag and let him talk! I reckon he has found something to say."

Vaniman heard louder groans. But Britt gave out no information.

"Back with the talk-tickler! Hold it closer! The same foot! We've got a good start on that one."

The man in the van felt his gorge rising, in spite of the fact that the victim was a relentless persecutor of others. The stifled accents of agony were dreadful.

After a time the short man spoke. Into three words he put the venom of a malice that would not be gainsaid. "Now, damn you!" His tone hinted at no regret for what had gone on before; it suggested that there was more to come; it was compelling demand that the captive should employ the respite that was offered.

Britt began to babble; there was a suggestion of partial mania in his tones. Vaniman could not understand what he was saying, but the sharp questions that were interjected by the manager of the affair—the queries that gimleted for additional information—suggested the line of confession that Britt was giving forth.

"Yes—in the bank! Where in the bank? . . . I heard that, but where? . . . In the basement, hey? Well, where in the basement? . . . Concrete block hey? . . . Come across! . . . Along here with that lamp, bo! . . . Exactly where is that block?"

Through Vaniman there flooded something that was almost a delirium of derring do. He did not know just what he would be able to perform—one against three. He did not dare to wait for any farther developments in the thing. He was possessed by the frantic fear that the knaves would use their information and beat him to the treasure. That the money was somewhere in the basement of Britt Block was enough for him at that juncture. He decided that the time for stealth was past. He would proclaim the news. He would tell his story. He would trust the case to the fair judgment of men.

He scrambled forward in the van and made a hasty survey of the situation. Britt was stretched on the ground. The two convicts were kneeling side by side, bending over their captive, and the short man was still plying Britt with questions. Their backs were toward the man in the van. Wagg was kneeling at Britt's feet, holding the carriage lamp, shielding the flare with a curved palm.

The posture of all three of them invited the attack that Vaniman instantly decided on. He could not hope that he would be offered a better opportunity.

He flung aside the flap, he leaped from the opening. Spreading his knees, he landed on the convicts, a knee on each back, and then he brought his hands toward each other with all his strength, cuffing their skulls together with a resounding crack. They fell across Britt. Vaniman was on his feet while Wagg was rising; the guard's slow mind was operating ineptly on his muscles. The young man felled Wagg with a vicious blow under the ear.

The convicts, knocked senseless, were on their faces, pinning Britt to the ground. The butts of the bulldog revolvers in their hip pockets were exposed. Vaniman snatched out the weapons. He aimed one of the revolvers at Wagg, who had struggled to his knees. "Your knife! Throw it to me! Quick!"

Under the menace of the gun Wagg obeyed.

The young man pocketed the guns for a moment. He rolled the reviving convicts off Britt and slashed the prisoner's bonds and tore the towel from his face. It was in his mind to force Britt to crawl into the van. He was regarding Britt as his chief witness and principal exhibit in the exposure he proposed to lay before the people of Egypt. In the back of Vaniman's head there may have been some sort of consideration for the man who had ruined him—scruples against leaving him with those renegades who had tortured him. However, the young man was conscious of the more compelling motive—to carry Britt along with him, to force Britt, before the eyes of men, to uncover the hiding place of the treasure.

He trained his guns on the three men, backing away from them in order to have them at a safe distance. Britt was on his knees. He was staring at Vaniman with unblinking eyes in which unmistakable mania was flaming. The attack on him in his bed that night, the blow that had stunned him so that the assailants might tie him up, the ride in the strange conveyance, the dreadful uncertainty of what it was all about—these matters had wrought cruelly upon the victim's wits. The torture by the flame had further unsettled his mind. And at that moment, coming down from the heavens, so it seemed, a dead man had appeared to him.

Britt's recent experience had rendered him incapable of surveying the thing from a normal viewpoint. He saw the man whom he had disgraced by plot and perjury, the man who was buried under tons of rock, so the state had officially reported, the man to whose return after seven years of punishment Britt had been looking forward with dread. He had slept more peacefully since that tragedy had been enacted at the prison. Britt was not admitting that this was a human being in the flesh. Already partially crazed by the manhandling from which he had suffered, he peered at this apparition, a mystic figure in the aura of the fog—the shade of Frank Vaniman, so his frantic belief insisted—and leaped up, screaming like a man who had gone stark, staring mad.

Before Vaniman had time to issue a command Britt ran away along the lane by which the van had entered the wood. He was an extraordinary figure in flight. His night robe fluttered behind as he ran. For the most part he hopped on one foot; he yelped with pain when he was obliged to set the blistered foot on the ground in order to recover his balance.

Holman Day

Vaniman did not stay to threaten the three men. He had their weapons and he did not fear them.

He ran after Britt.

CHAPTER XXIX

THE FOX WHO WAS RUN TO EARTH

Vaniman's first impulse was to overtake the fugitive. He wanted to have Britt in his grip, holding to him, forcing him to confess and restore.

But when Britt reached the highway and started in the direction of the village, saner second thought controlled the pursuer. Britt had become a self-operating proposition; Vaniman felt that, although sudden fright were spurring Britt, a fear more inherently characteristic was pulling the usurer on his race to the village—he had betrayed the hiding place of hard cash! He was rushing to protect it. By running to the treasure Britt would be betraying something of more moment to Vaniman than gold. The young man kept his distance, keeping the quarry in sight, running a few feet behind Britt in the fog.

In the mist the two were like the flitting figures of a fantasy. The road was still well filled with wains and pedestrians, following after those who had gone on ahead. The wains stopped; the pedestrians halted and gaped and gasped. Women cried out shrilly. Vaniman and Britt furnished an uncanny spectacle. The eyes which beheld them saw them only for an instant; the fog's curtain allowed each observer

Holman Day

scant time to determine what these figures were. Britt, hairless, his face sickly white, his night gear fluttering, was as starkly bodeful as if he were newly risen from the grave, garbed in death's cerements. Vaniman's presence on the scene added to the terrifying illusion produced by Britt.

This pursuer had been officially proclaimed dead. They who beheld believed they saw a dead man. The face was smutched with blood. The eyes were wide and were set straight ahead. Vaniman was taking no chances on losing the man whom he was chasing.

After the first thrill of horror, wild curiosity stung the men of Egypt. They dropped the reins, those who were driving horses, and joined those who had turned in their tracks and were following the phantoms of the night.

In this fashion, with the rout and rabble behind and Vaniman close on his heels, Tasper Britt arrived at Britt Block—and even the statue in its niche seemed to goggle with amazed stare.

Britt did not stop to lift the loop of the leather thong over his head; with a fierce tug he broke the cord. He unlocked the door and rushed in.

After Vaniman followed, the men outside hesitated only momentarily. Their numbers gave them courage. They crowded into the corridor. Some of them were carrying the lanterns which they had used to light the way of the procession of carts.

Britt did not enter his office; he ran the length of the corridor and flung open the door which led to the basement. The pursuers kept on at the heels of Vaniman. But they took the precaution to allow the men with the lanterns to go ahead.

Britt went frantically at his work, paying no attention to anybody. In fact, he did not seem to realize that others were present. There was a heap of furnace wood in one corner of the basement; he began to heave that wood in all directions. One of the lanterns was smashed by a billet. The men in the place were obliged to dodge the flying sticks. Britt worked as if he were alone in the place. He talked to himself. "Demons are after it. Demons and dead men! The demons sha'n't have it. I told 'em where it was. But I'll take it away. The demons brought hell fire to make me tell. They brought a dead man. But they sha'n't have it."

"He's gone raving crazy!" cried an onlooker in shrill tones.

"Come on, men! Let's catch him and tie him up," suggested somebody else.

But they were prevented by fears which were made effective by influences which did not seem to partake wholly of human qualities.

In their concentrated interest in the active Britt they had been disregarding Vaniman, who was restraining himself, standing outside the radiance of the lanterns.

The next instant he leaped into the sight of all of them. He stood between them and Britt. He pulled his weapons. His blood-spotted face seemed a vision of the unreal; but the guns were unmistakably the agents which a human being would employ in an emergency. And there was a business-like click in his tone. "Stand back, the whole of you! This is a show-down. Tasper Britt is confessing that he is a thief and a liar. Use your eyes."

They cowered back from the threat of the guns and did use their eyes. They saw Britt uncover a section of the basement floor of concrete. They saw him locate an iron ring that was cunningly concealed under a little square of concrete which he pried up with his finger nails. He tugged at the ring and lifted a slab. The men with the lanterns raised them high. The light glinted on gold—gold coins in bulk, naked of sacks.

A man had come thrusting through the crowd in the basement, hurrying in from the outside. It was Squire Amos Hexter. It was hard to determine from his expression which spectacle he found the more astounding—Frank Vaniman at bay, in the flesh, or the gold coins that Tasper Britt was dipping with both hands, sluicing them upon the concrete in jingling showers.

Squire Hexter did find his voice. "Good God!" he shouted.

"God is good!" said Vaniman. He threw the weapons into a far corner of the basement. "Squire Hexter, take charge of this thing. Here are plenty of witnesses."

The Squire went forward slowly. His lips moved without the sound of spoken word. He set the clutch of his hands on Vaniman's arms. He stared long and earnestly into the young man's eyes.

"I can't talk now," Vaniman quavered.

And the Squire seemed to know, out of his sympathy with men, that there was something for that case better than words. He put his arms around Vaniman and kissed him. "Come along home with me to Xoa, sonny."

Britt struggled to his feet, and groaned when his weight came on the tortured flesh. He looked about as if searching for something. "A basket!" he muttered. "I must find a basket."

He started forward and saw Vaniman in the hook of the Squire's arm. Whether increase of his mania or some sort of remorse prompted his utterance was not clear. "Take it back to Tophet with you! I didn't mean to keep it. I didn't know how to give it back. I took it so that they'd pen you up, out from under my feet. But even a thousand tons of rock can't pen you. I'm done trying. If this is what you're chasing me for, take it! Keep away from me."

He went through the crowd, beating his way with his fists.

"Shall we hold him, Squire?" called a man.

"Let him alone for just now! He can't go far in that shape. We'll attend to him after a little while." The Squire pulled himself together with the air of one who saw that the situation needed a commander. He singled responsible men from the crowd and ordered them to take charge of the coin.

"Come away with me," he urged Vaniman. "This is no place for our talk."

When they walked out of the building they saw no sign of Britt. "We'll let him alone," insisted the Squire. "There'll be no use in asking him questions till he's in his right mind. He'll probably get back his wits when he gets back his clothes."

"Squire Hexter, what's happening in this town to-night. What—"

"All in good time, sonny! Let's get home where Xoa is."

There were lights in the Squire's house. In spite of the fog, Vaniman perceived that there was a gray hint of dawn in the heavens. More acutely was he wondering what this universal vigil in Egypt signified. But reaction had overtaken him. He was in the mood to accept commands of any sort. He walked on in silence.

"You must stay out here till I break the thing to Xoa!"

The young man clung to the trellis of the porch for a few moments until Xoa flung wide the door. Supported in her embrace, he staggered into the sitting room.

"Cry, sonny! Cry a little," the Squire adjured him. "Put your head on Xoa's knee and have it out. It will tide you over till your own mother can comfort you."

But wild desire for knowledge burned the sudden tears out of Vaniman's eyes. "Where is Vona? What is happening?"

"We'll see to it mighty quick that Vona knows, sonny. The right word must get to her in the right way. Mother will know how. Mother, you'd better attend to it."

She agreed with that suggestion, but first she brought a basin and water and soft cloths and solicitously made more presentable the young man's face.

While she ministered to him he told them what had been happening in his affairs.

"You're alive. That's the main point. Now, Xoa," urged the Squire, "go to Vona before some lunatic tells her something to scare her to death!"

The good woman hastened away, her smile reassuring the lover.

For some time the Squire regarded Vaniman with an

expression into which some of the old notary's whimsical humor began to creep. "So it struck you, did it, that you had dropped back into town on a lively night? I was expecting quite a general stir, myself. But I'll confess that the thing hit me as livelier than what I had looked for when I was sitting here and heard a man holler outside that your ghost had chased Tasper Britt into his office. You see, the plan was not to have Tasper disturbed by any human beings this night. We all hoped he would sleep sound. Everybody proposed to tiptoe when passing in the neighborhood of the Harnden house. But to have a ghost come and chase Tasper around town was wholly outside the calculations of the human beings in Egypt this night."

"I'm afraid I don't see any joke hidden in this proposition, Squire," the young man complained.

"Son, it's a joke, but it's so big and ironic that only one of those gods on high Olympus is big enough and broad-minded enough to be able to laugh at it. Some day the folks of this town will be able to look back on this night and laugh, I do hope. But not now. They're too much wrought up. They're too busy. Hold on! I'm going to let another man explain the thing. He's in a position to pass out information more to the point than anything I can hand you. I'll simply say this. When you saw what you beheld in the fog this night, you were seeing a revised version of the Book of Exodus acted out in real life. The Children of Israel, of this day and date, are departing from the land of Pharaoh, current edition. With their flocks and their possessions, their wives and their children, they are on their way to The Promised Land. And now, if you'll step into the parlor with me I'll introduce you to the promiser."

Vaniman followed

Holman Day

CHAPTER XXX

THE PROMISED LAND

There was a big man in the parlor, a hearty-looking man, manifestly of the metropolis, patently of the "good sport" type. He was walking up and down. With his tweed knickerbockers, his belted jacket, his diamonds in his scarf and on his fingers, he was such an odd figure in the homely surroundings that he produced on Vaniman a surprise effect. The young man surveyed the stranger with the interest one might take in a queer animal in a circus van; the big man's restless pacing suggested a caged creature. But he took not the least interest in Vaniman, an unkempt individual without a coat.

"Hexter, what did happen, anyway? I thought you were never coming back. I had a good mind to chase you up, though it would be poor judgment for me to show myself to-night."

"This has happened!" The Squire pointed to Vaniman. The big man cocked an inquiring eyebrow, looking at the Squire's exhibit with indifference. "Colonel, this is Frank Vaniman. You know all about the case!"

The stranger stepped back so hastily that he knocked over a chair.

"Know about the case!" he bawled. "No, I don't know about it, either, if this is the man the mountain fell on—or whatever it was that happened. What kind of con is this you're giving me, Hexter?"

"This is the man, sir. What I mean by saying you know about the case is that you have agreed with me that an innocent man was railroaded into prison, after I gave you the facts. He is out through a trick worked by a prison guard. He'll give us the details later. Just now it's more important for you to be told that Tasper Britt, by his own acts, has confessed that he robbed the Egypt Trust Company."

"Well, I'll be damnationed!" blurted the big man, with such whole-souled astonishment that the mode of expression was pardonable. "And I thought that plenty and enough was happening in this town for one night!"

"Frank, this is Colonel Norman Wincott. He has well understood your case from what I have told him. Now he will understand better. Colonel, won't you allow Frank's story to wait? He is in a dreadfully nervous state, poor chap. And I'm afraid he'll go crazy on our hands if he isn't enlightened right away about what is going on here to-night."

Colonel Wincott strode across the room and slapped Vaniman cordially on the shoulder with one hand and pumphandled with the other. "Plenty of men have escaped from state prison. There's a special novelty about a story of that sort. But let me tell you that I'm the only man in the world who has ever put over a proposition such as this one that is on the docket right here and now. I don't blame you for being interested." It was plain that the colonel entertained no mean opinion of himself and his projects. "All is, Vaniman, I hope your making a two-ring affair of it hasn't taken the attention of the folks off the main show."

"It has only added to the general effect," affirmed the Squire. "It's a clincher. Folks don't care now because Tasper Britt is awake. He has got plenty of business of his own to attend to without calling in sheriffs to slap on attachments."

"Very good! The easier the better," returned Colonel Wincott. "But when I hired you to look after the law part, Hexter, I reckoned you could counter every crack he made. Sit down, Vaniman!" He picked up the chair he had overturned and took it for himself. "You have seen the parade, some of it?"

"I saw a great deal of it, sir."

"And you don't know where it's headed for?"

"No."

The colonel leaned back and regarded the Squire with the satisfied contentment of a cat who had tucked away the last morsel of the canary. Then he winked at Vaniman. "Young man, did you ever hear of Wincott's Pure Rye?"

"No, sir."

"Glad of it! Hope you never were familiar with any other brands. However, enough men did know about it in those dear, damp days beyond recall to make me independent of the pawnshop, to say the least. And, having cleaned up a good pot with whisky running down men's gullets, I reckoned I'd see what I could do with water running downhill. Do you get me at all so far?"

"No, sir."

"Didn't suppose you would. I'm only shuffling the deck. Now for the deal! Awhile ago I came up into this state from the

South and I bought the unorganized township that bounds this town on the north. It had gone begging for a buyer because it's mostly pond and water power. But it's what I wanted. And, having bought it, I used my check book and got some good lobbyists on the job and I got a conditional charter from the legislature. That is to say, it becomes a town charter automatically the moment I can report a certain number of inhabitants—not mere men, but families, regularly settled. Do you see?"

"I surely do begin to see, Colonel Wincott."

"Vaniman, if I had gone to the cities and advertised for settlers, what kind would I have got? Probably only a bunch of aliens dissatisfied already; if they weren't sore on general conditions I couldn't coax 'em to move. And aliens are always moving. I wanted some of the old breed of Yankee pioneers. That's what my folks were, 'way back. I took a sly peek into the town of Egypt. Good folks, but no opportunities here. Everything gone to seed. Up in my township a new deal with a fresh deck! Plenty of timber, plenty of rich land—and mills going up. Confound it! I propose to be boss of a real town—not a wild land plantation!"

He suddenly shifted his posture. He came forward in his chair and set his elbows on his knees. "Say, Vaniman, I got Hexter's opinion a few days ago when I opened up to him and hired him to attend to the law. But I want to ask you now what you think of my real-estate agent?"

The young man shifted his bewildered gaze from the colonel's jovial and inquiring visage to the Squire's equally cheerful countenance.

"Known to Pharaoh and the modern Children of Israel as the Prophet Elias, Frank," explained the notary. "I have heartily indorsed his good work. Furthermore, he knows well how to keep a secret and how to train others to keep one. Tasper Britt went to bed this night without one inkling of what was about to happen. He did not know that he was to be left here without men to toil and pay him his twelve per cent. He has town debts. He has the bare acres he has foreclosed on—he has the tumble-down houses. He has the paupers on the poor farm. He—"

"Hold on, Squire! I forgot about those paupers," broke in the colonel. "I want a town that's fully rounded out. A few paupers belong in a town so that they may serve to remind others folks that they must keep busy and avoid the poor farm. And even the paupers will wake up and go to work in my town! Work will be in the air. I'm going to send a wagon after those paupers. Britt is no sort of a man to be allowed pets; he'll let 'em starve."

"Undoubtedly," agreed the Squire. "I'll say, further, Frank, that when the Prophet started off last evening, blowing his trump to sound the signal for the migration, Britt stood and saw him go—and never guessed what it meant."

"I heard that horn—I wondered."

"He's a good blower," stated Colonel Wincott. "He blew all the props out from under the man Britt. Solidly grounded on texts, Elias is! Vaniman, a brand-new scheme needs a resourceful operator." He patted the top of his head. "Pardon me for flattering myself. I invented the system and the Prophet played it."

Then Colonel Wincott leaned back, stuck his thumbs into the armholes of his vest, and rocked on the hind legs of the chair. "I played a hunch," he went on. "I was going through Scollay Square in Boston one evening and I heard a street evangelist holding forth. He was preaching on the subject, 'Bondage.' Sin he called Pharaoh. And he was hammering the hearers with texts from Exodus. The idea hit me. I hung up beside the curb till he was through preaching, then I invited him to take a ride with me in my car. And a wise old bird I found him to be! No hypocrite! Doing his best to help his fellow-men, but always hep! Never out of a city till I pulled him up here. Likes the country now. Going to be the regular preacher in my new town. No more robe-and-umbrella business, of course. That was my idea. I'm inclined to be a little circusy in my notions. He stood for it. The scheme helped him to put over what he couldn't have got away with by ordinary means."

Vaniman remembered those flashes of worldly wisdom in the Prophet, and was enlightened. His countenance revealed his thoughts.

"Had you guessing?" demanded the colonel. "Nothing like starting folks to guessing. Keeps up the interest. One by one Elias snipped the cords that bound the folks to the soil of this place. Did a fine job. They're going to thrive after they are transplanted. Even Squire Hexter is going to bring up the rear guard, after he has finished here with the loose ends of the law needed in the case."

"It's to be a clean sweep, Frank," the Squire affirmed. "Even Usial and his press; the new town will be in his legislative class." Then he looked long at Colonel Wincott, who was rocking on the legs of his chair.

"I know mighty well what you want to say to me, Squire Hexter," stated the object of the regard. "You don't need to say a word, though. I'll do the saying. Vaniman, you have had a raw deal. But you'll soon be through the woods. I'm going to have a bank in my new town. You're going to be the boss of it."

"Just a moment before you say anything, Frank," expo-
stulated the Squire when Vaniman, choking with doubts and
gratitude both, attempted to speak. "I propose to start at once
for the shire town. I'll begin with the county attorney. I'll
have your name cleared inside of twenty-four hours."

"And don't bother with any Dobbins for that job," declared
the colonel. "Use my car. My chauffeur is hiding it in the
bush a little ways from here. And now, Vaniman, give me all
your attention," he went on, with the pride of a successful
performer. "I'll tell you what's going to happen over across
the line in my town. It's going to interest you. You have been
a man of affairs and you can grasp what I'm saying."

But Vaniman did not seem to be grasping even that
introduction of the subject. He had heard hurrying footsteps
outside the house.

"You'll never listen to anything that will stir your blood like
what I'm going to tell you of my plans for the future,"
insisted the colonel.

But a tremulous voice called: "Frank! Frank!"

Vaniman leaped from his chair and turned his back on the
man who proposed to stir the blood of the listener.

Squire Hexter hurried to Colonel Wincott and whispered
information which caused the master of The Promised Land
to elevate his eyebrows understandingly.

"Great Caesar! Why, sure!" he blurted, and popped up out of
his chair.

Following the Squire, he tiptoed to the door and stood on one side when the notary opened and peeped out.

"Vona!" called the Squire, gently. "The boy is in here. Come!"

She ran past them into the room.

Colonel Wincott ducked out and the Squire followed and closed the door. He closed it slowly, softly, reverently, and then turned a smiling face of compassionate understanding toward Xoa and the colonel.

CHAPTER XXXI

THROUGH THE GATES OF
THE DAWN INTO "LIBERTY"

There was a hush in the Squire's house. The three who were in the sitting room discussed affairs, subduing their tones almost to whispers.

When somebody tramped on to the porch and pounded on the door, the interruption was startling.

The Squire went and opened the door and disclosed Deputy-Warden Bangs of the state prison. But when Bangs made a step forward the notary bulked himself in the doorway with all the dignity his modest size would permit.

"I'm led to believe that you have in this house an escaped convict, name of Vaniman," declared the officer.

"Don't your prison records show that the convict named Vaniman is officially dead, sir?"

"I'll admit that; but if what I have heard since I was routed out of my bed is so, those records will have to be revised."

"I have no control over your records," returned the

Squire, grimly.

Mr. Bangs made another step forward.

"But I have full control over my own house, sir. You cannot come in."

"Do you stand in the way of a deputy warden of the state prison?"

"I certainly do until he presents himself in my door with a proper search warrant, instead of coming here on the strength of mere hearsay."

"I tried to get a warrant," the officer confessed. "But I can't locate the trial justice."

"I hear that he is moving," was the Squire's dry retort.

"You seem to be the only one in the place who isn't moving," said Bangs, craning his neck to peer past the keeper of the door.

"Oh, I'm simply delaying my departure a few days in order to close up some matters of business."

"Let me tell you that if you're concealing a convict in this house you'll have more business than what you plan on. I'm up here—"

"As you have reported to me and all others, you're up here to find two escaped prisoners, sir. Very well! They are not in my house. But I have heard from them. They were seen a very short time ago in the stretch of woods near here known as Baniman's Bower. If you hurry you may catch them."

Bangs displayed prompt interest. He showed more when the Squire added: "They may be already captured. I learned, also, that a man who has been a prison guard was in the same locality. You officials seem to be very vigilant!"

Mr. Bangs choked back some sort of a threatened explosion. He stood there, shifting from foot to foot. Then he blurted: "Say, you seem to be the most level-headed man in this town. I'll go chase those convicts if your tip is a straight one. But tell me! Am I having the nightmare, or are all these things really happening around here?"

However, Squire Hexter did not try to comfort the perturbed Mr. Bangs just then. The notary stepped out on the porch, closing his door behind him. He stared into the graying murk of the night and the fog. That fog was showing a light which was not that of the dawn. It was a spreading, baleful, reddening glare, and after a few moments it covered all the sky.

Then men began to shout. There was an especial uproar from one quarter. The Squire knew that in the direction of the hullabaloos were located the camps in which were lodged the imported workmen who had wrought into solid structure the plans of the mansion that Britt had held in pictured form before the eyes of Egypt.

The feet of running men pounded along the highway. Somebody cried, in clarion tones, "It's Tasp Britt's new house!"

The Squire ran into the road, and Bangs followed.

The notary hailed a little group of men who came rushing from the direction of the main part of the village. "Why aren't you bringing the tub? Fetch Hecla! Quick, men!"

"She's gone!" panted one of the group.

"Gone?"

"There wasn't any wagon left behind, Squire, and they had to haul that gold. They hove it into Hecly's water tank and formed a guard, and she's been a whole half hour gone!"

At that juncture a man came running to them from the direction of the fire. The Squire recognized him as the boss of the carpenters. "Mr. Britt is in that house. I saw him through a window. But it's a furnace from top to bottom."

The Squire opened his mouth as if query, urgently demanding utterance, had pried apart his jaws. "How do you think the fire—" But he promptly closed his mouth and set his lips tightly. He shook his head with the manner of one who did not require information. Then he turned and hurried to his house.

Colonel Wincott and Xoa were on the porch, lighted by the great, red torch whose radiance was flung afar by the reflector aid of the fog.

"It's Britt's house—and Britt is in it," he told them. "Colonel, your man Friday had over many times one text that fits this thing. 'Can a man take fire into his bosom, and his clothing not be burned?'"

He went to Xoa and patted her arm. "Better go inside, mother. It isn't a good thing to be looking at. Where are the children?"

Frank and Vona answered that question by appearing in the door. They were honestly affected by the news the Squire gave them. Vona hid her face against the young man's breast.

"It seems to be a self-operating proposition," stated Colonel Wincott. "And about all anybody can do is to let it flicker!"

Vaniman was clearly not the captain of his soul in those distressing circumstances. He was displaying symptoms of collapse. Squire Hexter noted and acted.

"Wincott, this boy must not stay here in this town any longer. If that prison guard runs afoul of him before I get matters under way at the shire, Frank will be galloped back to his cell in order to make a grandstand play. I've got to be going. Take Frank under your wing. Get him over the border."

"Surest thing in the world!" declared the hearty colonel. "Got a hitch?"

"My horse and double-seater. Come along to the stable— you, too, Frank. Xoa, bring him one of my coats and a hat!"

Vona leaped away from her lover and faced the Squire. "I shall go with him, wherever he may go!" she said, with the fire of one who expected to meet opposition.

But the Squire grinned. "Why, girl, of course you'll go! I wouldn't grab life-saving medicine away from a sick man. Take your mother along, and God bless the whole of you on the way."

That way was toward the north, on the heels of the wains and the flocks and the herds and the men and women and children of the migrating population of Egypt.

Colonel Wincott occupied the front seat with Mrs. Harnden. By the time he had teamed the Squire's fat little nag along for a mile he had succeeded in calming Mrs. Harnden's hysterical spirits. He induced her to quit looking over her shoulder at the great torch that lighted luridly the heavens above the deserted town. "It's a pillar of fire by night, madam, as you say! But that's as far as it fits in with the Exodus sentiment. It's behind us—and behind us let it stay."

At the end of another mile Mrs. Harnden was extolling the capability of her husband.

"I've heard about him," said the colonel. "Optimist? So am I. Get in touch with him and tell him to come to my new town. He'll have something that he can really optimize over."

Colonel Wincott sedulously kept his attention off the two who rode on the back seat; he obliged Mrs. Harnden to do the same.

After a time the trotting nag overtook the trailers of the procession. The colonel hailed and passed one wain after another, steadily calling, "Gangway!" They recognized his authority; they obeyed; they gave him half the road.

He had an especially hearty greeting for the hand tub, Hecla, trundling on its little wheels, men guarding its flanks, men pulling on the rope by which it was propelled. Ike Jones was one of the guards. He gave the colonel's party a return greeting by a flourish on the "tramboon."

"The stage starts from your town this morning, Colonel! Runs express through Egypt."

"Good idea! Nothing but scenery left there," agreed the colonel. "Take good care of that gold, boys! The receiver of the Egypt Trust Company will be able to cut *some* melon!"

But Prof. Almon Waite, toddling behind the treasure, had a metaphor of his own. "This gold will gloriously pave the streets of the New Jerusalem, sir!"

They went on in the growing dawn, threading their way among the vehicles and the folks on foot.

In all their progress they met only one party headed in the opposite direction, coming back toward the town that had been deserted. Vaniman beheld Bartley Wagg teaming along the two convicts. They were tied together and he was threatening them with a club. They merely flashed on the screen of the mist and were out of sight. It was evident that Mr. Wagg had determined to grab a couple of straws, at any rate, in a desperate attempt to buoy himself officially in the flood of his misfortunes.

The sun was burning away the mists when Colonel Wincott's turnout topped a hill; he waved his whip to invite the attention of his passengers. "There she lies, folks! I've been calling it my town. From now on it's our town. Some daisy on the breast of nature, eh?"

There was a lake on the facets of whose ripples the sunlight danced. White water tumbled down cascades. Beside the lake there was a nest of portable houses. "Homes till we build bigger ones," explained the master of The Promised Land. "I'm giving building lots free. The class of settlers warrants it!"

Then Colonel Wincott called their attention to something else—something that was not visible. He wrinkled his nose, but his sniff indicated gusto. "Smell it? It's food for the Children of Israel. Not manna. But it will fit the occasion, I hope. It's a barbecue. A whole ox and all the fixings."

Then they came to a high arch, fashioned from boughs of fir and spruce trees. The wains were rolling under it.

Frank and Vona lifted up their eyes. At the top of the arch, in great letters that were formed of pine tassels fastened to a stretch of canvas, was the word, "LIBERTY."

"The name of our new town," said the colonel.

But for the two on the rear seat it was more than the name of a town. Vaniman pressed the girl's trembling hand between his palms. They looked at each other through the lenses of grateful tears.

Just inside the arch stood Prophet Elias, welcoming all comers. He had put off his robe and had laid aside his fantastic umbrella. He wore the sober garb of a dominic, and his face, above his tie of white lawn, displayed shrewd and complete appreciation of the occasion.

He took off his hat and bowed low when Colonel Wincott's party passed under the arch. And this sonorous proclamation followed Frank and Vona:

"'And I will bring the blind by a way that they knew not; I will lead them in paths that they have not known; I will make darkness light before them, and crooked things straight. These things will I do unto them, and not forsake them.'"

"Amen!" responded Colonel Wincott, fervently.

The two persons on the rear seat did not speak. In silence they had reverently prostrated themselves at a shrine of thanksgiving in their souls.

Choose from Thousands of 1stWorldLibrary Classics By

A. M. Barnard
Ada Leverson
Adolphus William Ward
Aesop
Agatha Christie
Alexander Aaronsohn
Alexander Kielland
Alexandre Dumas
Alfred Gatty
Alfred Ollivant
Alice Duer Miller
Alice Turner Curtis
Alice Dunbar
Allen Chapman
Alleyne Ireland
Ambrose Bierce
Amelia E. Barr
Amory H. Bradford
Andrew Lang
Andrew McFarland Davis
Andy Adams
Angela Brazil
Anna Alice Chapin
Anna Sewell
Annie Besant
Annie Hamilton Donnell
Annie Payson Call
Annie Roe Carr
Annonaymous
Anton Chekhov
Archibald Lee Fletcher
Arnold Bennett
Arthur C. Benson
Arthur Conan Doyle
Arthur M. Winfield
Arthur Ransome
Arthur Schnitzler
Arthur Train
Atticus
B.H. Baden-Powell
B. M. Bower
B. C. Chatterjee
Baroness Emmuska Orczy
Baroness Orczy
Basil King
Bayard Taylor
Ben Macomber
Bertha Muzzy Bower
Bjornstjerne Bjornson

Booth Tarkington
Boyd Cable
Bram Stoker
C. Collodi
C. E. Orr
C. M. Ingleby
Carolyn Wells
Catherine Parr Traill
Charles A. Eastman
Charles Amory Beach
Charles Dickens
Charles Dudley Warner
Charles Farrar Browne
Charles Ives
Charles Kingsley
Charles Klein
Charles Hanson Towne
Charles Lathrop Pack
Charles Romyn Dake
Charles Whibley
Charles Willing Beale
Charlotte M. Braeme
Charlotte M. Yonge
Charlotte Perkins Stetson
Clair W. Hayes
Clarence Day Jr.
Clarence E. Mulford
Clemence Housman
Confucius
Coningsby Dawson
Cornelis DeWitt Wilcox
Cyril Burleigh
D. H. Lawrence
Daniel Defoe
David Garnett
Dinah Craik
Don Carlos Janes
Donald Keyhoe
Dorothy Kilner
Dougan Clark
Douglas Fairbanks
E. Nesbit
E. P. Roe
E. Phillips Oppenheim
E. S. Brooks
Earl Barnes
Edgar Rice Burroughs
Edith Van Dyne
Edith Wharton

Edward Everett Hale
Edward J. O'Biren
Edward S. Ellis
Edwin L. Arnold
Eleanor Atkins
Eleanor Hallowell Abbott
Eliot Gregory
Elizabeth Gaskell
Elizabeth McCracken
Elizabeth Von Arnim
Ellem Key
Emerson Hough
Emilie F. Carlen
Emily Bronte
Emily Dickinson
Enid Bagnold
Enilor Macartney Lane
Erasmus W. Jones
Ernie Howard Pie
Ethel May Dell
Ethel Turner
Ethel Watts Mumford
Eugene Sue
Eugenie Foa
Eugene Wood
Eustace Hale Ball
Evelyn Everett-green
Everard Cotes
F. H. Cheley
F. J. Cross
F. Marion Crawford
Fannie E. Newberry
Federick Austin Ogg
Ferdinand Ossendowski
Fergus Hume
Florence A. Kilpatrick
Fremont B. Deering
Francis Bacon
Francis Darwin
Frances Hodgson Burnett
Frances Parkinson Keyes
Frank Gee Patchin
Frank Harris
Frank Jewett Mather
Frank L. Packard
Frank V. Webster
Frederic Stewart Isham
Frederick Trevor Hill
Frederick Winslow Taylor

Friedrich Kerst
Friedrich Nietzsche
Fyodor Dostoyevsky
G.A. Henty
G.K. Chesterton
Gabrielle E. Jackson
Garrett P. Serviss
Gaston Leroux
George A. Warren
George Ade
Geroge Bernard Shaw
George Cary Eggleston
George Durston
George Ebers
George Eliot
George Gissing
George MacDonald
George Meredith
George Orwell
George Sylvester Viereck
George Tucker
George W. Cable
George Wharton James
Gertrude Atherton
Gordon Casserly
Grace E. King
Grace Gallatin
Grace Greenwood
Grant Allen
Guillermo A. Sherwell
Gulielma Zollinger
Gustav Flaubert
H. A. Cody
H. B. Irving
H.C. Bailey
H. G. Wells
H. H. Munro
H. Irving Hancock
H. R. Naylor
H. Rider Haggard
H. W. C. Davis
Haldeman Julius
Hall Caine
Hamilton Wright Mabie
Hans Christian Andersen
Harold Avery
Harold McGrath
Harriet Beecher Stowe
Harry Castlemon
Harry Coghill
Harry Houidini

Hayden Carruth
Helent Hunt Jackson
Helen Nicolay
Hendrik Conscience
Hendy David Thoreau
Henri Barbusse
Henrik Ibsen
Henry Adams
Henry Ford
Henry Frost
Henry James
Henry Jones Ford
Henry Seton Merriman
Henry W Longfellow
Herbert A. Giles
Herbert Carter
Herbert N. Casson
Herman Hesse
Hildegard G. Frey
Homer
Honore De Balzac
Horace B. Day
Horace Walpole
Horatio Alger Jr.
Howard Pyle
Howard R. Garis
Hugh Lofting
Hugh Walpole
Humphry Ward
Ian Maclaren
Inez Haynes Gillmore
Irving Bacheller
Isabel Cecilia Williams
Isabel Hornibrook
Israel Abrahams
Ivan Turgenev
J.G.Austin
J. Henri Fabre
J. M. Barrie
J. M. Walsh
J. Macdonald Oxley
J. R. Miller
J. S. Fletcher
J. S. Knowles
J. Storer Clouston
J. W. Duffield
Jack London
Jacob Abbott
James Allen
James Andrews
James Baldwin

James Branch Cabell
James DeMille
James Joyce
James Lane Allen
James Lane Allen
James Oliver Curwood
James Oppenheim
James Otis
James R. Driscoll
Jane Abbott
Jane Austen
Jane L. Stewart
Janet Aldridge
Jens Peter Jacobsen
Jerome K. Jerome
Jessie Graham Flower
John Buchan
John Burroughs
John Cournos
John F. Kennedy
John Gay
John Glasworthy
John Habberton
John Joy Bell
John Kendrick Bangs
John Milton
John Philip Sousa
John Taintor Foote
Jonas Lauritz Idemil Lie
Jonathan Swift
Joseph A. Altsheler
Joseph Carey
Joseph Conrad
Joseph E. Badger Jr
Joseph Hergesheimer
Joseph Jacobs
Jules Vernes
Julian Hawthrone
Julie A Lippmann
Justin Huntly McCarthy
Kakuzo Okakura
Karle Wilson Baker
Kate Chopin
Kenneth Grahame
Kenneth McGaffey
Kate Langley Bosher
Kate Langley Bosher
Katherine Cecil Thurston
Katherine Stokes
L. A. Abbot
L. T. Meade

L. Frank Baum
Latta Griswold
Laura Dent Crane
Laura Lee Hope
Laurence Housman
Lawrence Beasley
Leo Tolstoy
Leonid Andreyev
Lewis Carroll
Lewis Sperry Chafer
Lilian Bell
Lloyd Osbourne
Louis Hughes
Louis Joseph Vance
Louis Tracy
Louisa May Alcott
Lucy Fitch Perkins
Lucy Maud Montgomery
Luther Benson
Lydia Miller Middleton
Lyndon Orr
M. Corvus
M. H. Adams
Margaret E. Sangster
Margret Howth
Margaret Vandercook
Margaret W. Hungerford
Margret Penrose
Maria Edgeworth
Maria Thompson Daviess
Mariano Azuela
Marion Polk Angellotti
Mark Overton
Mark Twain
Mary Austin
Mary Catherine Crowley
Mary Cole
Mary Hastings Bradley
Mary Roberts Rinehart
Mary Rowlandson
M. Wollstonecraft Shelley
Maud Lindsay
Max Beerbohm
Myra Kelly
Nathaniel Hawthrone
Nicolo Machiavelli
O. F. Walton
Oscar Wilde

Owen Johnson
P.G. Wodehouse
Paul and Mabel Thorne
Paul G. Tomlinson
Paul Severing
Percy Brebner
Percy Keese Fitzhugh
Peter B. Kyne
Plato
Quincy Allen
R. Derby Holmes
R. L. Stevenson
R. S. Ball
Rabindranath Tagore
Rahul Alvares
Ralph Bonehill
Ralph Henry Barbour
Ralph Victor
Ralph Waldo Emmerson
Rene Descartes
Ray Cummings
Rex Beach
Rex E. Beach
Richard Harding Davis
Richard Jefferies
Richard Le Gallienne
Robert Barr
Robert Frost
Robert Gordon Anderson
Robert L. Drake
Robert Lansing
Robert Lynd
Robert Michael Ballantyne
Robert W. Chambers
Rosa Nouchette Carey
Rudyard Kipling
Saint Augustine
Samuel B. Allison
Samuel Hopkins Adams
Sarah Bernhardt
Sarah C. Hallowell
Selma Lagerlof
Sherwood Anderson
Sigmund Freud
Standish O'Grady
Stanley Weyman
Stella Benson
Stella M. Francis

Stephen Crane
Stewart Edward White
Stijn Streuvels
Swami Abhedananda
Swami Parmananda
T. S. Ackland
T. S. Arthur
The Princess Der Ling
Thomas A. Janvier
Thomas A Kempis
Thomas Anderton
Thomas Bailey Aldrich
Thomas Bulfinch
Thomas De Quincey
Thomas Dixon
Thomas H. Huxley
Thomas Hardy
Thomas More
Thornton W. Burgess
U. S. Grant
Upton Sinclair
Valentine Williams
Various Authors
Vaughan Kester
Victor Appleton
Victor G. Durham
Victoria Cross
Virginia Woolf
Wadsworth Camp
Walter Camp
Walter Scott
Washington Irving
Wilbur Lawton
Wilkie Collins
Willa Cather
Willard F. Baker
William Dean Howells
William le Queux
W. Makepeace Thackeray
William W. Walter
William Shakespeare
Winston Churchill
Yei Theodora Ozaki
Yogi Ramacharaka
Young E. Allison
Zane Grey

www.ingramcontent.com/pod-product-compliance
Lightning Source LLC
Chambersburg PA
CBHW021311250626
47155CB00002B/477